Alice Christiana Thompson Meynell

The Flower of the Mind

A Choice Among the Best Poems

Alice Christiana Thompson Meynell

The Flower of the Mind
A Choice Among the Best Poems

ISBN/EAN: 9783744710831

Printed in Europe, USA, Canada, Australia, Japan

Cover: Foto ©Thomas Meinert / pixelio.de

More available books at **www.hansebooks.com**

THE FLOWER
OF THE MIND

A Choice among the best Poems

MADE BY

ALICE MEYNELL

LONDON

GRANT RICHARDS

9 HENRIETTA STREET

1897

INTRODUCTION

PARTIAL collections of English poems, decided by a common subject or bounded by narrow dates and periods of literary history, are made at very short intervals, and the makers are safe from the reproach of proposing their own personal taste as a guide for the reading of others. But a general Anthology gathered from the whole of English literature—the whole from Chaucer to Wordsworth—by a gatherer intent upon nothing except the quality of poetry, is a more rare enterprise. It is hardly to be made without tempting the suspicion—nay, hardly without seeming to hazard the confession—of some measure of self-confidence. Nor can even the desire to enter upon that labour be a frequent one—the desire of the heart of one for whom poetry is veritably 'the complementary life' to set up a pale for inclusion and exclusion, to add honours, to multiply homage, to cherish, to restore, to protest, to proclaim, to depose; and to gain the consent of a multitude of readers to all those acts. Many years, then—some part of a century—may easily pass between the publication of one general anthology and the making of another.

The enterprise would be a sorry one if it were really arbitrary, and if an anthologist should give effect to passionate preferences without authority. An anthology that shall have any

Introduction

value must be made on the responsibility of
one but on the authority of many. There is no
caprice; the mind of the maker has been formed
for decision by the wisdom of many instructors.
It is the very study of criticism, and the grate-
ful and profitable study, that gives the justifica-
tion to work done upon the strongest personal
impulse, and done, finally, in the mental solitude
that cannot be escaped at the last. In another
order, moral education would be best crowned
if it proved to have quick and profound control
over the first impulses; its finished work would
be to set the soul in a state of law, delivered
from the delays of self-distrust; not action only,
but the desires would be in an old security, and
a wish would come to light already justified.
This would be the second—if it were not the
only—liberty. Even so an intellectual education
might assuredly confer freedom upon first and
solitary thoughts, and confidence and composure
upon the sallies of impetuous courage. In a
word, it should make a studious anthologist
quite sure about genius. And all who have
bestowed, or helped in bestowing, the liberating
education have given their student the authority
to be free. Personal and singular the choice in
such a book must be, not without right.

Claiming and disclaiming so much, the gatherers
may follow one another to harvest, and glean in
the same fields in different seasons, for the repetition of the work can never be altogether a
repetition. The general consent of criticism does
not stand still; and moreover, a mere accident

Introduction

has until now left a poet of genius of the past here and there to neglect or obscurity. This is not very likely to befall again; the time has come when there is little or nothing left to discover or rediscover in the sixteenth century or the seventeenth; we know that there does not lurk another Crashaw contemned, or another Henry Vaughan disregarded, or another George Herbert misplaced. There is now something like finality of knowledge at least; and therefore not a little error in the past is ready to be repaired. This is the result of time. Of the slow actions and reactions of critical taste there might be something to say, but nothing important. No loyal anthologist perhaps will consent to acknowledge these tides; he will hardly do his work well unless he believe it to be stable and perfect; nor, by the way, will he judge worthily in the name of others unless he be resolved to judge intrepidly for himself.

Inasmuch as even the best of all poems are the best upon innumerable degrees, the size of most anthologies has gone far to decide what degrees are to be gathered in and what left without. The best might make a very small volume, and be indeed the best, or a very large volume, and be still indeed the best. But my labour has been to do somewhat differently—to gather nothing that did not overpass a certain boundary-line of genius. Gray's *Elegy*, for instance, would rightly be placed at the head of everything below that mark. It is, in fact, so near to the work of genius as to be most directly, closely, and immediately rebuked by genius; it meets genius at close quarters and almost deserves that Shakespeare himself should defeat it. Mediocrity said its own true word in the *Elegy* :

> 'Full many a flower is born to blush unseen,
> And waste its sweetness on the desert air.'

But greatness had said its own word also in a sonnet :

> 'The summer flower is to the summer sweet
> Though to itself it only live and die.'

The reproof here is too sure; not always does it touch so quick, but it is not seldom manifest, and it makes exclusion a simple task. Inclusion, on the other hand, cannot be so completely fulfilled. The impossibility of taking in poems of great length, however purely lyrical, is a mechanical barrier, even on the plan of the present volume; in the case of Spenser's *Prothalamion*, the unmanageably autobiographical and local passage makes it inappropriate; some exquisite things of Landor's are lyrics in blank verse, and the necessary rule against blank verse shuts them out. No extracts have been made from any poem, but in a very few instances a stanza or a passage has been dropped out. No poem has been put in for the sake of a single perfectly fine passage; it would be too much to say that no poem has been put in for the sake of two splendid passages or so. The Scottish ballad poetry is represented by examples that are to my mind finer than anything left out; still, it is but represented; and as the song of this multitude of unknown poets overflows by its quantity a collection of lyrics of genius, so does

Introduction

severally the song of Wordsworth, Crashaw, and Shelley. It has been necessary, in considering traditional songs of evidently mingled authorship, to reject some one invaluable stanza or burden—the original and ancient surviving matter of a spoilt song—because it was necessary to reject the sequel that has cumbered it since some sentimentalist took it for his own. An example, which makes the heart ache, is that burden of keen and remote poetry:

> 'O the broom, the bonnie, bonnie broom,
> The broom of Cowdenknowes!'

Perhaps some hand will gather all such precious fragments as these together one day, freed from what is alien in the work of the restorer. It is inexplicable that a generation resolved to forbid the restoration of ancient buildings should approve the eighteenth century restoration of ancient poems; nay, the architectural 'restorer' is immeasurably the more respectful. In order to give us again the ancient fragments, it is happily not necessary to break up the composite songs which, since the time of Burns, have gained a national love. Let them be, but let the old verses be also; and let them have, for those who desire it, the solitariness of their state of ruin. Even in the cases—and they are not few—where Burns is proved to have given beauty and music to the ancient fragment itself, his work upon the old stanza is immeasurably finer than his work in his own new stanzas following, and it would be less than impiety to part the two.

Introduction

I have obeyed a profound conviction which I have reason to hope will be more commended in the future than perhaps it can be now, in leaving aside a multitude of composite songs —anachronisms, and worse than mere anachronisms, as I think them to be, for they patch wild feeling with sentiment of the sentimentalist. There are some exceptions. The one fine stanza of a song which both Sir Walter Scott and Burns restored is given with the restorations of both, those restorations being severally beautiful; and the burden, 'Hame, hame, hame,' is printed with the Jacobite song that carries it; this song seems so mingled and various in date and origin that no apology is needed for placing it amongst the bundle of Scottish ballads of days before the Jacobites. *Sir Patrick Spens* is treated here as an ancient song. It is to be noted that the modern, or comparatively modern, additions to old songs full of quantitative metre—'Hame, hame, hame,' is one of these—full of long notes, rests, and interlinear pauses, are almost always written in anapæsts. The later writer has slipped away from the fine, various, and subtle metre of the older. Assuredly the popularity of the metre which, for want of a term suiting the English rules of verse, must be called anapæstic, has done more than any other thing to vulgarise the national sense of rhythm and to silence the finer rhythms. Anapæsts came quite suddenly into English poetry and brought coarseness, glibness, volubility, dapper and fatuous effects. A master may use it well, but as a popular measure it has been disastrous. I would be bound to find the modern stanzas in an old song by this very habit of anapæsts and this very misunderstanding of the long words and interlinear pauses of the older stanzas. This, for instance, is the old metre:

'Hame, hame, hame! O hame fain wad I be!'

and this the lamentable anapæstic line (from the same song):

'Yet the sun through the mirk seems to promise to me——.'

It has been difficult to refuse myself the delight of including *A Divine Love* of Carew, but it seemed too bold to leave out four stanzas of a poem of seven, and the last four are of the poorest argument. This passage at least shall speak for the first three:

'Thou didst appear
A glorious mystery, so dark, so clear,
As Nature did intend
All should confess, but none might comprehend.'

From *Christ's Victory in Heaven* of Giles Fletcher (out of reach for its length) it is a happiness to extract here at least the passage upon 'Justice,' who looks 'as the eagle

that hath so oft compared
Her eye with heaven's';

from Marlowe's poem, also unmanageable, that in which Love ran to the priestess

'And laid his childish head upon her breast';

Introduction

with that which tells how Night,

> 'deep-drenched in misty Acheron,
> Heaved up her head, and half the world upon
> Breathed darkness forth';

from Robert Greene two lines of a lovely passage:

> 'Cupid abroad was lated in the night,
> His wings were wet with ranging in the rain';

from Ben Jonson's *Hue and Cry* (not throughout fine) the stanza:

> 'Beauties, have ye seen a toy,
> Called Love, a little boy,
> Almost naked, wanton, blind;
> Cruel now, and then as kind?
> If he be amongst ye, say;
> He is Venus' run-away';

from Francis Davison:

> 'Her angry eyes are great with tears'

from George Wither:

> 'I can go rest
> On her sweet breast
> That is the pride of Cynthia's train';

from Cowley:

> . 'Return, return, gay planet of mine east'!

The poems in which these are cannot make part of the volume, but the citation of the fragments is a relieving act of love.

At the very beginning, Skelton's song to 'Mistress Margery Wentworth' had almost taken a place; but its charm is hardly fine enough.

If it is necessary to answer the inevitable

Introduction

question in regard to Byron, let me say that in another Anthology, a secondary Anthology, the one in which Gray's *Elegy* would have an honourable place, some more of Byron's lyrics would certainly be found; and except this there is no apology. If the last stanza of the 'Dying Gladiator' passage, or the last stanza on the cascade rainbow at Terni,

'Love watching madness with unalterable mien,'

had been separate poems instead of parts of *Childe Harold*, they would have been amongst the poems that are here collected in no spirit of arrogance, or of caprice, of diffidence or doubt.

The volume closes some time before the middle of the century and the death of Wordsworth.

A. M

CONTENTS

Contents

Contents

b　　　　xvii

Contents

Contents

xix

Contents

Contents

Contents

xxii

Contents

Contents

ANONYMOUS

13TH CENTURY

THE FIRST CAROL

SUMMER is y-comen in!
  Loud sing cuckoo!
Groweth seed and bloweth mead,
  And springeth the wood new.
    Sing cuckoo! cuckoo!

Ewe bleateth after lamb,
Loweth cow after calf;
Bullock starteth, buck verteth;
  Merry sing cuckoo!
    Cuckoo! cuckoo!
  Nor cease thou ever now.
Sing cuckoo now!
    Sing cuckoo!

SIR WALTER RALEIGH

1552-1618

VERSES BEFORE DEATH

EVEN such is time, that takes in trust
  Our youth, our joys, our all we have,
And pays us but with earth and dust;
  Who, in the dark and silent grave,

A   1

Edmund Spenser

When we have wandered all our ways,
Shuts up the story of our days;
But from this earth, this grave, this dust,
My God shall raise me up, I trust!

EDMUND SPENSER

1553-1599

EASTER

MOST glorious Lord of life! that on this day
   Didst make thy triumph over death and sin;
And, having harrowed hell, didst bring away
   Captivity then captive, us to win:
This glorious day, dear Lord, with joy begin,
   And grant that we, for whom thou diddest die,
Being with thy dear blood clean washed from sin,
   May live for ever in felicity!

And that thy love we weighing worthily,
   May likewise love thee for the same again;
And for thy sake, that all like dear didst buy,
   With love may one another entertain.
So let us love, dear Love, like as we ought;
Love is the lesson which the Lord us taught.

FRESH SPRING

FRESH Spring, the herald of love's mighty king,
   In whose coat-armour richly are displayed
All sorts of flowers, the which on earth do spring
   In goodly colours gloriously arrayed:

2

Edmund Spenser

Go to my love, where she is careless laid,
    Yet in her winter bower not well awake ;
Tell her the joyous time will not be stayed,
    Unless she do him by the forelock take ;

Bid her therefore herself soon ready make,
    To wait on Love amongst his lovely crew ;
Where every one that misseth there her make
    Shall be by him amerced with penance due.
Make haste therefore, sweet love, whilst it is prime,
For none can call again the passed time.

LIKE AS A SHIP

LIKE as a ship, that through the ocean wide,
    By conduct of some star doth make her way,
When, as a storm hath dimmed her trusty guide,
    Out of her course doth wander far astray !
So I, whose star, that wont with her bright ray
    Me to direct, with clouds is overcast,
Do wander now, in darkness and dismay,
    Through hidden perils round about me placed ;

Yet hope I well that, when this storm is past,
    My Helice, the loadstar of my life,
Will shine again, and look on me at last,
    With lovely light to clear my cloudy grief :
Till then I wander, careful, comfortless,
In secret sorrow and sad pensiveness.

EPITHALAMION

YE learned sisters, which have oftentimes
Been to me aiding, others to adorn,
Whom ye thought worthy of your graceful rhymes,
That even the greatest did not greatly scorn

3

Edmund Spenser

To hear their names sung in your simple lays,
But joyed in their praise;
And when ye list your own mishaps to mourn,
Which death, or love, or fortune's wreck did raise,
Your string could soon to sadder tenor turn,
And teach the woods and waters to lament
Your doleful dreariment:
Now lay those sorrowful complaints aside;
And, having all your heads with garlands crowned,
Help me mine own love's praises to resound;
Ne let the same of any be envíed:
So Orpheus did for his own bride!
So I unto myself alone will sing;
The woods shall to me answer, and my echo ring.

Early, before the world's light-giving lamp
His golden beam upon the hills doth spread,
Having dispersed the night's uncheerful damp,
Do ye awake; and, with fresh lusty-head,
Go to the bower of my beloved love,
My truest turtle dove;
Bid her awake; for Hymen is awake,
And long since ready forth his mask to move,
With his bright tead that flames with many a flake,
And many a bachelor to wait on him,
In their fresh garments trim.
Bid her awake therefore, and soon her dight,
For lo! the wished day is come at last,
That shall, for all the pains and sorrows past,
Pay to her usury of long delight:
And, whilst she doth her dight,
Do ye to her of joy and solace sing,
That all the woods may answer, and your echo ring.

4

Edmund Spenser

Bring with you all the Nymphs that you can hear
Both of the rivers and the forests green,
And of the sea that neighbours to her near:
All with gay garlands goodly well beseen.
And let them also with them bring in hand
Another gay garland,
For my fair love, of lilies and of roses,
Bound truelove wise, with a blue silk riband.
And let them make great store of bridal posies,
And let them eke bring store of other flowers,
To deck the bridal bowers.
And let the ground whereas her foot shall tread,
For fear the stones her tender foot should wrong,
Be strewed with fragrant flowers all along,
And diapred like the discoloured mead.
Which done, do at her chamber door await,
For she will waken straight;
The whiles do ye this song unto her sing,
The woods shall to you answer, and your echo ring.

Ye Nymphs of Mulla, which with careful heed
The silver scaly trouts do tend full well,
And greedy pikes which use therein to feed
(Those trouts and pikes all others do excel);
And ye likewise, which keep the rushy lake,
Where none do fishes take;
Bind up the locks the which hang scattered light,
And in his waters, which your mirror make,
Behold your faces as the crystal bright,
That when you come whereas my love doth lie,
No blemish she may spy.
And eke, ye lightfoot maids, which keep the door,
That on the hoary mountain used to tower;
And the wild wolves, which seek them to devour,

Edmund Spenser

With your steel darts do chase from coming near;
Be also present here,
To help to deck her, and to help to sing,
That all the woods may answer, and your echo ring.

Wake now, my love, awake! for it is time:
The Rosy Morn long since left Tithon's bed,
All ready to her silver coach to climb;
And Phœbus 'gins to show his glorious head.
Hark! how the cheerful birds do chant their lays
And carol of love's praise.
The merry Lark her matins sings aloft;
The Thrush replies; the Mavis descant plays:
The Ouzel shrills; the Ruddock warbles soft;
So goodly all agree, with sweet consent,
To this day's merriment.
Ah! my dear love, why do ye sleep thus long,
When meeter were that ye should now awake,
T' await the coming of your joyous make,
And hearken to the birds' love-learned song,
The dewy leaves among?
For they of joy and pleasance to you sing,
That all the woods them answer, and their echo ring.

My love is now awake out of her dreams,
And her fair eyes, like stars that dimmed were
With darksome cloud, now show their goodly beams
More bright than Hesperus his head doth rear.
Come now, ye damsels, daughters of delight,
Help quickly her to dight!
But first come, ye fair hours, which were begot,
In Jove's sweet paradise, of Day and Night;
Which do the seasons of the year allot,

Edmund Spenser

And all, that ever in this world is fair,
Do make and still repair :
And ye three handmaids of the Cyprian Queen,
The which do still adorn her beauty's pride,
Help to adorn my beautifullest bride :
And, as ye her array, still throw between
Some graces to be seen ;
And, as ye use to Venus, to her sing,
The whiles the woods shall answer, and your echo ring.

Now is my love all ready forth to come :
Let all the virgins therefore well await :
And ye, fresh boys, that tend upon her groom,
Prepare yourselves, for he is coming straight.
Set all your things in seemly good array,
Fit for so joyful day :
The joyfullest day that ever Sun did see.
Fair Sun ! show forth thy favourable ray,
And let thy life-full heat not fervent be,
For fear of burning her sunshiny face,
Her beauty to disgrace.
O fairest Phœbus ! father of the Muse !
If ever I did honour thee aright,
Or sing the thing that mote thy mind delight,
Do not thy servant's simple boon refuse ;
But let this day, let this one day, be mine ;
Let all the rest be thine.
Then I thy sovereign praises loud will sing,
That all the woods shall answer, and their echo ring.

Hark ! how the minstrels 'gin to shrill aloud
Their merry Music that resounds from far,
The pipe, the tabor, and the trembling crowd,
That well agree withouten breach or jar.

7

Edmund Spenser

But, most of all, the damsels do delight
When they their timbrels smite,
And thereunto do dance and carol sweet,
That all the senses they do ravish quite ;
The whiles the boys run up and down the street,
Crying aloud with strong confused noise,
As if it were one voice,
Hymen! iö Hymen! Hymen, they do shout ;
That even to the heavens their shouting shrill
Doth reach, and all the firmament doth fill ;
To which the people standing all about,
As in approvance, do thereto applaud,
And loud advance her laud ;
And evermore they Hymen, Hymen! sing,
That all the woods them answer, and their echo ring.

Lo! where she comes along with portly pace,
Like Phœbe, from her chamber of the East,
Arising forth to run her mighty race,
Clad all in white, that seems a virgin best.
So well it her beseems, that ye would ween
Some angel she had been.
Her long loose yellow locks like golden wire,
Sprinkled with pearl, and pearling flowers atween,
Do like a golden mantle her attire ;
And, being crowned with a garland green,
Seem like some maiden Queen.
Her modest eyes, abashed to behold
So many gazers as on her do stare,
Upon the lowly ground affixed are ;
Ne dare lift up her countenance too bold,
But blush to hear her praises sung so loud,
So far from being proud.

Edmund Spenser

Nathless, do ye still loud her praises sing,
That all the woods may answer, and your echo ring.

Tell me, ye merchants' daughters, did ye see
So fair a creature in your town before ;
So sweet, so lovely, and so mild as she,
Adorned with beauty's grace and virtue's store ?
Her goodly eyes like sapphires shining bright,
Her forehead ivory white,
Her cheeks like apples which the sun hath ruddied,
Her lips like cherries charming men to bite,
Her breast like to a bowl of cream uncrudded,
Her paps like lilies budded,
Her snowy neck like to a marble tower ;
And all her body like a palace fair,
Ascending up, with many a stately stair,
To honour's seat and chastity's sweet bower.
Why stand ye still, ye virgins, in amaze,
Upon her so to gaze,
Whiles ye forget your former lay to sing,
To which the woods did answer, and your echo ring ?

But if ye saw that which no eyes can see,
The inward beauty of her lively spright,
Garnished with heavenly gifts of high degree,
Much more then would ye wonder at that sight,
And stand astonished like to those which read
Medusa's mazeful head.
There dwells sweet love, and constant chastity,
Unspotted faith, and comely womanhood,
Regard of honour, and mild modesty ;
There virtue reigns as Queen in royal throne,
And giveth laws alone,

Edmund Spenser

The which the base affections do obey,
And yield their services unto her will;
Ne thought of thing uncomely ever may
Thereto approach to tempt her mind to ill.
Had ye once seen these her celestial treasures
And unrevealed pleasures,
Then would ye wonder, and her praises sing,
That all the woods should answer, and your echo ring.

Open the temple gates unto my love,
Open them wide that she may enter in,
And all the posts adorn as doth behove,
And all the pillars deck with garlands trim,
For to receive this Saint with honour due,
That cometh in to you.
With trembling steps, and humble reverence,
She cometh in before th' Almighty's view;
Of her ye virgins learn obedience,
When so ye come into those holy places,
To humble your proud faces:
Bring her up to th' high altar, that she may
The sacred ceremonies there partake,
The which do endless matrimony make;
And let the roaring organs loudly play
The praises of the Lord in lively notes;
The whiles, with hollow throats,
The choristers the joyous anthem sing,
That all the woods may answer, and their echo ring.

Behold, whiles she before the altar stands,
Hearing the holy priest that to her speaks,
And blesseth her with his two happy hands,
How the red roses flush up in her cheeks,

Edmund Spenser

And the pure snow with goodly vermeil stain,
Like crimson dyed in grain :
That even th' Angels, which continually
About the sacred altar do remain,
Forget their service and about her fly,
Oft peeping in her face, that seems more fair,
The more they on it stare.
But her sad eyes, still fastened on the ground,
Are governed with goodly modesty,
That suffers not one look to glance awry,
Which may let in a little thought unsound.
Why blush ye, love, to give to me your hand,
The pledge of all our band ?
Sing, ye sweet Angels, Alleluja sing,
That all the woods may answer, and your echo ring.

Now all is done : bring home the Bride again ;
Bring home the triumph of our victory :
Bring home with you the glory of her gain,
With joyance bring her and with jollity.
Never had man more joyful day than this,
Whom heaven would heap with bliss.
Make feast therefore now all this live-long day ;
This day for ever to me holy is.
Pour out the wine without restraint or stay,
Pour not by cups, but by the bellyful !
Pour out to all that wull,   .
And sprinkle all the posts and walls with wine,
That they may sweat, and drunken be withal.
Crown ye God Bacchus with a coronal,
And Hymen also crown with wreaths of vine ;
And let the Graces dance unto the rest,
For they can do it best :

Edmund Spenser

The whiles the maidens do their carol sing,
To which the woods shall answer, and their echo ring.

Ring ye the bells, ye young men of the town,
And leave your wonted labours for this day :
This day is holy ; do ye write it down,
That ye for ever it remember may.
This day the sun is in his chiefest height,
With Barnaby the bright,
From whence declining daily by degrees,
He somewhat loseth of his heat and light,
When once the Crab behind his back he sees.
But for this time it ill ordained was,
To choose the longest day in all the year,
And shortest night, when longest fitter were :
Yet never day so long, but late would pass.
Ring ye the bells, to make it wear away,
And bonfires make all day ;
And dance about them, and about them sing,
That all the woods may answer, and your echo ring !

Ah ! when will this long weary day have end,
And lend me leave to come unto my love ?
How slowly do the hours their numbers spend ;
How slowly does sad Time his feathers move !
Haste thee, O fairest Planet, to thy home,
Within the Western foam :
Thy tired steeds long since have need of rest.
Long though it be, at last I see it gloom,
And the bright evening-star with golden crest
Appear out of the East.
Fair child of beauty ! glorious lamp of love !
That all the host of heaven in ranks dost lead,
And guidest lovers through the night's sad dread,

Edmund Spenser

How cheerfully thou lookest from above,
And seem'st to laugh atween thy twinkling light,
As joying in the sight
Of these glad many, which for joy do sing,
That all the woods them answer, and their echo ring !

Now cease, ye damsels, your delights forepast ;
Enough it is that all the day was yours :
Now day is done, and night is nighing fast,
Now bring the Bride into the bridal bowers.
The night is come ; now soon her disarray,
And in her bed her lay ;
Lay her in lilies and in violets,
And silken curtains over her display,
And odoured sheets, and arras coverlets.
Behold how goodly my fair love does lie,
In proud humility !
Like unto Maia, when as Jove her took
In Tempe, lying on the flowery grass,
'Twixt sleep and wake, after she weary was,
With bathing in the Acidalian brook.
Now it is night, ye damsels may be gone,
And leave my love alone,
And leave likewise your former lay to sing :
The woods no more shall answer, nor your echo ring.

Now welcome, night ! thou night so long expected,
That long day's labour dost at last defray,
And all my cares, which cruel Love collected,
Hast summed in one, and cancelled for aye :
Spread thy broad wing over my love and me,
That no man may us see ;
And in thy sable mantle us enwrap,
From fear of peril and foul horror free.

13

Edmund Spenser

Let no false treason seek us to entrap,
Nor any dread disquiet once annoy
The safety of our joy;
But let the night be calm, and quietsome,
Without tempestuous storms or sad affray :
Like as when Jove with fair Alcmena lay,
When he begot the great Tirynthian groom :
Or like as when he with thy self did lie
And begot Majesty.
And let the maids and young men cease to sing ;
Ne let the woods them answer, nor their echo ring.

Let no lamenting cries nor doleful tears
Be heard all night within, nor yet without ;
Ne let false whispers, breeding hidden fears,
Break gentle sleep with misconceived doubt.
Let no deluding dreams, nor dreadful sights,
Make sudden sad affrights ;
Ne let house-fires, nor lightning's helpless harms,
Ne let the Pouke, nor other evil sprights,
Ne let mischievous witches with their charms,
Ne let hobgoblins, names whose sense we see not,
Fray us with things that be not :
Let not the shriek-owl nor the stork be heard,
Nor the night raven, that still deadly yells ;
Nor damned ghosts, called up with mighty spells,
Nor grisly vultures, make us once afeard :
Ne let the unpleasant choir of frogs still croaking
Make us to wish their choking !
Let none of these their dreary accents sing ;
Ne let the woods them answer, nor their echo ring.

But let still Silence true night-watches keep,
That sacred Peace may in assurance reign,

Edmund Spenser

And timely Sleep, when it is time to sleep,
May pour his limbs forth on your pleasant plain ;
The whiles an hundred little winged loves,
Like divers-feathered doves,
Shall fly and flutter round about your bed,
And in the secret dark, that none reproves,
Their pretty stealths shall work, and snares shall spread
To filch away sweet snatches of delight,
Concealed through covert night.
Ye sons of Venus, play your sports at will !
For greedy Pleasure, careless of your toys,
Thinks more upon her paradise of joys,
Then what ye do, albeit good or ill !
All night therefore attend your merry play,
For it will soon be day :
Now none doth hinder you, that say or sing ;
Ne will the woods now answer, nor your echo ring.

Who is the same, which at my window peeps,
Or whose is that fair face that shines so bright ?
Is it not Cynthia, she that never sleeps,
But walks about high heaven all the night ?
O ! fairest goddess, do thou not envý
My love with me to spy :
For thou likewise didst love, though now unthought,
And for a fleece of wool, which privily
The Latmian shepherd once unto thee brought,
His pleasures with thee wrought !
Therefore to us be favourable now ;   .
And sith of women's labours thou hast charge,
And generation goodly dost enlarge,
Incline thy will to effect our wishful vow,
And the chaste womb inform with timely seed,
That may our comfort breed :

15

Edmund Spenser

Till which we cease our hopeful hap to sing ;
Ne let the woods us answer, nor our echo ring.

And thou, great Juno ! which with awful might
The laws of wedlock still dost patronize,
And the religion of the faith first plight
With sacred rites hast taught to solemnize ;
And eke for comfort often called art
Of women in their smart ;
Eternally bind thou this lovely band,
And all thy blessings unto us impart.
And thou, glad Genius ! in whose gentle hand
The bridal bower and genial bed remain,
Without blemish or stain ;
And the sweet pleasures of their love's delight
With secret aid dost succour and supply,
Till they bring forth the fruitful progeny ;
Send us the timely fruit of this same night.
And thou, fair Hebe ! and thou, Hymen free !
Grant that it may so be.
Till which we cease your further praise to sing ;
Ne any woods shall answer, nor your echo ring.

And ye high heavens, the Temple of the Gods,
In which a thousand torches flaming bright
Do burn, that to us wretched earthly clods
In dreadful darkness lend desired light ;
And all ye powers which in the same remain,
More than we men can feign !
Pour out your blessing on us plenteously,
And happy influence upon us rain,
That we may raise a large posterity,
Which from the earth, which they may long possess
With lasting happiness,

John Lyly

Up to your haughty palaces may mount;
And, for the guerdon of their glorious merit,
May heavenly tabernacles there inherit,
Of blessed saints for to increase the count.
So let us rest, sweet Love, in hope of this,
And cease till then our timely joys to sing:
The woods no more us answer, nor our echo ring!

Song! made in lieu of many ornaments,
With which my Love should duly have been decked,
Which cutting off through hasty accidents,
Ye would not stay your due time to expect,
But promised both to recompense;
Be unto her a goodly ornament,
And for short time an endless monument.

JOHN LYLY

1554 (?)-1606

THE SPRING

WHAT bird so sings, yet does so wail?
O, 'tis the ravished nightingale!
'Jug, jug, jug, jug, tereu,' she cries,
And still her woes at midnight rise.
Brave prick-song! who is 't now we hear?
None but the lark so shrill and clear;
Now at heaven's gate she claps her wings,
The morn not waking till she sings.
Hark, hark, with what a pretty throat
Poor robin-redbreast tunes his note;
Hark, how the jolly cuckoos sing!
Cuckoo to welcome in the spring,
Cuckoo to welcome in the spring!

B   17

SIR PHILIP SIDNEY

1554-1586

TRUE LOVE

My true-love hath my heart, and I have his,
By just exchange one for the other given:
I hold his dear, and mine he cannot miss,
There never was a better bargain driven:
His heart in me keeps him and me in one,
My heart in him his thoughts and senses guides:
He loves my heart, for once it was his own,
I cherish his because in me it bides:
His heart his wound received from my sight;
My heart was wounded with his wounded heart;
For as from me on him his hurt did light,
So still methought in me his hurt did smart:
   Both, equal hurt, in this change sought our bliss.
   My true-love hath my heart, and I have his.

THE MOON

With how sad steps, O Moon, thou climb'st the skies!
How silently, and with how wan a face!
What, may it be that e'en in heavenly place
That busy archer his sharp arrows tries!
Sure, if that long-with-love-acquainted eyes
Can judge of love, thou feel'st a lover's case;
I read it in thy looks; thy languished grace,
To me, that feel the like, thy state descries.

18

Sir Philip Sidney

Then, e'en of fellowship, O Moon, tell me,
Is constant love deemed there but want of wit?
Are beauties there as proud as here they be?
Do they above love to be loved, and yet
    Those lovers scorn whom that love doth possess?
    Do they call virtue, there, ungratefulness?

KISS

LOVE still a boy and oft a wanton is,
Schooled only by his mother's tender eye;
What wonder, then, if he his lesson miss,
When for so soft a rod dear play he try?
And yet my Star, because a sugared kiss
In sport I sucked while she asleep did lie,
Doth lower, nay chide, nay threat, for only this.—
Sweet, it was saucy Love, not humble I!
But no 'scuse serves; she makes her wrath appear
In Beauty's throne; see now, who dares come near
Those scarlet judges, threatening bloody pain!
O heavenly fool, thy most kiss-worthy face
Anger invests with such a lovely grace,
That Anger's self I needs must kiss again.

SWEET JUDGE

ALAS! whence comes this change of looks? If I
Have changed desert, let mine own conscience be
A still-felt plague to self-condemning me,
Let woe gripe on my heart, shame load mine eye;
But if all faith, like spotless ermine, lie
Safe in my soul, which only doth to thee,

Sir Philip Sidney

As his sole object of felicity,
With wings of love in air of wonder fly,
O ease your hand, treat not so hard your slave;
In justice, pains come not till faults do call:
Or if I needs, sweet Judge, must torments have,
Use something else to chasten me withal
    Than those blest eyes, where all my hopes do dwell:
    No doom should make one's heaven become his hell.

SLEEP

COME, Sleep! O Sleep, the certain knot of peace,
The baiting-place of wit, the balm of woe,
The poor man's wealth, the prisoner's release,
The indifferent judge between the high and low;
With shield of proof shield me from out the prease
Of those fierce darts Despair at me doth throw:
O make in me those civil wars to cease;
I will good tribute pay, if thou do so.
Take thou of me smooth pillows, sweetest bed,
A chamber deaf of noise and blind of light,
A rosy garland and a weary head:
And if these things, as being thine in right,
    Move not thy heavy grace, thou shalt in me
    Livelier than elsewhere Stella's image see.

WAT'RED WAS MY WINE

LATE tired with woe, even ready for to pine,
With rage of love, I called my love unkind;
She in whose eyes love, though unfelt, doth shine,
Sweet said that I true love in her should find.

20

Thomas Lodge

I joyed; but straight thus wat'red was my wine,
That love she did, but loved a love not blind;
Which would not let me, whom she loved, decline
From nobler course, fit for my birth and mind:
And therefore, by her love's authority,
Wiled me these tempests of vain love to fly,
And anchor fast myself on virtue's shore.
Alas, if this the only metal be
Of love new-coined to help my beggary,
Dear, love me not, that you may love me more.

THOMAS LODGE
1556-1625

ROSALYND'S MADRIGAL

Love in my bosom, like a bee,
    Doth suck his sweet;
Now with his wings he plays with me,
    Now with his feet.
  Within mines eyes he makes his nest,
  His bed amidst my tender breast;
  My kisses are his daily feast,
  And yet he robs me of my rest:
    Ah! wanton, will ye?

And if I sleep, then percheth he
    With pretty flight,
And makes his pillow of my knee
    The livelong night.
  Strike I my lute, he tunes the string;
  He music plays if so I sing:
  He lends me every lovely thing,
  Yet cruel he my heart doth sting:
    Whist, wanton, will ye?

Thomas Lodge

Else I with roses every day
 Will whip you hence,
And bind you, when you long to play,
 For your offence ;
 I 'll shut my eyes to keep you in,
 I 'll make you fast it for your sin,
 I 'll count your power not worth a pin :
 Alas ! what hereby shall I win,
 If he gainsay me ?

What if I beat the wanton boy
 With many a rod ?
He will repay me with annoy,
 Because a god.
 Then sit thou safely on my knee,
 And let thy bower my bosom be ;
 Lurk in mine eyes, I like of thee !
 O Cupid ! so thou pity me,
 Spare not, but play thee !

ROSALINE

LIKE to the clear in highest sphere
Where all imperial glory shines,
Of selfsame colour is her hair
Whether unfolded, or in twines :
 Heigh ho, fair Rosaline !
Her eyes are sapphires set in snow,
Resembling heaven by every wink ;
The gods do fear whenas they glow,
And I do tremble when I think—
 Heigh ho, would she were mine !

Thomas Lodge

Her cheeks are like the blushing cloud
That beautifies Aurora's face,
Or like the silver crimson shroud
That Phœbus' smiling looks doth grace;
   Heigh ho, fair Rosaline!
Her lips are like two budded roses
Whom ranks of lilies neighbour nigh,
Within which bounds she balm encloses
Apt to entice a deity:
   Heigh ho, would she were mine!

Her neck is like a stately tower
Where Love himself imprisoned lies,
To watch for glances every hour
From her divine and sacred eyes:
   Heigh ho, fair Rosaline!
Her paps are centres of delight,
Her breasts are orbs of heavenly frame,
Where Nature moulds the dew of light
To feed perfection with the same:
   Heigh ho, would she were mine!

With orient pearl, with ruby red,
With marble white, with sapphire blue
Her body every way is fed,
Yet soft in touch and sweet in view:
   Heigh ho, fair Rosaline!
Nature herself her shape admires;
The gods are wounded in her sight;
And Love forsakes his heavenly fires
And at her eyes his brand doth light:
   Heigh ho, would she were mine!

Anonymous

Then muse not, Nymphs, though I bemoan
The absence of fair Rosaline,
Since for a fair there's fairer none,
Nor for her virtues so divine:
    Heigh ho, fair Rosaline;
Heigh ho, my heart! would God that she were mine!

THE SOLITARY SHEPHERD'S SONG

O SHADY vale, O fair enriched meads,
    O sacred woods, sweet fields, and rising mountains;
O painted flowers, green herbs where Flora treads,
    Refreshed by wanton winds and watery fountains!

O all ye winged choristers of wood,
    That perched aloft, your former pains report;
And straight again recount with pleasant mood
    Your present joys in sweet and seemly sort!

O all you creatures whosoever thrive
    On mother earth, in seas, by air, by fire;
More blest are you than I here under sun!
    Love dies in me, whenas he doth revive
In you; I perish under Beauty's ire,
    Where after storms, winds, frosts, your life is won.

ANONYMOUS

I SAW MY LADY WEEP

I SAW my Lady weep,
And Sorrow proud to be advanced so
In those fair eyes where all perfections keep.
    Her face was full of woe,
But such a woe (believe me) as wins more hearts
Than Mirth can do with her enticing parts.

24

George Peele

Sorrow was there made fair,
And Passion, wise; Tears, a delightful thing;
Silence, beyond all speech, a wisdom rare :
　　She made her sighs to sing,
And all things with so sweet a sadness move
As made my heart at once both grieve and love.

　　O fairer than aught else
The world can show, leave off in time to grieve!
Enough, enough : your joyful look excels :
　　Tears kill the heart, believe.
O strive not to be excellent in woe,
Which only breeds your beauty's overthrow.

GEORGE PEELE

1558 (?)-1597

FAREWELL TO ARMS

His golden locks time hath to silver turned ;
　　O time too swift ! O swiftness never ceasing !
His youth 'gainst age, and age at time, hath spurned,
　　But spurned in vain ; youth waneth by increasing :
Beauty, strength, youth, are flowers but fading seen ;
Duty, faith, love, are roots and ever green.

His helmet now shall make an hive for bees,
　　And lovers' sonnets turn to holy psalms ;
A man-at-arms must now serve on his knees,
　　And feed on prayers, that are old age's alms :
But though from court to cottage he depart,
His saint is sure of his unspotted heart.

25

And when he saddest sits in homely cell,
  He'll teach his swains this carol for a song,—
'Blessed be the hearts that wish my sovereign well,
  Cursed be the souls that think her any wrong!'
Goddess, allow this aged man his right
To be your beadsman now that was your knight.

ROBERT GREENE

1560 (?)-1592

FAWNIA

Ah, were she pitiful as she is fair,
  Or but as mild as she is seeming so,
Then were my hopes greater than my despair,
  Then all the world were heaven, nothing woe!
Ah, were her heart relenting as her hand,
  That seems to melt even with the mildest touch,
Then knew I where to seat me in a land
  Under wide heavens, but yet I know not such.
So as she shows, she seems the budding rose,
  Yet sweeter far than is an earthly flower,
Sovereign of beauty, like the spray she grows,
  Compassed she is with thorns and cankered flower;
Yet were she willing to be plucked and worn,
She would be gathered, though she grew on thorn.

Ah, when she sings, all music else be still,
  For none must be compared to her note;
Ne'er breathed such glee from Philomela's bill,
  Nor from the morning-singer's swelling throat.

26

Robert Greene

Ah, when she riseth from her blissful bed,
   She comforts all the world, as doth the sun,
And at her sight the night's foul vapour 's fled ;
   When she is set, the gladsome day is done.
O glorious sun, imagine me thy west,
Shine in mine arms, and set thou in my breast !

SEPHESTIA'S SONG TO HER CHILD

WEEP not, my wanton, smile upon my knee,
When thou art old there 's grief enough for thee.
    Mother's wag, pretty boy,
    Father's sorrow, father's joy ;
    When thy father first did see
    Such a boy by him and me,
    He was glad, I was woe,
    Fortune changed made him so,
    When he left his pretty boy
    Last his sorrow, first his joy.

Weep not, my wanton, smile upon my knee,
When thou art old there 's grief enough for thee.
    Streaming tears that never stint,
    Like pearl drops from a flint,
    Fell by course from his eyes,
    That one another's place supplies ;
    Thus he grieved in every part,
    Tears of blood fell from his heart,
    When he left his pretty boy;
    Father's sorrow, father's joy.

Weep not, my wanton, smile upon my knee,
When thou art old, there 's grief enough for thee.
    The wanton smiled, father wept,
    Mother cried, baby leapt ;

More he crowed, more we cried,
Nature could not sorrow hide:
He must go, he must kiss
Child and mother, baby bless,
For he left his pretty boy,
Father's sorrow, father's joy.
Weep not, my wanton, smile upon my knee,
When thou art old, there's grief enough for thee.

CHRISTOPHER MARLOWE

1562-1593

THE PASSIONATE SHEPHERD TO HIS LOVE

COME live with me and be my Love,
And we will all the pleasures prove
That hills and valleys, dale and field,
And all the craggy mountains yield.

There will we sit upon the rocks
And see the shepherds feed their flocks,
By shallow rivers, to whose falls
Melodious birds sing madrigals.

There will I make thee beds of roses
And a thousand fragrant posies,
A cap of flowers, and a kirtle
Embroidered all with leaves of myrtle.

A gown made of the finest wool,
Which from our pretty lambs we pull,
Fair lined slippers for the cold,
With buckles of the purest gold.

Samuel Daniel

A belt of straw and ivy buds
With coral clasps and amber studs :
And if these pleasures may thee move,
Come live with me and be my Love.

Thy silver dishes for thy meat
As precious as the gods do eat,
Shall on an ivory table be
Prepared each day for thee and me.

The shepherd swains shall dance and sing
For thy delight each May-morning ;
If these delights thy mind may move,
Then live with me and be my Love.

SAMUEL DANIEL

1562-1619

SLEEP

CARE-CHARMER Sleep, son of the sable Night,
Brother to Death, in silent darkness born,
Relieve my languish, and restore the light ;
With dark forgetting of my care return.
And let the day be time enough to mourn
The shipwreck of my ill-adventured youth :
Let waking eyes suffice to wail their scorn,
Without the torment of the night's untruth.
Cease, dreams, the images of day-desires,
To model forth the passions of the morrow ;
Never let rising Sun approve you liars,
To add more grief to aggravate my sorrow :
    Still let me sleep, embracing clouds in vain,
    And never wake to feel the day's disdain.

Michael Drayton

MY SPOTLESS LOVE

MY spotless love hovers with purest wings
About the temple of the proudest frame,
Where blaze those lights, fairest of earthly things,
Which clear our clouded world with brightest flame.
My ambitious thoughts, confined in her face,
Affect no honour but what she can give;
My hopes do rest in limits of her grace;
I weigh no comfort unless she relieve.
For she that can my heart imparadise,
Holds in her fairest hand what dearest is,
My fortune's wheel's the circle of her eyes,
Whose rolling grace deign once a turn of bliss!
    All my life's sweet consists in her alone;
    So much I love the most Unloving One.

MICHAEL DRAYTON

1563-1631

SINCE THERE'S NO HELP

SINCE there's no help, come let us kiss and part,—
Nay I have done, you get no more of me;
And I am glad, yea, glad with all my heart,
That thus so cleanly I myself can free;
Shake hands for ever, cancel all our vows,
And when we meet at any time again,
Be it not seen in either of our brows,
That we one jot of former love retain.

Joshua Sylvester

Now at the last gasp of love's latest breath,
When, his pulse failing, passion speechless lies,
When faith is kneeling by his bed of death,
And innocence is closing up his eyes,
    —Now if thou would'st, when all have given him
      over,
    From death to life thou might'st him yet recover!

JOSHUA SYLVESTER

1563-1618

WERE I AS BASE

WERE I as base as is the lowly plain,
And you, my Love, as high as heaven above,
Yet should the thoughts of me your humble swain
Ascend to heaven, in honour of my Love.
Were I as high as heaven above the plain,
And you, my Love, as humble and as low
As are the deepest bottoms of the main,
Wheresoe'er you were, with you my love should
    go.
Were you the earth, dear Love, and I the skies,
My love should shine on you like to the sun,
And look upon you with ten thousand eyes
Till heaven waxed blind, and till the world were
    done.
    Wheresoe'er I am, below, or else above you,
    Wheresoe'er you are, my heart shall truly love
      you.

William Shakespeare

WILLIAM SHAKESPEARE
1564-1616

POOR Soul, the centre of my sinful earth,
[Foiled by] those rebel powers that thee array,
Why dost thou pine within, and suffer dearth,
Painting thy outward walls so costly gay?
Why so large cost, having so short a lease,
Dost thou upon thy fading mansion spend?
Shall worms, inheritors of this excess,
Eat up thy charge? is this thy body's end?
Then, Soul, live thou upon thy servant's loss,
And let that pine to aggravate thy store;
Buy terms divine in selling hours of dross;
Within be fed, without be rich no more :—
   So shalt thou feed on death, that feeds on men,
   And death once dead, there's no more dying then.

O ME! what eyes hath Love put in my head
Which have no correspondence with true sight;
Or if they have, where is my judgment fled
That censures falsely what they see aright?
If that be fair whereon my false eyes dote,
What means the world to say it is not so?
If it be not, then love doth well denote
Love's eye is not so true as all men's : No,
How can it? O how can love's eye be true,
That is so vexed with watching and with tears?
No marvel then though I mistake my view :
The sun itself sees not till heaven clears.

William Shakespeare

O cunning Love! with tears thou keep'st me
blind,
Lest eyes well-seeing thy foul faults should
find!

SHALL I compare thee to a summer's day?
Thou art more lovely and more temperate:
Rough winds do shake the darling buds of May,
And summer's lease hath all too short a date:
Sometimes too hot the eye of heaven shines,
And often is his gold complexion dimmed;
And every fair from fair sometime declines,
By chance, or nature's changing course, un-
trimmed.
But thy eternal summer shall not fade
Nor lose possession of that fair thou owest;
Nor shall Death brag thou wanderest in his
shade,
When in eternal lines to time thou growest:—
So long as men can breathe, or eyes can see,
So long lives this, and this gives life to thee.

WHEN in the chronicle of wasted time
I see descriptions of the fairest wights,
And beauty making beautiful old rhyme
In praise of ladies dead, and lovely knights;
Then in the blazon of sweet beauty's best
Of hand, of foot, of lip, of eye, of brow,
I see their antique pen would have exprest
Ev'n such a beauty as you master now.

c   33

William Shakespeare

So all their praises are but prophecies
Of this our time, all, you prefiguring;
And for they looked but with divining eyes,
They had not skill enough your worth to sing:
   For we, which now behold these present days,
     Have eyes to wonder, but lack tongues to
     praise.

THAT time of year thou may'st in me behold
When yellow leaves, or none, or few, do hang
Upon those boughs which shake against the cold,
Bare ruined choirs, where late the sweet birds
    sang:
In me thou see'st the twilight of such day
As after sunset fadeth in the west,
Which by and by black night doth take away,
Death's second self, that seals up all in rest:
In me thou see'st the glowing of such fire
That on the ashes of his youth doth lie,
As the death-bed whereon it must expire,
Consumed with that which it was nourished by:
   This thou perceiv'st, which makes thy love more
     strong,
   To love that well which thou must leave ere
     long.

How like a winter hath my absence been
From thee the pleasure of the fleeting year!
What freezings have I felt, what dark days seen,
What old December's bareness everywhere!

William Shakespeare

And yet this time removed was summer's time :
The teeming autumn, big with rich increase,
Bearing the wanton burden of the prime
Like widowed wombs after their lord's decease :
Yet this abundant issue seemed to me
But hope of orphans, and unfathered fruit ;
For summer and his pleasures wait on thee,
And, thou away, the very birds are mute ;
   Or if they sing, 'tis with so dull a cheer,
   That leaves look pale, dreading the winter's
    near.

BEING your slave, what should I do but tend
Upon the hours and times of your desire?
I have no precious time at all to spend
Nor services to do, till you require :
Nor dare I chide the world-without-end-hour
Whilst I, my sovereign, watch the clock for you,
Nor think the bitterness of absence sour
When you have bid your servant once adieu :
Nor dare I question with my jealous thought
Where you may be, or your affairs suppose,
But like a sad slave, stay and think of nought
Save, where you are how happy you make those ;—
   So true a fool is love, that in your will
   Though you do anything, he thinks no ill.

WHEN in disgrace with fortune and men's eyes
I all alone beweep my outcast state,
And trouble deaf Heaven with my bootless cries,
And look upon myself and curse my fate ;

William Shakespeare

Wishing me like to one more rich in hope,
Featured like him, like him with friends possessed,
Desiring this man's heart, and that man's scope,
With what I most enjoy contented least;
Yet in these thoughts myself almost despising,
Haply I think on Thee—and then my state,
Like to the lark at break of day arising
From sullen earth sings hymns at heaven's gate:
    For thy sweet love remembered such wealth
      brings
    That then I scorn to change my state with
      kings.

THEY that have power to hurt, and will do
    none,
That do not do the thing they most do show,
Who, moving others, are themselves as stone,
Unmoved, cold, and to temptation slow,—
They rightly do inherit heaven's graces,
And husband nature's riches from expense;
They are the lords and owners of their faces,
Others, but stewards of their excellence.
The summer's flower is to the summer sweet,
Though to itself it only live and die;
But if that flower with base infection meet,
The basest weed outbraves his dignity:
    For sweetest things turn sourest by their
      deeds;
    Lilies that fester smell far worse than weeds.

William Shakespeare

FAREWELL! thou art too dear for my possessing,
And like enough thou know'st thy estimate:
The charter of thy worth gives thee releasing;
My bonds in thee are all determinate.
For how do I hold thee but by thy granting?
And for that riches where is my deserving?
The cause of this fair gift in me is wanting,
And so my patent back again is swerving.
Thyself thou gav'st, thy own worth then not
    knowing,
Or me, to whom thou gav'st it, else mistaking;
So thy great gift, upon misprision growing,
Comes home again, on better judgment making.
  Thus have I had thee as a dream doth flatter;
  In sleep, a king; but waking, no such matter.

WHEN to the sessions of sweet silent thought
I summon up remembrance of things past,
I sigh the lack of many a thing I sought,
And with old woes new wail my dear time's
    waste;
Then can I drown an eye, unused to flow,
For precious friends hid in death's dateless night,
And weep afresh love's long-since-cancelled woe,
And moan the expense of many a vanished sight.
Then can I grieve at grievances foregone,
And heavily from woe to woe tell o'er

William Shakespeare

The sad account of fore-bemoanèd moan,
Which I new pay as if not paid before :
   But if the while I think on thee, dear friend,
   All losses are restored, and sorrows end.

DID not the heavenly rhetoric of thine eye
'Gainst whom the world could not hold argument,
Persuade my heart to this false perjury?
Vows for thee broke deserve not punishment.
A woman I forswore; but I will prove,
Thou being a goddess, I forswore not thee :
My vow was earthly, thou a heavenly love;
Thy grace being gained cures all disgrace in me.
My vow was breath, and breath a vapour is;
Then, thou fair sun, that on this earth doth shine,
Exhale this vapour vow ; in thee it is:
If broken, then it is no fault of mine.
   If by me broke, what fool is not so wise
   To break an oath, to win a paradise?

THE forward violet thus did I chide :
Sweet thief, whence didst thou steal thy sweet
    that smells,
If not from my love's breath ? The purple pride
Which on thy soft cheek for complexion dwells
In my love's veins thou hast too grossly dyed.
The lily I condemned for thy hand,
And buds of marjoram had stol'n thy hair :
The roses fearfully on thorns did stand,
One blushing shame, another white despair ;

William Shakespeare

A third, nor red nor white, had stol'n of both
And to his robbery had annexed thy breath;
But, for his theft, in pride of all his growth
A vengeful canker eat him up to death.
    More flowers I noted, yet I none could see
    But sweet or colour it had stol'n from thee.

O, LEST the world should task you to recite
What merit lived in me, that you should love
After my death, dear love, forget me quite,
For you in me can nothing worthy prove;
Unless you would devise some virtuous lie,
To do more for me than mine own desert,
And hang more praise upon deceased I
Than niggard truth would willingly impart:
O, lest your true love may seem false in this,
That you for love speak well of me untrue,
My name be buried where my body is,
And live no more to shame nor me nor you.
    For I am shamed by that which I bring forth,
    And so should you, to love things nothing worth.

LET me not to the marriage of true minds
Admit impediments.   Love is not love
Which alters when it alteration finds,
Or bends with the remover to remove:
O, no! it is an ever-fixed mark
That looks on tempests and is never shaken;
It is the star to every wandering bark,
Whose worth's unknown, although his height be taken.

William Shakespeare

Love's not Time's fool, though rosy lips and cheeks
Within his bending sickle's compass come ;
Love alters not with his brief hours and weeks,
But bears it out even to the edge of doom.
   If this be error and upon me proved,
    I never writ, nor no man ever loved.

How oft, when thou, my music, music play'st,
Upon that blessed wood whose motion sounds
With thy sweet fingers, when thou gently sway'st
The wiry concord that mine ear confounds,
Do I envy those jacks that nimble leap
To kiss the tender inward of thy hand,
Whilst my poor lips, which should that harvest reap,
At the wood's boldness by thee blushing stand !
To be so tickled, they would change their state
And situation with those dancing chips,
O'er whom thy fingers walk with gentle gait,
Making dead wood more blest than living lips.
   Since saucy jacks so happy are in this,
    Give them thy fingers, me thy lips to kiss.

FULL many a glorious morning have I seen
Flatter the mountain-tops with sovereign eye,
Kissing with golden face the meadows green,
Gilding pale streams with heavenly alchemy ;
Anon permit the basest clouds to ride
With ugly rack on his celestial face,
And from the forlorn world his visage hide,
Stealing unseen to west with this disgrace :

William Shakespeare

Even so my sun one early morn did shine
With all-triumphant splendour on my brow ;
But out, alack ! he was but one hour mine ;
The region cloud hath masked him from me now.
   Yet him for this my love no whit disdaineth :
   Suns of the world may stain when heaven's sun staineth.

THE expense of spirit in a waste of shame
Is lust in action ; and till action, lust
Is perjured, murderous, bloody, full of blame,
Savage, extreme, rude, cruel, not to trust,
Enjoyed no sooner but despised straight,
Past reason hunted, and no sooner had
Past reason hated, as a swallow'd bait
On purpose laid to make the taker mad ;
Mad in pursuit and in possession so ;
Had, having, and in quest to have, extreme ;
A bliss in proof, and proved, a very woe ;
Before, a joy proposed ; behind, a dream.
   All this the world well knows ; yet none knows well
   To shun the heaven that leads men to this hell.

FANCY

   TELL me where is Fancy bred,
   Or in the heart, or in the head ?
   How begot, how nourished ?
     Reply, reply.

   It is engendered in the eyes ;
   With gazing fed ; and Fancy dies
   In the cradle where it lies :
   Let us all ring Fancy's knell ;
   I 'll begin it,—Ding, dong, bell.
     Ding, dong, bell.

William Shakespeare

UNDER THE GREENWOOD TREE

UNDER the greenwood tree
Who loves to lie with me,
And tune his merry note
Unto the sweet bird's throat—
Come hither, come hither, come hither !
Here shall he see
No enemy
But winter and rough weather.

Who doth ambition shun
And loves to live i' the sun,
Seeking the food he eats
And pleased with what he gets—
Come hither, come hither, come hither !
Here shall he see
No enemy
But winter and rough weather.

FAIRIES

COME unto these yellow sands,
And then take hands :
Courtsied when you have, and kissed,
The wild waves whist,
Foot it featly here and there ;
And sweet Sprites the burthen bear.
Hark, hark !
Bow-bow.
The watch-dogs bark :
Bow-wow.
Hark, hark ! I hear
The strain of strutting chanticleer
Cry, Cock-a-diddle-dow !

William Shakespeare

COME away, come away, Death,
And in sad cypres let me be laid;
  Fly away, fly away, breath;
I am slain by a fair cruel maid.
My shroud of white, stuck all with yew,
    O prepare it!
My part of death, no one so true
    Did share it.

  Not a flower, not a flower sweet
On my black coffin let there be strown;
  Not a friend, not a friend greet
My poor corpse, where my bones shall be thrown;
A thousand, thousand sighs to save,
    Lay me, O where
Sad true lover ne'er may find my grave
    To weep there.

FULL FATHOM FIVE

FULL fathom five thy father lies;
  Of his bones are coral made;
Those are pearls that were his eyes:
  Nothing of him that doth fade,
But doth suffer a sea-change
Into something rich and strange.
Sea-nymphs hourly ring his knell:
  Hark! now I hear them,—
    Ding, dong, bell.

William Shakespeare

FEAR no more the heat o' the sun
  Nor the furious winter's rages;
Thou thy worldly task hast done,
  Home art gone and ta'en thy wages:
Golden lads and girls all must,
As chimney-sweepers, come to dust.

Fear no more the frown o' the great,
  Thou art past the tyrant's stroke;
Care no more to clothe and eat;
  To thee the reed is as the oak:
The sceptre, learning, physic, must
All follow this, and come to dust.

Fear no more the lightning-flash
  Nor the all-dreaded thunder-stone;
Fear not slander, censure rash;
  Thou hast finished joy and moan:
All lovers young, all lovers must
Consign to thee, and come to dust.

SONG

TAKE, O take those lips away
That so sweetly were forsworn,
And those eyes, the break of day,
Lights that do mislead the morn:
But my kisses bring again,
    Bring again—
Seals of love, but sealed in vain,
    Sealed in vain!

Anonymous

Hide, O hide those hills of snow,
  Which thy frozen bosom bears,
On whose tops the pinks that grow
  Are of those that April wears.
But first set my poor heart free
Bound in those icy chains by thee.

SONG

How should I your true love know
  From another one?
By his cockle hat and staff
  And his sandal shoon.

He is dead and gone, lady,
  He is dead and gone;
And at his head a green grass turf
  And at his heels a stone.

White his shroud as mountain snow,
  Larded with sweet showers,
Which bewept to the grave did go,
  With true love showers.

ANONYMOUS

TOM O' BEDLAM

THE morn's my constant mistress,
  And the lovely owl my marrow;
    The flaming drake,
    And the night-crow, make
  Me music to my sorrow.

45

Thomas Campion

I know more than Apollo;
  For oft when he lies sleeping,
    I behold the stars
    At mortal wars,
  And the rounded welkin weeping.

The moon embraces her shepherd,
  And the Queen of Love her warrior;
    While the first does horn
    The stars of the morn,
  And the next the heavenly farrier.

With a heart of furious fancies,
  Whereof I am commander:
    With a burning spear,
    And a horse of air,
  To the wilderness I wander;

With a Knight of ghosts and shadows,
  I summoned am to Tourney:
    Ten leagues beyond
    The wide world's end;
  Methinks it is no journey.

THOMAS CAMPION

Circ. 1567-1620

KIND ARE HER ANSWERS

KIND are her answers,
But her performance keeps no day;
Breaks time, as dancers
From their own music when they stray.
All her free favours and smooth words
Wing my hopes in vain.

Thomas Campion

O, did ever voice so sweet but only feign?
  Can true love yield such delay,
  Converting joy to pain?

  Lost is our freedom
  When we submit to women so:
  Why do we need 'em
  When, in their best, they work our woe?
  There is no wisdom
  Can alter ends by fate prefixt.
O, why is the good of man with evil mixt?
  Never were days yet called two
  But one night went betwixt.

LAURA

ROSE-CHEEKED Laura, come;
Sing thou smoothly with thy beauty's
Silent music, either other
    Sweetly gracing.

Lovely forms do flow
From concent divinely framed;
Heaven is music, and thy beauty's
    Birth is heavenly.

These dull notes we sing
Discords need for helps to grace them,
Only beauty purely loving
    Knows no discord.

But still moves delight,
Like clear springs renewed by flowing,
Ever perfect, ever in them-
    Selves eternal.

47

Thomas Campion

HER SACRED BOWER

WHERE she her sacred bower adorns
   The rivers clearly flow,
The groves and meadows swell with flowers,
   The winds all gently blow.
Her sun-like beauty shines so fair,
   Her spring can never fade.
Who then can blame the life that strives
   To harbour in her shade?

Her grace I sought, her love I wooed;
   Her love though I obtain,
No time, no toil, no vow, no faith
   Her wished grace can gain.
Yet truth can tell my heart is hers
   And her will I adore;
And from that love when I depart
   Let heaven view me no more!

Her roses with my prayers shall spring;
   And when her trees I praise,
Their boughs shall blossom, mellow fruit
   Shall straw her pleasant ways.
The words of hearty zeal have power
   High wonders to effect;
O, why should then her princely ear
   My words or zeal neglect?

If she my faith misdeems, or worth,
   Woe worth my hapless fate!
For though time can my truth reveal,
   That time will come too late.

Thomas Campion

And who can glory in the worth
  That cannot yield him grace?
Content in everything is not,
  Nor joy in every place.

But from her Bower of Joy since I
  Must now excluded be,
And she will not relieve my cares,
  Which none can help but she;
My comfort in her love shall dwell,
  Her love lodge in my breast,
And though not in her bower, yet I
  Shall in her temple rest.

FOLLOW

Follow thy fair sun, unhappy shadow,
  Though thou be black as night,
  And she made all of light;
Yet follow thy fair sun, unhappy shadow!

Follow her whose light thy light depriveth;
  Though here thou live disgraced
  And she in heaven is placed;
Yet follow her whose light the world reviveth.

Follow those pure beams whose beauty burneth
  That so have scorched thee
  As thou still black must be,
Till her kind beams thy black to brightness turneth.

Follow her while yet her glory shineth;
  There comes a luckless night
  That will dim all her light;
And this the black unhappy shade divineth.

D   49

Thomas Campion

Follow still since so thy fates ordained;
 The sun must have his shade,
 Till both at once do fade;
The sun still proved, the shadow still disdained.

WHEN THOU MUST HOME

WHEN thou must home to shades of underground,
 And there arrived, a new admired guest,
The beauteous spirits do engird thee round,
 White Iope, blithe Helen, and the rest,
To hear the stories of thy finished love,
 From that smooth tongue whose music hell can move;
Then wilt thou speak of banqueting delights,
 Of masks and revels which sweet youth did make,
Of tourneys and great challenges of knights,
 And all these triumphs for thy beauties' sake:
When thou hast told these honours done to thee,
Then tell, O tell, how thou didst murther me.

WESTERN WIND

THE peaceful western wind
 The winter storms hath tamed,
And nature in each kind
 The kind heat hath inflamed:
The forward buds so sweetly breathe
 Out of their earthly bowers,
That heav'n, which views their pomp beneath,
 Would fain be decked with flowers.

See how the morning smiles
 On her bright eastern hill,
And with soft steps beguiles
 Them that lie slumbering still!

Thomas Campion

The music-loving birds are come
    From cliffs and rocks unknown,
To see the trees and briars bloom
    That late were overflown.

What Saturn did destroy,
    Love's Queen revives again;
And now her naked boy
    Doth in the fields remain,
Where he such pleasing change doth view
    In every living thing,
As if the world were born anew
    To gratify the Spring.

If all things life present,
    Why die my comforts then?
Why suffers my content?
    Am I the worst of men?
O beauty, be not thou accus'd
    Too justly in this case!
Unkindly if true love be used,
    'Twill yield thee little grace.

FOLLOW YOUR SAINT

FOLLOW your saint, follow with accents sweet!
Haste you, sad notes, fall at her flying feet!
There, wrapped in cloud of sorrow, pity move,
And tell the ravisher of my soul I perish for her love;
But if she scorns my never-ceasing pain,
Then burst with sighing in her sight and ne'er return
    again.

Thomas Campion

All that I sang still to her praise did tend,
Still she was first, still she my songs did end ;
Yet she my love and music both doth fly,
The music that her echo is and beauty's sympathy.
Then let my notes pursue her scornful flight !
It shall suffice that they were breathed and died for her
delight.

CHERRY-RIPE

THERE is a garden in her face
    Where roses and white lilies blow ;
A heavenly paradise is that place,
    Wherein all pleasant fruits do grow ;
There cherries grow that none may buy,
Till Cherry-Ripe themselves do cry.

Those cherries fairly do enclose
    Of orient pearl a double row,
Which when her lovely laughter shows,
    They look like rosebuds filled with snow :
Yet them no peer nor prince may buy,
Till Cherry-Ripe themselves do cry.

Her eyes like angels watch them still ;
    Her brows like bended bows do stand,
Threat'ning with piercing frowns to kill
    All that approach with eye or hand
These sacred cherries to come nigh,
Till Cherry-Ripe themselves do cry !

THOMAS NASH
1567-1601
SPRING

SPRING, the sweet Spring, is the year's pleasant king ;
Then blooms each thing, then maids dance in a ring ;
Cold doth not sting, the pretty birds do sing,
Cuckoo, jug-jug, pu-we, tu-witta-woo.

The palm and may make country-houses gay,
Lambs frisk and play, the shepherds pipe all day,
And hear we aye birds tune this merry lay,
Cuckoo, jug-jug, pu-we, tu-witta-woo.

The fields breathe sweet, the daisies kiss our feet,
Young lovers meet, old wives a-sunning sit ;
In every street these tunes our ears do greet,
Cuckoo, jug-jug, pu-we, tu-witta-woo.
        Spring, the sweet Spring !

JOHN DONNE
1573-1631
THIS HAPPY DREAM

DEAR love, for nothing less than thee
Would I have broke this happy dream ;
        It was a theme
For reason, much too strong for fantasy.
Therefore thou wak'dst me wisely ; yet
My dream thou brok'st not but continu'dst it :

John Donne

Thou art so true, that thoughts of thee suffice
To make dreams truth, and fables histories;
Enter these arms, for since thou thought'st it best
Not to dream all my dream, let's act the rest.

As lightning or a taper's light,
Thine eyes, and not thy noise, waked me.
          Yet I thought thee
(For thou lov'st truth) an angel at first sight;
But when I saw thou saw'st my heart,
And knew'st my thoughts beyond an angel's art,
When thou knew'st what I dreamt, then thou knew'st
          when
Excess of joy would wake me, and cam'st then;
I must confess, it could not choose but be
Profane to think thee anything but thee.

Coming and staying showed thee thee,
But rising makes me doubt, that now
          Thou art not thou.
That love is weak, where fear's as strong as he;
'Tis not all spirit, pure and brave,
If mixture it of fear, shame, honour, have.
Perchance as torches, which must ready be,
Men light and put out, so thou deal'st with me;
Thou cam'st to kindle, goest to come : then I
Will dream that hope again, but else would die.

DEATH

DEATH, be not proud, though some have called thee
Mighty and dreadful, for thou art not so;
For those whom thou think'st thou dost overthrow
Die not, poor Death, nor yet canst thou kill me.

John Donne

From rest and sleep which but thy picture be,
Much pleasure, then from thee much more must flow ;
And soonest our best men with thee do go,
Rest of their bones, and soul's delivery.

Thou 'rt slave to fate, chance, kings, and desperate men,
And dost with poison, war, and sickness dwell,
And poppy or charms can make us sleep as well,
And better than thy stroke.   Why swell'st thou then ?

One short sleep past, we wake eternally,
And Death shall be no more ; Death, thou shalt die.

HYMN TO GOD THE FATHER

WILT Thou forgive that sin where I begun,
  Which was my sin, though it were done before ?
Wilt Thou forgive that sin through which I run,
  And do run still, though still I do deplore ?
When Thou hast done, Thou hast not done ;
      For I have more.

Wilt Thou forgive that sin, which I have won
  Others to sin, and made my sins their door ?
Wilt Thou forgive that sin which I did shun
  A year or two and wallowed in a score ?
When Thou hast done, Thou hast not done ;
      For I have more.

I have a sin of fear, that when I've spun
  My last thread, I shall perish on the shore ;
But swear by Thyself that at my death Thy Son
  Shall shine, as He shines now and heretofore.
And having done that, Thou hast done ;
      I fear no more.

John Donne

WHOEVER comes to shroud me, do not harm
　　　Nor question much
That subtle wreath of hair about mine arm;
The mystery, the sign, you must not touch,
　　　For 'tis my outward soul,
Viceroy to that which, unto heaven being gone,
　　　Will leave this to control
And keep these limbs, her provinces, from dissolution.

But if the sinewy thread my brain lets fall
　　　Through every part,
Can tie those parts and make me one of all;
The hairs, which upward grew, and strength and art
　　　Have from a better brain,
Can better do 't; except she meant that I
　　　By this should know my pain,
As prisoners are manacled when they 're condemned to
　　die.

Whate'er she meant by 't, bury it with me;
　　　For since I am
Love's martyr, it might breed idolatry
If into others' hands these relics came.
　　　As 'twas humility
To afford to it all that a soul can do,
　　　So 'twas some bravery
That since you would have none of me, I bury some of
　　you.

Richard Barnefield

RICHARD BARNEFIELD

1574 (?) —— (?)

THE NIGHTINGALE

As it fell upon a day
In the merry month of May,
Sitting in a pleasant shade
Which a grove of myrtles made,
Beasts did leap and birds did sing,
Trees did grow and plants did spring;
Everything did banish moan
Save the Nightingale alone.
She, poor bird, as all forlorn,
Leaned her breast up-till a thorn,
And there sung the dolefull'st ditty
That to hear it was great pity.
Fie, fie, fie, now would she cry;
Teru, teru, by and by:
That to hear her so complain
Scarce I could from tears refrain;
For her griefs so lively shown
Made me think upon mine own.
—Ah, thought I, thou mourn'st in vain,
None takes pity on thy pain:
Senseless trees, they cannot hear thee,
Ruthless beasts, they will not cheer thee;
King Pandion, he is dead,
All thy friends are lapped in lead:
All thy fellow birds do sing
Careless of thy sorrowing:
Even so, poor bird, like thee
None alive will pity me.

57

BEN JONSON

1574-1637

CHARIS' TRIUMPH

SEE the chariot at hand here of Love,
    Wherein my lady rideth !
Each that draws is a swan or a dove,
    And well the car Love guideth.
As she goes all hearts do duty
        Unto her beauty ;
And enamoured do wish, so they might
        But enjoy such a sight,
That they still were to run by her side,
Through swords, through seas, whither she would
        ride.

Do but look on her eyes, they do light
    All that love's world compriseth !
Do but look on her, she is bright
    As love's star when it riseth !
Do but mark, her forehead 's smoother
        Than words that soothe her !
And from her arched brows, such a grace
        Sheds itself through the face,
As alone there triumphs to the life
All the gain, all the good of the elements' strife.

Have you seen but a bright lily grow
    Before rude hands have touched it ?
Have you marked but the fall of the snow
    Before the soil hath smutched it ?
Have you felt the wool of the beaver,
        Or swan's down ever ?

Ben Jonson

Or have smelled o' the bud o' the brier?
Or the nard in the fire?
Or have tasted the bag of the bee?
O so white! O so soft! O so sweet is she!

JEALOUSY

WRETCHED and foolish jealousy,
How cam'st thou thus to enter me?
I ne'er was of thy kind:
Nor have I yet the narrow mind
To vent that poor desire,
That others should not warm them at my fire:
I wish the sun should shine
On all men's fruits and flowers as well as mine.

But under the disguise of love,
Thou say'st thou only cam'st to prove
What my affections were.
Think'st thou that love is helped by fear?
Go, get thee quickly forth,
Love's sickness and his noted want of worth,
Seek doubting men to please.
I ne'er will owe my health to a disease.

EPITAPH ON ELIZABETH L. H.

WOULDST thou hear what many say
In a little?—reader, stay.

Underneath this stone doth lie
As much beauty as could die;
Which in life did harbour give
To more virtue than doth live.

Ben Jonson

If at all she had a fault,
Leave it buried in this vault.
One name was Elizabeth,
The other, let it sleep with death:
Fitter where it died to tell
Than that it lived at all.   Farewell!

HYMN TO DIANA

QUEEN and Huntress, chaste and fair,
    Now the sun is laid to sleep,
Seated in thy silver chair
    State in wonted manner keep:
        Hesperus entreats thy light,
        Goddess excellently bright!

Earth, let not thy envious shade
    Dare itself to interpose;
Cynthia's shining orb was made
    Heaven to clear when day did close:
        Bless us then with wished sight,
        Goddess excellently bright!

Lay thy bow of pearl apart,
    And thy crystal-shining quiver;
Give unto the flying hart
    Space to breathe, how short soever:
        Thou that mak'st a day of night,
        Goddess excellently bright!

ON MY FIRST DAUGHTER

HERE lies to each her parent's ruth,
Mary, the daughter of their youth:

Ben Jonson

Yet all heaven's gifts being heaven's due,
It makes the father less to rue.
At six months' end she parted hence
With safety of her innocence ;
Whose soul Heaven's Queen (whose name she bears),
In comfort of her mother's tears,
Hath placed among her virgin train :
Where, while that severed doth remain,
This grave partakes the fleshly birth,
Which cover lightly, gentle earth.

ECHO'S LAMENT FOR NARCISSUS

SLOW, slow, fresh fount, keep time with my salt tears ;
   Yet, slower yet; O faintly, gentle springs ;
List to the heavy part the music bears ;
   Woe weeps out her division when she sings.
        Droop herbs and flowers ;
        Fall grief in showers,
        Our beauties are not ours ;
        O, I could still,
Like melting snow upon some craggy hill,
        Drop, drop, drop, drop,
Since nature's pride is now a withered daffodil.

AN EPITAPH ON SALATHIEL PAVY, A CHILD OF
QUEEN ELIZABETH'S CHAPEL

    WEEP with me, all you that read
        This little story ;
    And know, for whom a tear you shed
        Death's self is sorry.

John Fletcher

It was a child that so did thrive
    In grace and feature,
As Heaven and Nature seemed to strive
    Which owned the creature.
Years he numbered scarce thirteen
    When fates turned cruel,
Yet three filled zodiacs had he been
    The stage's jewel;
And did act (what now we moan)
    Old men so duly,
Ah, sooth, the Parcae thought him one—
    He played so truly.
So by error to his fate
    They all consented,
But viewing him since, alas, too late
    They have repented;
And have sought, to give new birth,
    In baths to steep him;
But being much too good for earth,
    Heaven vows to keep him.

JOHN FLETCHER

1579-1625

INVOCATION TO SLEEP, FROM VALENTINIAN

CARE-CHARMING Sleep, thou easer of all woes,
Brother to Death, sweetly thyself dispose
On this afflicted prince; fall like a cloud
In gentle showers; give nothing that is loud
Or painful to his slumbers;—easy, sweet,
And as a purling stream, thou son of Night,
Pass by his troubled senses; sing his pain
Like hollow murmuring wind or silver rain;

John Webster

Into this prince gently, oh, gently slide
And kiss him into slumbers like a bride !

TO BACCHUS

God Lyæus, ever young,
Ever honoured, ever sung ;
Stained with blood of lusty grapes
In a thousand lusty shapes ;
Dance upon the mazer's brim,
In the crimson liquor swim ;
From thy plenteous hand divine,
Let a river run with wine :
   God of Youth, let this day here
   Enter neither care nor fear.

JOHN WEBSTER
(?)-1625

SONG FROM THE DUCHESS OF MALFI

Hark, now everything is still,
The screech-owl and the whistler shrill
Call upon our dame aloud,
And bid her quickly don her shroud :

Much you had of land and rent,
Your length in clay 's now competent ;
A long war disturbed your mind,
Here your perfect peace is signed. ·
Of what is 't fools make such vain keeping ?
Sin their conception, their birth weeping,
Their life a general mist of error,
Their death a hideous storm of terror.
Strew your hair with powders sweet,
Don clean linen, bathe your feet,

John Webster

And (the foul fiend more to check)
A crucifix let bless your neck ;
'Tis now full tide 'tween night and day ;
End your groan and come away.

SONG FROM THE DEVIL'S LAW-CASE

ALL the flowers of the spring
Meet to perfume our burying ;
These have but their growing prime,
And man does flourish but his time.
Survey our progress from our birth ;
We're set, we grow, we turn to earth,
Courts adieu, and all delights,
All bewitching appetites !
Sweetest breath and clearest eye,
Like perfumes, go out and die ;
And consequently this is done
As shadows wait upon the sun.
Vain the ambition of kings
Who seek by trophies and dead things
To leave a living name behind,
And weave but nets to catch the wind.

IN EARTH, DIRGE FROM VITTORIA COROMBONA

CALL for the robin-redbreast and the wren,
Since o'er shady groves they hover,
And with leaves and flowers do cover
The friendless bodies of unburied men.
Call unto his funeral dole
The ant, the field-mouse, and the mole
To rear him hillocks that shall keep him warm
And (when gay tombs are robbed) sustain no harm ;
But keep the wolf far thence, that's foe to men,
For with his nails he'll dig them up again.

WILLIAM DRUMMOND OF HAWTHORNDEN

1585-1649

SONG

PHŒBUS, arise!
And paint the sable skies
With azure, white, and red:
Rouse Memnon's mother from her Tithon's bed
That she thy càreer may with roses spread:
The nightingales thy coming each-where sing:
Make an eternal Spring!
Give life to this dark world which lieth dead;
Spread forth thy golden hair
In larger locks than thou wast wont before,
And emperor-like decore
With diadem of pearl thy temples fair:
Chase hence the ugly night
Which serves but to make dear thy glorious light.

This is that happy morn,
That day, long-wished day
Of all my life so dark
(If cruel stars have not my ruin sworn
And fates not hope betray),
Which, purely white, deserves
An everlasting diamond should it mark.
This is the morn should bring unto this grove
My Love, to hear and recompense my love.
Fair king, who all preserves,
But show thy blushing beams,
And thou two sweeter eyes

E   65

William Drummond of Hawthornden

Shalt see than those which by Peneus' streams
Did once thy heart surprise.
Nay, suns, which shine as clear
As thou, when two thou didst to Rome appear.
Now, Flora, deck thyself in fairest guise :
If that ye winds would hear
A voice surpassing far Amphion's lyre,
Your stormy chiding stay ;
Let Zephyr only breathe,
And with her tresses play,
Kissing sometimes these purple ports of death.
—The winds all silent are,
And Phœbus in his chair
Ensaffroning sea and air
Makes vanish every star :
Night like a drunkard reels
Beyond the hills, to shun his flaming wheels :
The fields with flowers are decked in every hue,ʹ
The clouds with orient gold spangle their blue ;
Here is the pleasant place—
And nothing wanting is, save She, alas !

SLEEP, SILENCE' CHILD

SLEEP, Silence' child, sweet father of soft rest,
Prince, whose approach peace to all mortals brings,
Indifferent host to shepherds and to kings,
Sole comforter of minds with grief oppressed ;
Lo, by thy charming rod all breathing things
Lie slumb'ring, with forgetfulness possessed,
And yet o'er me to spread thy drowsy wings
Thou sparest, alas ! who cannot be thy guest.
Since I am thine, O come, but with that face
To inward light which thou art wont to show ;

66

William Drummond of Hawthornden

With feigned solace ease a true-felt woe ;
Or if, deaf god, thou do deny that grace,
   Come as thou wilt, and what thou wilt bequeath :
   I long to kiss the image of my death.

TO THE NIGHTINGALE

DEAR chorister, who from these shadows sends,
Ere that the blushing morn dare show her light,
Such sad lamenting strains, that night attends,
Become all ear, stars stay to hear thy plight:
If one whose grief even reach of thought transcends,
Who ne'er, not in a dream, did taste delight,
May thee importune who like care pretends,
And seems to joy in woe, in woe's despite ;
Tell me (so may thou fortune milder try,
And long, long sing) for what thou thus complains,
Sith, winter gone, the sun in dappled sky
Now smiles on meadows, mountains, woods, and plains?
   The bird, as if my question did her move,
   With trembling wings sobbed forth, 'I love! I love!'

MADRIGAL I

   LIKE the Idalian queen,
   Her hair about her eyne,
With neck and breast's ripe apples to be seen,
   At first glance of the morn,
In Cyprus' gardens gathering those fair flowers
   Which of her blood were born,
I saw, but fainting saw, my paramours.
The graces naked danced about the place,
   The winds and trees amazed
   With silence on her gazed ;

The flowers did smile, like those upon her face,
And as their aspen stalks those fingers band,
   That she might read my case
A hyacinth I wished me in her hand.

MADRIGAL II

  THE beauty and the life
Of life's and beauty's fairest paragon,
O tears! O grief! hung at a feeble thread
To which pale Atropos had set her knife;
   The soul with many a groan
   Had left each outward part,
And now did take its last leave of the heart;
Nought else did want, save death, even to be dead;
When the afflicted band about her bed,
Seeing so fair him come in lips, cheeks, eyes,
Cried, 'Ah! and can death enter paradise?'

BEAUMONT AND FLETCHER

1586-1616   1579-1625

I DIED TRUE

  LAY a garland on my hearse
    Of the dismal yew;
  Maidens willow branches bear;
    Say, I die true.

  My love was false, but I was firm
    From my hour of birth.
  Upon my buried body lie
    Lightly, gentle earth.

FRANCIS BEAUMONT

1586-1616

ON THE TOMBS IN WESTMINSTER ABBEY

MORTALITY, behold and fear!
What a change of flesh is here!
Think how many royal bones
Sleep within these heaps of stones;
Here they lie, had realms and lands,
Who now want strength to stir their hands;
Where from their pulpits sealed with dust
They preach, 'In greatness is no trust.'
Here's an acre sown indeed
With the richest royallest seed
That the earth did e'er suck in
Since the first man died for sin:
Here the bones of birth have cried,
'Though gods they were, as men they died!'
Here are sands, ignoble things,
Dropt from the ruined sides of kings:
Here's a world of pomp and state
Buried in dust, once dead by fate.

SIR FRANCIS KYNASTON

1587-1642 .

TO CYNTHIA, ON CONCEALMENT OF HER BEAUTY

Do not conceal those radiant eyes,
The starlight of serenest skies;
Lest, wanting of their heavenly light,
They turn to chaos' endless night!

Sir Francis Kynaston

Do not conceal those tresses fair,
The silken snares of thy curled hair
Lest, finding neither gold nor ore,
The curious silk-worm work no more.

Do not conceal those breasts of thine,
More snow-white than the Apennine;
Lest, if there be like cold and frost,
The lily be for ever lost.

Do not conceal that fragrant scent,
Thy breath, which to all flowers hath lent
Perfumes; lest, it being supprest,
No spices grow in all the rest.

Do not conceal thy heavenly voice,
Which makes the hearts of gods rejoice;
Lest, music hearing no such thing,
The nightingale forget to sing.

Do not conceal, nor yet eclipse,
Thy pearly teeth with coral lips;
Lest that the seas cease to bring forth
Gems which from thee have all thy worth.

Do not conceal no beauty, grace,
That's either in thy mind or face;
Lest virtue overcome by vice
Make men believe no Paradise.

NATHANIEL FIELD

1587-1638

MATIN SONG

Rise, Lady Mistress, rise!
  The night hath tedious been;
No sleep hath fallen into mine eyes
  Nor slumbers made me sin.
Is not she a saint then, say,
Thoughts of whom keep sin away?

Rise, Madam! rise and give me light,
  Whom darkness still will cover,
And ignorance, darker than night,
  Till thou smile on thy lover.
All want day till thy beauty rise;
For the grey morn breaks from thine eyes.

GEORGE WITHER

1588-1667

SLEEP, BABY, SLEEP!

Sleep, baby, sleep! what ails my dear,
  What ails my darling thus to cry?
Be still, my child, and lend thine ear,
  To hear me sing thy lullaby.
My pretty lamb, forbear to weep;
Be still, my dear; sweet baby, sleep.

71

George Wither

Thou blessed soul, what canst thou fear?
  What thing to thee can mischief do?
Thy God is now thy father dear,
  His holy Spouse thy mother too.
Sweet baby, then forbear to weep;
Be still, my babe; sweet baby, sleep.

Though thy conception was in sin,
  A sacred bathing thou hast had;
And though thy birth unclean hath been,
  A blameless babe thou now art made.
Sweet baby, then forbear to weep;
Be still, my babe; sweet baby, sleep.

While thus thy lullaby I sing,
  For thee great blessings ripening be;
Thine Eldest Brother is a king,
  And hath a kingdom bought for thee.
Sweet baby, then forbear to weep;
Be still, my babe; sweet baby, sleep.

Sweet baby, sleep, and nothing fear;
  For whosoever thee offends
By thy protector threaten'd are,
  And God and angels are thy friends.
Sweet baby, then forbear to weep;
Be still, my babe; sweet baby, sleep.

When God with us was dwelling here,
  In little babes He took delight;
Such innocents as thou, my dear,
  Are ever precious in His sight.
Sweet baby, then forbear to weep;
Be still, my babe; sweet baby, sleep.

George Wither

A little infant once was He;
    And strength in weakness then was laid
Upon His Virgin Mother's knee,
    That power to thee might be convey'd.
Sweet baby, then forbear to weep;
Be still, my babe; sweet baby, sleep.

In this thy frailty and thy need
    He friends and helpers doth prepare,
Which thee shall cherish, clothe, and feed,
    For of thy weal they tender are.
Sweet baby, then forbear to weep;
Be still, my babe; sweet baby, sleep.

The King of kings, when He was born,
    Had not so much for outward ease;
By Him such dressings were not worn,
    Nor such like swaddling-clothes as these.
Sweet baby, then forbear to weep;
Be still, my babe; sweet baby, sleep.

Within a manger lodged thy Lord,
    Where oxen lay and asses fed:
Warm rooms we do to thee afford,
    An easy cradle or a bed.
Sweet baby, then forbear to weep;
Be still, my babe; sweet baby, sleep.

The wants that He did then sustain
    Have purchased wealth, my babe, for thee;
And by His torments and His pain
    Thy rest and ease secured be.
My baby, then forbear to weep;
Be still, my babe; sweet baby, sleep.

Thomas Carew

Thou hast, yet more, to perfect this,
   A promise and an earnest got
Of gaining everlasting bliss,
   Though thou, my babe, perceiv'st it not.
Sweet baby, then forbear to weep;
Be still, my babe; sweet baby, sleep.

THOMAS CAREW

1589-1639

SONG

Ask me no more where Jove bestows,
When June is past, the fading rose;
For in your beauties, orient deep,
These flowers, as in their causes, sleep.

Ask me no more whither do stray
The golden atoms of the day;
For in pure love heaven did prepare
Those powders to enrich your hair.

Ask me no more whither doth haste
The nightingale when May is past;
For in your sweet dividing throat
She winters, and keeps warm her note.

Ask me no more if east or west
The phœnix builds her spicy nest;
For unto you at last she flies,
And in your fragrant bosom dies!

Thomas Carew

WHEN thou, poor Excommunicate
  From all the joys of Love, shalt see
The full reward and glorious fate
  Which my strong faith shall purchase me,
  Then curse thine own Inconstancy.

A fairer hand than thine shall cure
  That heart which thy false oaths did wound;
And to my soul a soul more pure
  Than thine shall by Love's hand be bound,
  And both with equal glory crowned.

Then shalt thou weep, entreat, complain
  To Love, as I did once to thee:
When all thy tears shall be as vain
  As mine were then: for thou shalt be
  Damned for thy false Apostacy.

AN HYMENEAL DIALOGUE

Groom.—TELL me, my Love, since Hymen tied
    The holy knot, hast thou not felt
  A new-infused spirit slide
    Into thy breast, whilst mine did melt?

Bride.—First tell me, Sweet, whose words were those?
    For though your voice the air did break,
  Yet did my soul the sense compose,
    And through your lips my heart did speak.

75

Thomas Carew

Groom.—Then I perceive, when from the flame
    Of love my scorched soul did retire,
    Your frozen heart in that place came,
    And sweetly melted in that fire.

Bride.—'Tis true, for when that mutual change
    Of souls was made, with equal gain,
    I straight might feel diffused a strange
    But gentle heat through every vein.

Bride.—Thy bosom then I'll make my nest,
    Since there my willing soul doth perch.
Groom.—And for my heart, in thy chaste breast,
    I'll make an everlasting search.

    O blest disunion, that doth so
        Our bodies from our souls divide;
    As two to one, and one four grow,
        Each by contraction multiplied.

INGRATEFUL BEAUTY THREATENED

Know, Celia (since thou art so proud),
    'Twas I that gave thee thy renown!
Thou hadst in the forgotten crowd
    Of common beauties lived unknown,
Had not my verse exhaled thy name,
And with it imped the wings of fame.

That killing power is none of thine;
    I gave it to thy voice and eyes;
Thy sweets, thy graces, all are mine;
    Thou art my star, shin'st in my skies;
Then dart not from thy borrowed sphere
Lightning on him that fixed thee there.

Thomas Dekker

Tempt me with such affrights no more,
    Lest what I made I uncreate !
Let fools thy mystic forms adore ;
    I 'll know thee in thy mortal state.
Wise poets, that wrapped the truth in tales,
Knew her themselves through all her veils.

THOMAS DEKKER

Circa 1570-1641

LULLABY

GOLDEN slumbers kiss your eyes,
Smiles awake you when you rise.
Sleep, pretty wantons, do not cry,
And I will sing a lullaby.
Rock them, rock a lullaby.

Care is heavy, therefore sleep you,
You are care, and care must keep you.
Sleep, pretty wantons, do not cry,
And I will sing a lullaby.
Rock them, rock a lullaby.

SWEET CONTENT

ART thou poor, yet hast thou golden slumbers ?
    O sweet content !
Art thou rich, yet is thy mind perplexed ?
    O punishment !
Dost thou laugh to see how fools are vexed
To add to golden numbers, golden numbers ?

Thomas Heywood

O sweet content! O sweet, O sweet content!
  Work apace, apace, apace, apace;
  Honest labour bears a lovely face;
  Then hey nonny nonny, hey nonny nonny!

Canst drink the waters of the crisped spring?
          O sweet content!
Swimm'st thou in wealth, yet sink'st in thine own tears?
          O punishment!
Then he that patiently want's burden bears
No burden bears, but is a king, a king!
O sweet content! O sweet, O sweet content!
  Work apace, apace, apace, apace;
  Honest labour bears a lovely face;
  Then hey nonny nonny, hey nonny nonny!

THOMAS HEYWOOD

—-1649?

GOOD-MORROW

PACK, clouds, away, and welcome day,
  With night we banish sorrow;
Sweet air blow soft, mount larks aloft
  To give my Love good-morrow!
Wings from the wind to please her mind,
  Notes from the lark I'll borrow;
Bird, prune thy wing, nightingale sing,
  To give my Love good-morrow;
  To give my Love good-morrow,
  Notes from them both I'll borrow.

78

Robert Herrick

Wake from thy nest, Robin-redbreast,
　Sing, birds, in every furrow;
And from each hill, let music shrill
　Give my fair Love good-morrow!
Blackbird and thrush in every bush,
　Stare, linnet, and cock-sparrow!
You pretty elves, amongst yourselves,
　Sing my fair Love good-morrow;
　To give my Love good-morrow
　Sing, birds, in every furrow!

ROBERT HERRICK

1591-1674

TO DIANEME

SWEET, be not proud of those two eyes
Which star-like sparkle in their skies;
Nor be you proud, that you can see
All hearts your captives; yours yet free.
Be you not proud of that rich hair
Which wantons with the love-sick air;
Whenas that ruby which you wear,
Sunk from the tip of your soft ear,
Will last to be a precious stone
When all your world of beauty's gone.

TO MEADOWS

YE have been fresh and green,
　Ye have been filled with flowers;
And ye the walks have been
　Where maids have spent their hours.

79

Robert Herrick

Ye have beheld how they
   With wicker arks did come
To kiss and bear away
   The richer cowslips home.

You've heard them sweetly sing,
   And seen them in a round,
Each virgin, like a Spring,
   With honeysuckles crowned.

But now we see none here
   Whose silvery feet did tread,
And with dishevelled hair
   Adorned this smoother mead.

Like unthrifts, having spent
   Your stock, and needy grown,
You're left here to lament
   Your poor estates alone.

TO BLOSSOMS

FAIR pledges of a fruitful tree,
   Why do ye fall so fast?
   Your date is not so past,
But you may stay yet here awhile
   To blush and gently smile,
     And go at last.

What, were ye born to be
   An hour or half's delight,
   And so to bid good-night?
'Twas pity Nature brought ye forth
   Merely to show your worth,
     And lose you quite!

Robert Herrick

But you are lovely leaves, where we
  May read how soon things have
  Their end, though ne'er so brave:
And after they have shown their pride
  Like you, awhile, they glide
    Into the grave.

TO DAFFODILS

FAIR Daffodils, we weep to see
  You haste away so soon:
As yet the early-rising Sun
  Has not attained his noon.
      Stay, stay,
  Until the hasting day
      Has run
  But to the even-song;
And, having prayed together, we
  Will go with you along.

We have short time to stay, as you,
  We have as short a Spring;
As quick a growth to meet decay
  As you, or any thing.
      We die,
  As your hours do, and dry
      Away,
  Like to the Summer's rain,
Or as the pearls of morning's dew,
  Ne'er to be found again.

Robert Herrick

WELCOME, Maids of Honour!
  You do bring
  In the Spring,
And wait upon her.

She has Virgins many,
  Fresh and fair ;
  Yet you are
More sweet than any.

Ye are the Maiden Posies,
  And so graced
  To be placed
'Fore damask roses.

But, though thus respected,
  By and by
  Ye do lie,
Poor girls, neglected.

TO PRIMROSES

WHY do ye weep, sweet babes? can tears
    Speak grief in you,
    Who were but born
  Just as the modest morn
  Teemed her refreshing dew?
Alas, you have not known that shower
    That mars a flower ;
    Nor felt th' unkind
  Breath of a blasting wind ;
  Nor are ye worn with years ;

Robert Herrick

Or warped as we,
Who think it strange to see
Such pretty flowers, like to orphans young,
To speak by tears, before ye have a tongue.

Speak, whimp'ring younglings, and make known
The reason, why
Ye droop and weep;
Is it for want of sleep?
Or childish lullaby?
Or that ye have not seen as yet
The violet?
Or brought a kiss
From that sweetheart to this?
No, no, this sorrow shown
By your tears shed,
Would have this lecture read,
That things of greatest, so of meanest, worth,
Conceived with care are, and with tears brought
forth.

TO DAISIES, NOT TO SHUT SO SOON

Shut not so soon; the dull-eyed night
Hath not as yet begun
To make a seizure on the light,
Or to seal up the sun.

No marigolds yet closed are,
No shadows great appear;
Nor doth the early shepherd's star
Shine like a spangle here.

Robert Herrick

Stay but till my Julia close
   Her life-begetting eye,
And let the whole world then dispose
   Itself to live or die.

TO THE VIRGINS, TO MAKE MUCH OF TIME

GATHER ye rose-buds while ye may,
   Old Time is still a-flying:
And this same flower that smiles to-day
   To-morrow will be dying.

The glorious Lamp of Heaven, the Sun,
   The higher he's a-getting,
The sooner will his race be run,
   And nearer he's to setting.

That age is best which is the first,
   When youth and blood are warmer;
But being spent, the worse, and worst
   Times still succeed the former.

Then be not coy, but use your time;
   And while ye may, go marry:
For having lost but once your prime,
   You may for ever tarry.

DRESS

A SWEET disorder in the dress
Kindles in clothes a wantonness:—
A lawn about the shoulders thrown
Into a fine distraction,—

Robert Herrick

An erring lace, which here and there
Enthrals the crimson stomacher,—
A cuff neglectful, and thereby
Ribbands to flow confusedly,—
A winning wave, deserving note,
In the tempestuous petticoat,—
A careless shoe-string, in whose tie
I see a wild civility,—
Do more bewitch me, than when art
Is too precise in every part.

IN SILKS

WHENAS in silks my Julia goes,
Then, then (methinks) how sweetly flows
That liquefaction of her clothes.

Next, when I cast mine eyes and see
That brave vibration each way free;
O how that glittering taketh me!

CORINNA'S GOING A-MAYING

GET up, get up for shame! The blooming morn
Upon her wings presents the god unshorn.
    See how Aurora throws her fair
    Fresh-quilted colours through the air!
    Get up, sweet Slug-a-bed, and see
    The dew bespangling herb and tree.
Each flower has wept, and bowed toward the east,
Above an hour since; yet you not drest—
    Nay! not so much as out of bed,
    When all the birds have matins said,

Robert Herrick

And sung their thankful hymns : 'tis sin,
Nay, profanation, to keep in—
Whenas a thousand virgins on this day
Spring, sooner than the lark, to fetch in May.

Rise, and put on your foliage, and be seen
To come forth, like the Spring-time, fresh and green,
    And sweet as Flora.   Take no care
    For jewels for your gown or hair :
    Fear not ; the leaves will strew
    Gems in abundance upon you :
Besides, the childhood of the day has kept,
Against you come, some orient pearls unwept :
    Come, and receive them while the light
    Hangs on the dew-locks of the night :
    And Titan on the eastern hill
    Retires himself, or else stands still
Till you come forth.   Wash, dress, be brief in
    praying :
Few beads are best, when once we go a-Maying.

Come, my Corinna, come ! and coming, mark
How each field turns a street, each street a park
    Made green, and trimmed with trees : see how
    Devotion gives each house a bough
    Or branch : each porch, each door, ere this,
    An ark, a tabernacle is,
Made up of white-thorn neatly interwove,
As if here were those cooler shades of love.
    Can such delights be in the street
    And open fields, and we not see 't ?
    Come, we 'll abroad : and let 's obey
    The proclamation made for May :

Robert Herrick

And sin no more, as we have done, by staying:
But, my Corinna, come! let's go a-Maying.

There's not a budding boy or girl, this day,
But is got up, and gone to bring in May.
    A deal of youth, ere this, is come
    Back, and with white-thorn laden home.
    Some have despatched their cakes and cream,
    Before that we have left to dream:
And some have wept, and wooed, and plighted troth
And chose their priest, ere we can cast off sloth:
    Many a green-gown has been given;
    Many a kiss, both odd and even:
    Many a glance, too, has been sent
    From out the eye, Love's firmament:
Many a jest told of the keys betraying
This night, and locks picked:—Yet we're not a-
    Maying.

Come! let us go, while we are in our prime,
And take the harmless folly of the time!
    We shall grow old apace, and die
    Before we know our liberty.
    Our life is short; and our days run
    As fast away as does the sun:
And as a vapour, or a drop of rain
Once lost, can ne'er be found again;
    So when or you or I are made
    A fable, song, or fleeting shade,
    All love, all liking, all delight
    Lies drowned with us in endless night.
Then while time serves, and we are but decaying,
Come, my Corinna, come! let's go a-Maying.

Robert Herrick

GRACE FOR A CHILD

HERE, a little child, I stand,
Heaving up my either hand :
Cold as paddocks though they be,
Here I lift them up to Thee,
For a benison to fall
On our meat and on our all.   Amen.

BEN JONSON

AH, Ben !
Say how, or when,
Shall we thy guests
Meet at those lyric feasts
Made at the Sun,
The Dog, the Triple Tun ?
Where we such clusters had
As made us nobly wild, not mad ;
And yet each verse of thine
Out-did the meat, out-did the frolic wine.

My Ben !
Or come again
Or send to us
Thy wit's great over-plus ;
But teach us yet
Wisely to husband it,
Lest we that talent spend :
And having once brought to an end
That precious stock, the store
Of such a wit, the world should have no more.

George Herbert

GEORGE HERBERT

1593-1632

HOLY BAPTISM

SINCE, Lord, to Thee
A narrow way and little gate
Is all the passage, on my infancy
Thou didst lay hold, and antedate
My faith in me.

O, let me still
Write Thee 'great God,' and me 'a child';
Let me be soft and supple to Thy will,
Small to myself, to others mild,
Behither ill.

Although by stealth
My flesh get on; yet let her sister,
My soul, bid nothing but preserve her wealth:
The growth of flesh is but a blister;
Childhood is health.

VIRTUE

SWEET day, so cool, so calm, so bright,
The bridal of the earth and sky,
The dew shall weep thy fall to-night,
      For thou must die.

Sweet rose, whose hue, angry and brave,
Bids the rash gazer wipe his eye,
Thy root is ever in its grave,
      And thou must die.

George Herbert

Sweet Spring, full of sweet days and roses,
A box where sweets compacted lie,
My music shows ye have your closes,
    And all must die.

Only a sweet and virtuous soul,
Like seasoned timber, never gives ;
But though the whole world turn to coal,
    Then chiefly lives.

UNKINDNESS

LORD, make me coy and tender to offend :
In friendship, first I think if that agree
    Which I intend
Unto my friend's intent and end ;
I would not use a friend as I use Thee.

If any touch my friend or his good name,
It is my honour and my love to free
    His blasted fame
From the least spot or thought of blame ;
I could not use a friend as I use Thee.

My friend may spit upon my curious floor ;
Would he have gold ? I lend it instantly ;
    But let the poor,
And Thee within them, starve at door ;
I cannot use a friend as I use Thee.

When that my friend pretendeth to a place,
I quit my interest, and leave it free ;
    But when Thy grace
Sues for my heart, I Thee displace ;
Nor would I use a friend as I use Thee.

George Herbert

Yet can a friend what Thou hast done fulfil?
O, write in brass, 'My God upon a tree
    His blood did spill,
  Only to purchase my good-will';
Yet use I not my foes as I use Thee.

LOVE

LOVE bade me welcome; yet my soul drew back,
    Guilty of dust and sin.
But quick-eyed Love, observing me grow slack
    From my first entrance in,
Drew nearer to me, sweetly questioning
    If I lacked anything.

'A guest,' I answered, 'worthy to be here':
    Love said, 'You shall be he.'
'I, the unkind, ungrateful? Ah, my dear!
    I cannot look on thee.'
Love took my hand, and smiling did reply,
    'Who made the eyes but I?'

'Truth, Lord; but I have marred them; let my shame
    Go where it doth deserve.'
'And know you not,' says Love, 'who bore the blame?
    'My dear, then I will serve.'
'You must sit down,' says Love, 'and taste my meat.'
    So I did sit and eat.

THE PULLEY

  WHEN God at first made man,
Having a glass of blessings standing by,
'Let us,' said He, 'pour on him all we can;
Let the world's riches, which dispersed lie,
    Contract into a span.'

George Herbert

So strength first made a way,
Then beauty flowed, then wisdom, honour
    pleasure;
When almost all was out, God made a stay,
Perceiving that, alone of all His treasure,
    Rest in the bottom lay.

'For if I should,' said He,
'Bestow this jewel also on My creature,
He would adore My gifts instead of Me,
And rest in Nature, not the God of Nature:
    So both should losers be.

'Yet let him keep the rest,
But keep them with repining restlessness;
Let him be rich and weary, that at least,
If goodness lead him not, yet weariness
    May toss him to My breast.'

THE COLLAR

I struck the board, and cried, 'No more;
    I will abroad.
What, shall I ever sigh and pine?
My lines and life are free; free as the road,
Loose as the wind, as large as store.
    Shall I be still in suit?
Have I no harvest but a thorn
To let me blood, and not restore
What I have lost with cordial fruit?
    Sure there was wine
Before my sighs did dry it; there was corn
Before my tears did drown it;

George Herbert

Is the year only lost to me ?
Have I no bays to crown it,
No flowers, no garlands gay ? all blasted,
     All wasted ?
Not so, my heart ; but there is fruit,
     And thou hast hands.
Recover all thy sigh-blown age
On double pleasures ; leave thy cold dispute
Of what is fit and not ; forsake thy cage,
     Thy rope of sands,
Which petty thoughts have made ; and made to
    thee
Good cable, to enforce and draw,
     And be thy law,
While thou didst wink and wouldst not see.
       Away ! take heed ;
       I will abroad.
Call in thy death's-head there, tie up thy fears ;
       He that forbears
To suit and serve his need
       Deserves his load.'
But as I raved and grew more fierce and wild
       At every word,
Methought I heard one calling, ' Child ' ;
       And I replied, ' My Lord.'

LIFE

I MADE a posy while the day ran by :
Here will I smell my remnant out, and tie
   My life within this band ;
But Time did beckon to the flowers, and they
By noon most cunningly did steal away,
   And withered in my hand.

George Herbert

My hand was next to them, and then my heart;
I took, without more thinking, in good part
   Time's gentle admonition ;
Who did so sweetly Death's sad taste convey,
Making my mind to smell my fatal day,
   Yet sugaring the suspicion.

Farewell, dear flowers; sweetly your time ye spent,
Fit while ye lived for smell or ornament,
   And after death for cures.
I follow straight, without complaints or grief,
Since if my scent be good, I care not if
   It be as short as yours.

MISERY

LORD, let the angels praise Thy name:
   Man is a foolish thing, a foolish thing ;
Folly and sin play all his game ;
   His house still burns, and yet he still doth sing—
      Man is but grass,
      He knows it—' Fill the glass.'

How canst Thou brook his foolishness ?
   Why, he 'll not lose a cup of drink for Thee:
Bid him but temper his excess,
   Not he: he knows where he can better be—
      As he will swear—
      Than to serve Thee in fear.

What strange pollutions doth he wed,
   And make his own ! as if none knew but he.

George Herbert

No man shall beat into his head
  That Thou within his curtains drawn canst see:
    'They are of cloth
    Where never yet came moth.'

The best of men, turn but Thy hand
  For one poor minute, stumble at a pin;
They would not have their actions scanned,
  Nor any sorrow tell them that they sin,
    Though it be small,
    And measure not the fall.

They quarrel Thee, and would give over
  The bargain made to serve Thee; but Thy love
Holds them unto it, and doth cover
  Their follies with the wings of Thy mild Dove,
    Not suffering those
    Who would, to be Thy foes.

My God, man cannot praise Thy name:
  Thou art all brightness, perfect purity;
The sun holds down his head for shame,
  Dead with eclipses, when we speak of Thee:
    How shall infection
    Presume on Thy perfection?

As dirty hands foul all they touch,
  And those things most which are most pure and
    fine,
So our clay-hearts, even when we crouch
  To sing Thy praises, make them less divine:
    Yet either this
    Or none Thy portion is.

George Herbert

Man cannot serve Thee : let him go
   And serve the swine—there, that is his delight:
He doth not like this virtue, no ;
   Give him his dirt to wallow in all night:
       ' These preachers make
      His head to shoot and ache.'

O foolish man ! where are thine eyes ?
   How hast thou lost them in a crowd of cares !
Thou pull'st the rug, and wilt not rise,
   No, not to purchase the whole pack of stars:
      ' There let them shine ;
      Thou must go sleep or dine.'

The bird that sees a dainty bower
   Made in the tree, where she was wont to sit,
Wonders and sings, but not His power
   Who made the arbour ; this exceeds her wit.
      But man doth know
      The Spring whence all things flow :

And yet, as though he knew it not,
   His knowledge winks, and lets his humours reign ;
They make his life a constant blot,
   And all the blood of God to run in vain.
      Ah, wretch ! what verse
      Can thy strange ways rehearse ?

Indeed, at first man was a treasure,
   A box of jewels, shop of rarities,
A ring whose posy was ' my pleasure ';
   He was a garden in a Paradise ;
      Glory and grace
      Did crown his heart and face.

James Shirley

But sin hath fooled him; now he is
  A lump of flesh, without a foot or wing
To raise him to a glimpse of bliss;
  A sick-tossed vessel, dashing on each thing,
    Nay, his own shelf:
    My God, I mean myself.

JAMES SHIRLEY

1596-1666

EQUALITY

THE glories of our blood and state
  Are shadows, not substantial things;
There is no armour against fate;
  Death lays his icy hand on kings:
    Sceptre and Crown
    Must tumble down,
And in the dust be equal made
With the poor crooked scythe and spade.

Some men with swords may reap the field,
  And plant fresh laurels where they kill:
But their strong nerves at last must yield;
  They tame but one another still:
    Early or late
    They stoop to fate,
And must give up their murmuring breath
When they, pale captives, creep to death.

The garlands wither on your brow;
  Then boast no more your mighty deeds;
Upon Death's purple altar now
  See where the victor-victim bleeds:

Anonymous

Your heads must come
To the cold tomb ;
Only the actions of the just
Smell sweet, and blossom in their dust.

ANONYMOUS

Circa 1603

LULLABY

WEEP you no more, sad fountains ;
What need you flow so fast ?
Look how the snowy mountains
Heaven's sun doth gently waste.
But my sun's heavenly eyes
View not your weeping,
That now lies sleeping
Softly, now softly lies
Sleeping.

Sleep is a reconciling,
. A rest that peace begets ;
Doth not the sun rise smiling
When fair at eve he sets ?
Rest you, then, rest, sad eyes,
Melt not in weeping,
While she lies sleeping
Softly, now softly lies
Sleeping.

98

SIR WILLIAM DAVENANT

1605-1668

MORNING

THE lark now leaves his watery nest,
  And climbing shakes his dewy wings,
He takes your window for the east,
  And to implore your light, he sings;
Awake, awake, the morn will never rise,
Till she can dress her beauty at your eyes.

The merchant bows unto the seaman's star,
  The ploughman from the sun his season takes;
But still the lover wonders what they are,
  Who look for day before his mistress wakes;
Awake, awake, break through your veils of lawn!
Then draw your curtains and begin the dawn.

EDMUND WALLER

1605-1687

THE ROSE

Go, lovely rose!
Tell her that wastes her time and me,
  That now she knows,
When I resemble her to thee,
How sweet and fair she seems to be.

99

Thomas Randolph

Tell her that's young
And shuns to have her graces spied,
That hadst thou sprung
In deserts, where no men abide,
Thou must have uncommended died.

Small is the worth
Of beauty from the light retired;
Bid her come forth,
Suffer herself to be desired,
And not blush so to be admired.

Then die! that she
The common fate of all things rare
May read in thee:
How small a part of time they share
That are so wondrous sweet and fair!

THOMAS RANDOLPH

1606-1634?

HIS MISTRESS

I HAVE a mistress, for perfections rare
In every eye, but in my thoughts most fair.
Like tapers on the altar shine her eyes;
Her breath is the perfume of sacrifice;
And wheresoe'er my fancy would begin,
Still her perfection lets religion in.
We sit and talk, and kiss away the hours
As chastely as the morning dews kiss flowers.
I touch her, like my beads, with devout care,
And come unto my courtship as my prayer.

CHARLES BEST

17TH CENTURY

A SONNET OF THE MOON

LOOK how the pale Queen of the silent night
  Doth cause the ocean to attend upon her,
And he, as long as she is in his sight,
  With his full tide is ready her to honour:

But when the silver waggon of the Moon
  Is mounted up so high he cannot follow,
The sea calls home his crystal waves to moan,
  And with low ebb doth manifest his sorrow.

So you that are the sovereign of my heart,
  Have all my joys attending on your will,
My joys low ebbing when you do depart,
  When you return, their tide my heart doth fill.

So as you come, and as you do depart,
Joys ebb and flow within my tender heart.

JOHN MILTON

1608-1674

HYMN ON CHRIST'S NATIVITY

IT was the winter wild
While the heaven-born Child
All meanly wrapt in the rude manger lies;
Nature in awe to Him
Had doffed her gaudy trim,

101

John Milton

With her great Master so to sympathise :
It was no season then for her
To wanton with the sun, her lusty paramour.

Only with speeches fair
She woos the gentle air
To hide her guilty front with innocent snow ;
And on her naked shame,
Pollute with sinful blame,
The saintly veil of maiden white to throw ;
Confounded, that her Maker's eyes
Should look so near upon her foul deformities.

But He, her fears to cease,
Sent down the meek-eyed Peace ;
She, crowned with olive green, came softly sliding
Down through the turning sphere,
His ready harbinger,
With turtle wing the amorous clouds dividing ;
And waving wide her myrtle wand,
She strikes a universal peace through sea and land.

No war, or battle's sound
Was heard the world around :
The idle spear and shield were high uphung ;
The hooked chariot stood
Unstained with hostile blood ;
The trumpet spake not to the armed throng ;
And kings sat still with awful eye,
As if they surely knew their sovran Lord was by.

But peaceful was the night
Wherein the Prince of Light

John Milton

His reign of peace upon the earth began :
 The winds, with wonder whist,
 Smoothly the waters kist,
Whispering new joys to the mild ocèan,   ′
Who now hath quite forgot to rave,
While birds of calm sit brooding on the charmed wave.

 The stars, with deep amaze,
 Stand fixed in steadfast gaze,
Bending one way their precious influence ;
 And will not take their flight
 For all the morning light,
Or Lucifer that often warned them thence ;
But in their glimmering orbs did glow,
Until their Lord Himself bespake, and bid them go.

 And though the shady gloom
 Had given day her room,
The sun himself withheld his wonted speed,
 And hid his head for shame,
 As his inferior flame
The new-enlightened world no more should need ;
He saw a greater Sun appear
Than his bright throne or burning axletree could bear.

 The shepherds on the lawn,
 Or ere the point of dawn,
Sat simply chatting in a rustic row ;
 Full little thought they than
 That the mighty Pan
Was kindly come to live with them below ;
Perhaps their loves, or else their sheep,
Was all that did their silly thoughts so busy keep.

John Milton

When such music sweet
Their hearts and ears did greet
As never was by mortal fingers strook—
Divinely-warbled voice
Answering the stringed noise,
As all their souls in blissful rapture took;
The air, such pleasure loth to lose,
With thousand echoes still prolongs each heavenly
close.

Nature, that heard such sound
Beneath the hollow round
Of Cynthia's seat the airy region thrilling,
Now was almost won
To think her part was done,
And that her reign had here its last fulfilling;
She knew such harmony alone
Could hold all Heaven and Earth in happier union.

At last surrounds their sight
A globe of circular light,
That with long beams the shamefaced night
arrayed;
The helmed Cherubim
And sworded Seraphim
Are seen in glittering ranks with wings displayed,
Harping in loud and solemn quire,
With unexpressive notes, to Heaven's new-born Heir.

Such music (as 'tis said)
Before was never made
But when of old the Sons of Morning sung,
While the Creator great
His constellations set,

John Milton

And the well-balanced world on hinges hung ;
And cast the dark foundations deep,
And bid the weltering waves their oozy channel keep.

     Ring out, ye crystal spheres !
     Once bless our human ears,
If ye have power to touch our senses so ;
      And let your silver chime
      Move in melodious time ;
And let the bass of heaven's deep organ blow ;
And with your ninefold harmony
Make up full consort to the angelic symphony.

     For if such holy song
     Enwrap our fancy long,
Time will run back and fetch the age of gold ;
      And speckled Vanity
      Will sicken soon and die,
And leprous Sin will melt from earthly mould ;
And Hell itself will pass away,
And leave her dolorous mansions to the peering day.

     Yea, Truth and Justice then
     Will down return to men,
Orbed in a rainbow ; and, like glories wearing,
      Mercy will sit between
      Throned in celestial sheen,
With radiant feet the tissued clouds down steering;
And Heaven, as at some festival,
Will open wide the gates of her high palace-hall.

     But wisest Fate says No;
     This must not yet be so;
     The Babe yet lies in smiling infancy

John Milton

That on the bitter cross
Must redeem our loss;
So both Himself and us to glorify:
Yet first, to those ychained in sleep,
The wakeful trump of doom must thunder through the
deep,

With such a horrid clang
As on Mount Sinai rang,
While the red fire and smouldering clouds out-
brake:
The aged Earth aghast
With terror of that blast
Shall from the surface to the centre shake,
When, at the world's last session,
The dreadful Judge in middle air shall spread His throne.

And then at last our bliss
Full and perfect is,
But now begins; for from this happy day
The old Dragon under ground,
In straiter limits bound,
Not half so far casts his usurped sway;
And, wroth to see his kingdom fail,
Swinges the scaly horror of his folded tail.

The Oracles are dumb;
No voice or hideous hum
Runs through the arched roof in words deceiving.
Apollo from his shrine
Can no more divine,
With hollow shriek the steep of Delphos leaving:
No nightly trance or breathed spell
Inspires the pale-eyed priest from the prophetic cell.

John Milton

The lonely mountains o'er
And the resounding shore
A voice of weeping heard and loud lament;
From haunted spring and dale
Edged with poplar pale,
The parting Genius is with sighing sent;
With flower-inwoven tresses torn
The Nymphs in twilight shade of tangled thickets
mourn.

In consecrated earth
And on the holy hearth
The Lars and Lemures moan with midnight plaint;
In urns, and altars round,
A drear and dying sound
Affrights the Flamens at their service quaint;
And the chill marble seems to sweat,
While each peculiar Power forgoes his wonted seat.

Peor and Baalim
Forsake their temples dim,
With that twice-battered god of Palestine;
And mooned Ashtaroth,
Heaven's queen and mother both,
Now sits not girt with tapers' holy shine;
The Lybic Hammon shrinks his horn:
In vain the Tyrian maids their wounded Thammuz
mourn.

And sullen Moloch, fled,
Hath left in shadows dread
His burning idol all of blackest hue;
In vain with cymbals' ring
They call the grisly king,

John Milton

In dismal dance about the furnace blue ;
The brutish gods of Nile as fast,
Isis, and Orus, and the dog Anubis, haste.

Nor is Osiris seen
In Memphian grove or green,
Trampling the unshowered grass with lowings loud:
Nor can he be at rest
Within his sacred chest ;
Nought but profoundest Hell can be his shroud ;
In vain with timbrelled anthems dark
The sable-stoled sorcerers bear his worshipped ark.

He feels from Juda's land
The dreaded Infant's hand ;
The rays of Bethlehem blind his dusky eyn ;
Nor all the gods beside
Longer dare abide,
Not Typhon huge ending in snaky twine :
Our Babe, to show His Godhead true,
Can in His swaddling bands control the damned crew.

So, when the sun in bed,
Curtained with cloudy red,
Pillows his chin upon an orient wave,
The flocking shadows pale
Troop to the infernal jail,
Each fettered ghost slips to his several grave ;
And the yellow-skirted fays
Fly after the night-steeds, leaving their moon-loved
maze.

But see ! the Virgin blest
Hath laid her Babe to rest ;

John Milton

Time is, our tedious song should here have ending:
 Heaven's youngest-teemed star
 Hath fixed her polished car,
Her sleeping Lord with handmaid lamp attending:
And all about the courtly stable
Bright-harnessed Angels sit in order serviceable.

HENCE, loathed Melancholy,
 Of Cerberus and blackest Midnight born
In Stygian cave forlorn,
 'Mongst horrid shapes, and shrieks, and sights un-
 holy!
Find out some uncouth cell
 Where brooding Darkness spreads his jealous wings
And the night-raven sings;
 There under ebon shades, and low-browed rocks
As ragged as thy locks,
 In dark Cimmerian desert ever dwell.

 But come, thou goddess fair and free,
 In heaven yclept Euphrosyne,
 And by men, heart-easing Mirth,
 Whom lovely Venus at a birth
 With two sister Graces more
 To ivy-crowned Bacchus bore;
 Or whether (as some sager sing)
 The frolic wind that breathes the spring,
 Zephyr, with Aurora playing,
 As he met her once a-Maying—
 There on beds of violets blue
 And fresh-blown roses washed in dew

John Milton

Filled her with thee, a daughter fair,
So buxom, blithe, and debonair.
  Haste thee, Nymph, and bring with thee
Jest, and youthful jollity,
Quips, and cranks, and wanton wiles,
Nods, and becks, and wreathed smiles,
Such as hang on Hebe's cheek,
And love to live in dimple sleek ;
Sport that wrinkled Care derides,
And Laughter holding both his sides :—
Come, and trip it as you go
On the light fantastic toe ;
And in thy right hand lead with thee
The mountain-nymph, sweet Liberty ;
And if I give thee honour due,
Mirth, admit me of thy crew,
To live with her, and live with thee
In unreproved pleasures free ;
To hear the lark begin his flight
And singing startle the dull night
From his watch-tower in the skies,
Till the dappled dawn doth rise ;
Then to come, in spite of sorrow,
And at my window bid good-morrow
Through the sweetbriar, or the vine,
Or the twisted eglantine :
While the cock with lively din
Scatters the rear of darkness thin,
And to the stack, or the barn-door,
Stoutly struts his dames before :
Oft listening how the hounds and horn
Cheerly rouse the slumbering morn,
From the side of some hoar hill,
Through the high wood echoing shrill :

John Milton

Sometime walking, not unseen,
By hedge-row elms, on hillocks green,
Right against the eastern gate
Where the great Sun begins his state
Robed in flames and amber light,
The clouds in thousand liveries dight ;
While the ploughman, near at hand,
Whistles o'er the furrowed land,
And the milkmaid singeth blithe,
And the mower whets his scythe,
And every shepherd tells his tale
Under the hawthorn in the dale.

   Straight mine eye hath caught new pleasures
Whilst the landscape round it measures ;
Russet lawns, and fallows gray,
Where the nibbling flocks do stray ;
Mountains, on whose barren breast
The labouring clouds do often rest ;
Meadows trim with daisies pied,
Shallow brooks, and rivers wide ;
Towers and battlements it sees
Bosomed high in tufted trees,
Where perhaps some Beauty lies,
The cynosure of neighbouring eyes.

   Hard by, a cottage chimney smokes
From betwixt two aged oaks,
Where Corydon and Thyrsis, met,
Are at their savoury dinner set
Of herbs, and other country messes,
Which the neat-handed Phillis dresses ;
And then in haste her bower she leaves,
With Thestylis to bind the sheaves ;
Or, if the earlier season lead,
To the tanned haycock in the mead.

John Milton

Sometimes with secure delight
The upland hamlets will invite,
When the merry bells ring round,
And the jocund rebecks sound
To many a youth and many a maid,
Dancing in the chequered shade;
And young and old come forth to play
On a sunshine holiday,
Till the live-long day-light fail:
Then to the spicy nut-brown ale,
With stories told of many a feat,
How Faery Mab the junkets eat:—
She was pinched and pulled, she said;
And he by Friar's lantern led;
Tells how the grudging Goblin sweat
To earn his cream-bowl duly set,
When in one night, ere glimpse of morn,
His shadowy flail hath threshed the corn
That ten day-labourers could not end;
Then lies him down the lubber fiend,
And, stretched out all the chimney's length,
Basks at the fire his hairy strength;
And crop-full out of doors he flings,
Ere the first cock his matin rings.
  Thus done the tales, to bed they creep,
By whispering winds soon lulled asleep.
  Towered cities please us then
And the busy hum of men,
Where throngs of knights and barons bold,
In weeds of peace, high triumphs hold,
With store of ladies, whose bright eyes
Rain influence, and judge the prize
Of wit or arms, while both contend
To win her grace, whom all commend.

John Milton

There let Hymen oft appear
In saffron robe, with taper clear,
And pomp, and feast, and revelry,
With mask, and antique pageantry ;
Such sights as youthful poets dream
On summer eves by haunted stream.
Then to the well-trod stage anon,
If Jonson's learned sock be on,
Or sweetest Shakespeare, Fancy's child,
Warble his native wood-notes wild.

    And ever against eating cares
Lap me in soft Lydian airs
Married to immortal verse,
Such as the meeting soul may pierce
In notes, with many a winding bout
Of linked sweetness long drawn out,
With wanton heed and giddy cunning,
The melting voice through mazes running,
Untwisting all the chains that tie
The hidden soul of harmony ;
That Orpheus' self may heave his head
From golden slumber, on a bed
Of heaped Elysian flowers, and hear
Such strains as would have won the ear
Of Pluto, to have quite set free
His half-regained Eurydice.

    These delights if thou canst give,
Mirth, with thee I mean to live.

IL PENSEROSO

HENCE, vain deluding Joys,
    The brood of Folly without father bred !

John Milton

How little you bestead
    Or fill the fixed mind with all your toys!
Dwell in some idle brain,
    And fancies fond with gaudy shapes possess
As thick and numberless
    As the gay motes that people the sunbeams,
Or likest hovering dreams,
    The fickle pensioners of Morpheus' train.

    But hail, thou goddess sage and holy,
Hail, divinest Melancholy!
Whose saintly visage is too bright
To hit the sense of human sight,
And therefore to our weaker view
O'erlaid with black, staid Wisdom's hue;
Black, but such as in esteem
Prince Memnon's sister might beseem,
Or that starred Ethiop queen that strove
To set her beauty's praise above
The sea-nymphs, and their powers offended:
Yet thou art higher far descended:
Thee bright-haired Vesta, long of yore,
To solitary Saturn bore;
His daughter she; in Saturn's reign
Such mixture was not held a stain:
Oft in glimmering bowers and glades
He met her, and in secret shades
Of woody Ida's inmost grove,
While yet there was no fear of Jove.
    Come, pensive Nun, devout and pure,
Sober, steadfast, and demure,
All in a robe of darkest grain
Flowing with majestic train

114

John Milton

And sable stole of Cipres lawn
Over thy decent shoulders drawn :
Come, but keep thy wonted state,
With even step and musing gait,
And looks commercing with the skies,
Thy rapt soul sitting in thine eyes :
There, held in holy passion still,
Forget thyself to marble, till
With a sad leaden downward cast
Thou fix them on the earth as fast :
And join with thee calm Peace, and Quiet,
Spare Fast, that oft with gods doth diet,
And hears the Muses in a ring
Aye round about Jove's altar sing :
And add to these retired Leisure
That in trim gardens takes his pleasure :—
But first and chiefest, with thee bring
Him that yon soars on golden wing,
Guiding the fiery-wheeled throne,
The cherub Contemplation;
And the mute Silence hist along,
'Less Philomel will deign a song
In her sweetest, saddest plight,
Smoothing the rugged brow of Night,
While Cynthia checks her dragon yoke
Gently o'er the accustomed oak.
    Sweet bird, that shunn'st the noise of folly,
Most musical, most melancholy !.
Thee, chauntress, oft the woods among,
I woo to hear thy even-song ;
And missing thee, I walk unseen
On the dry smooth-shaven green,
To behold the wandering Moon
Riding near her highest noon,

John Milton

Like one that had been led astray
Through the heaven's wide pathless way,
And oft, as if her head she bowed,
Stooping through a fleecy cloud.

   Oft on a plat of rising ground
I hear the far-off curfew sound
Over some wide-watered shore,
Swinging slow with sullen roar;
Or, if the air will not permit,
Some still, removed place will fit,
Where glowing embers through the room
Teach light to counterfeit a gloom;
Far from all resort of mirth,
Save the cricket on the hearth,
Or the bellman's drowsy charm
To bless the doors from nightly harm.

   Or let my lamp at midnight hour
Be seen in some high lonely tower,
Where I may oft out-watch the Bear
With thrice-great Hermes, or unsphere
The spirit of Plato, to unfold
What worlds or what vast regions hold
The immortal mind, that hath forsook
Her mansion in this fleshly nook:
And of those demons that are found
In fire, air, flood, or under ground,
Whose power hath a true consent
With planet, or with element.
Sometime let gorgeous Tragedy
In sceptered pall come sweeping by,
Presenting Thebes, or Pelops' line,
Or the tale of Troy divine;
Or what (though rare) of later age
Ennobled hath the buskined stage.

John Milton

But, O sad Virgin, that thy power
Might raise Musaeus from his bower,
Or bid the soul of Orpheus sing
Such notes as, warbled to the string,
Drew iron tears down Pluto's cheek
And made Hell grant what Love did seek !
Or call up him that left half-told
The story of Cambuscan bold,
Of Camball, and of Algarsife,
And who had Canace to wife
That owned the virtuous ring and glass ;
And of the wondrous horse of brass
On which the Tartar king did ride :
And if aught else great bards beside
In sage and solemn tunes have sung
Of tourneys and of trophies hung,
Of forests and enchantments drear,
Where more is meant than meets the ear.
   Thus, Night, oft see me in thy pale career,
Till civil-suited Morn appear,
Not tricked and frounced as she was wont
With the Attic Boy to hunt,
But kercheft in a comely cloud
While rocking winds are piping loud,
Or ushered with a shower still,
When the gust hath blown his fill,
Ending on the rustling leaves
With minute drops from off the eaves.
And when the sun begins to fling
His flaring beams, me, goddess, bring
To arched walks of twilight groves,
And shadows brown, that Sylvan loves,
Of pine, or monumental oak,
Where the rude axe, with heaved stroke,

John Milton

Was never heard the nymphs to daunt,
Or fright them from their hallowed haunt.
There in close covert by some brook,
Where no profaner eye may look,
Hide me from day's garish eye,
While the bee with honeyed thigh,
That at her flowery work doth sing,
And the waters murmuring,
With such consort as they keep
Entice the dewy-feathered Sleep;
And let some strange mysterious dream
Wave at his wings in airy stream
Of lively portraiture displayed,
Softly on my eyelids laid:
And, as I wake, sweet music breathe
Above, about, or underneath,
Sent by some Spirit to mortals good,
Or the unseen Genius of the wood.
   But let my due feet never fail
To walk the studious cloister's pale,
And love the high-embowed roof,
With antique pillars massy proof,
And storied windows richly dight
Casting a dim religious light.
There let the pealing organ blow
To the full-voiced quire below
In service high and anthems clear,
As may with sweetness, through mine ear,
Dissolve me into ecstasies,
And bring all Heaven before mine eyes.
   And may at last my weary age
Find out the peaceful hermitage,
The hairy gown and mossy cell
Where I may sit and rightly spell

John Milton

Of every star that heaven doth shew,
And every herb that sips the dew;
Till old experience do attain
To something like prophetic strain.
    These pleasures, Melancholy, give,
And I with thee will choose to live.

LYCIDAS

Elegy on a Friend drowned in the Irish Channel, 1637

YET once more, O ye laurels, and once more
Ye myrtles brown, with ivy never sere,
I come to pluck your berries harsh and crude,
And with forced fingers rude
Shatter your leaves before the mellowing year.
Bitter constraint and sad occasion dear
Compels me to disturb your season due:
For Lycidas is dead, dead ere his prime,
Young Lycidas, and hath not left his peer.
Who would not sing for Lycidas? he knew
Himself to sing, and build the lofty rhyme.
He must not float upon his watery bier
Unwept, and welter to the parching wind,
Without the meed of some melodious tear.

    Begin, then, Sisters of the sacred well
That from beneath the seat of Jove doth spring;
Begin, and somewhat loudly sweep the string.
Hence withdenial vain and coy excuse:
So may some gentle Muse
With lucky words favour my destined urn;
And, as he passes, turn
And bid fair peace be to my sable shroud.

John Milton

For we were nursed upon the self-same hill,
Fed the same flock by fountain, shade, and rill:
Together both, ere the high lawns appeared
Under the opening eyelids of the Morn,
We drove a-field, and both together heard
What time the grey-fly winds her sultry horn,
Battening our flocks with the fresh dews of night,
Oft till the star that rose at evening bright
Toward heaven's descent had sloped his westering
    wheel.
Meanwhile the rural ditties were not mute,
Tempered to the oaten flute,
Rough Satyrs danced, and Fauns with cloven heel
From the glad sound would not be absent long;
And old Damoetas loved to hear our song.

But, oh! the heavy change, now thou art gone,
Now thou art gone and never must return!
Thee, Shepherd, thee the woods and desert caves
With wild thyme and the gadding vine o'ergrown,
And all their echoes, mourn:
The willows and the hazel copses green
Shall now no more be seen
Fanning their joyous leaves to thy soft lays.
As killing as the canker to the rose,
Or taint-worm to the weanling herds that graze,
Or frost to flowers, that their gay wardrobe wear
When first the white-thorn blows;
Such, Lycidas, thy loss to shepherd's ear.

Where were ye, Nymphs, when the remorseless deep
Closed o'er the head of your loved Lycidas?
For neither were ye playing on the steep

John Milton

Where your old bards, the famous Druids, lie,
Nor on the shaggy top of Mona high,
Nor yet where Deva spreads her wizard stream :
Ay me ! I fondly dream—
Had ye been there . . . For what could that have done ?
What could the Muse herself that Orpheus bore,
The Muse herself, for her enchanting son,
Whom universal nature did lament,
When by the rout that made the hideous roar
His gory visage down the stream was sent,
Down the swift Hebrus to the Lesbian shore ?

Alas ! what boots it with incessant care
To tend the homely, slighted, shepherd's trade,
And strictly meditate the thankless Muse?
Were it not better done, as others use,
To sport with Amaryllis in the shade,
Or with the tangles of Neaera's hair ?
Fame is the spur that the clear spirit doth raise
(That last infirmity of noble mind)
To scorn delights, and live laborious days ;
But the fair guerdon when we hope to find,
And think to burst out into sudden blaze,
Comes the blind Fury with the abhorred shears,
And slits the thin-spun life.   ' But not the praise,'
Phoebus replied, and touched my trembling ears ;
' Fame is no plant that grows on mortal soil,
Nor in the glistering foil
Set off to the world, nor in broad rumour lies :
But lives and spreads aloft by those pure eyes
And perfect witness of all-judging Jove ;
As he pronounces lastly on each deed,
Of so much fame in heaven expect thy meed.'

John Milton

O fountain Arethuse, and thou honoured flood,
Smooth-sliding Mincius, crowned with vocal reeds,
That strain I heard was of a higher mood.
But now my oat proceeds,
And listens to the herald of the sea
That came in Neptune's plea.
He asked the waves, and asked the felon winds,
What hard mishap hath doomed this gentle swain?
And questioned every gust of rugged wings
That blows from off each beaked promontory.
They knew not of his story;
And sage Hippotades their answer brings,
That not a blast was from his dungeon strayed;
The air was calm, and on the level brine
Sleek Panope with all her sisters played.
It was that fatal and perfidious bark
Built in the eclipse, and rigged with curses dark,
That sunk so low that sacred head of thine.

Next Camus, reverend sire, went footing slow,
His mantle hairy, and his bonnet sedge
Inwrought with figures dim, and on the edge
Like to that sanguine flower inscribed with woe.
'Ah! who hath reft,' quoth he, 'my dearest pledge?'
Last came, and last did go
The Pilot of the Galilean lake;
Two massy keys he bore of metals twain
(The golden opes, the iron shuts amain);
He shook his mitred locks, and stern bespake:
'How well could I have spared for thee, young swain,
Enow of such, as for their bellies' sake
Creep and intrude and climb into the fold!
Of other care they little reckoning make
Than how to scramble at the shearers' feast,

John Milton

And shove away the worthy bidden guest.
Blind mouths! that scarce themselves know how to
    hold
A sheep-hook, or have learned aught else the least
That to the faithful herdman's art belongs!
What recks it them? What need they? They are
    sped;
And when they list, their lean and flashy songs
Grate on their scrannel pipes of wretched straw;
The hungry sheep look up, and are not fed,
But, swoln with wind and the rank mist they draw,
Rot inwardly, and foul contagion spread:
Besides what the grim wolf with privy paw
Daily devours apace, and nothing said:
But that two-handed engine at the door
Stands ready to smite once, and smite no more.'

    Return, Alpheus; the dread voice is past
That shrunk thy streams; return, Sicilian Muse,
And call the vales, and bid them hither cast
Their bells and flowerets of a thousand hues.
Ye valleys low, where the mild whispers use
Of shades, and wanton winds, and gushing brooks
On whose fresh lap the swart star sparely looks;
Throw hither all your quaint enamelled eyes
That on the green turf suck the honeyed showers
And purple all the ground with vernal flowers.
Bring the rathe primrose that forsaken dies,
The tufted crow-toe, and pale jessamine,
The white pink, and the pansy freaked with jet,
The glowing violet,
The musk-rose, and the well-attired woodbine,
With cowslips wan that hang the pensive head,
And every flower that sad embroidery wears:

John Milton

Bid amaranthus all his beauty shed,
And daffadillies fill their cups with tears,
To strew the laureate hearse where Lycid lies.
For so to interpose a little ease,
Let our frail thoughts dally with false surmise :—
Ay me ! whilst thee the shores and sounding seas
Wash far away, where'er thy bones are hurled,
Whether beyond the stormy Hebrides,
Where thou perhaps, under the whelming tide,
Visitest the bottom of the monstrous world ;
Or whether thou, to our moist vows denied,
Sleep'st by the fable of Bellerus old,
Where the great Vision of the guarded mount
Looks toward Namancos and Bayona's hold :
Look homeward, Angel, now, and melt with ruth :
And, O ye dolphins, waft the hapless youth !

  Weep no more, woeful shepherds, weep no more,
For Lycidas, your sorrow, is not dead,
Sunk though he be beneath the watery floor :
So sinks the day-star in the ocean bed,
And yet anon repairs his drooping head
And tricks his beams, and with new-spangled ore
Flames in the forehead of the morning sky :
So Lycidas sunk low, but mounted high
Through the dear might of Him that walked the waves ;
Where, other groves and other streams along,
With nectar pure his oozy locks he laves,
And hears the unexpressive nuptial song
In the blest kingdoms meek of joy and love.
There entertain him all the Saints above,
In solemn troops, and sweet societies,
That sing, and singing in their glory move,
And wipe the tears for ever from his eyes.

124

John Milton

Now, Lycidas, the shepherds weep no more;
Henceforth thou art the Genius of the shore,
In thy large recompense, and shalt be good
To all that wander in that perilous flood.

    Thus sang the uncouth swain to the oaks and rills,
While the still morn went out with sandals grey;
He touched the tender stops of various quills,
With eager thought warbling his Doric lay:
And now the sun had stretched out all the hills,
And now was dropt into the western bay:
At last he rose, and twitched his mantle blue:
To-morrow to fresh woods, and pastures new.

ON HIS BLINDNESS

WHEN I consider how my light is spent
  Ere half my days, in this dark world and wide,
  And that one talent which is death to hide
Lodged with me useless, though my soul more bent
To serve therewith my Maker, and present
  My true account, lest He returning chide,—
  Doth God exact day-labour, light denied?
I fondly ask:—But Patience, to prevent
That murmur, soon replies: God doth not need
  Either man's work, or His own gifts; who best
    Bear His mild yoke, they serve Him best: His state
Is kingly; thousands at His bidding speed
  And post o'er land and ocean without rest:
    They also serve who only stand and wait.

125

John Milton

METHOUGHT I saw my late espoused saint
   Brought to me like Alkestis from the grave,
   Whom Jove's great son to her glad husband gave,
Rescued from death by force, though pale and faint.
Mine, as whom washed from spot of child-bed taint
   Purification in the Old Law did save,
   And such as yet once more I trust to have
Full sight of her in Heaven without restraint,
Came vested all in white, pure as her mind ;
   Her face was veiled, yet to my fancied sight
Love, sweetness, goodness in her person shined
   So clear as in no face with more delight.
But oh ! as to embrace me she inclined,
   I waked, she fled, and day brought back my night.

WHAT needs my Shakespeare, for his honoured bones,
The labour of an age in piled stones?
Or that his hallowed reliques should be hid
Under a star-y-pointing pyramid?
Dear son of memory, great heir of fame,
What need'st thou such weak witness of thy name?
Thou in our wonder and astonishment
Hast built thyself a live-long monument.
For whilst, to shame of slow-endeavouring art
Thy easy numbers flow, and that each heart
Hath from the leaves of thy unvalued book
Those Delphic lines with deep impression took,
Then thou, our fancy of itself bereaving,
Dost make us marble with too much conceiving ;
And so sepulchered in such pomp dost lie,
That kings for such a tomb would wish to die.

John Milton

SONG ON MAY MORNING

Now the bright morning star, day's harbinger,
Comes dancing from the East, and leads with her
The flowery May, who from her green lap throws
The yellow cowslip and the pale primrose.
    Hail, bounteous May, that dost inspire
    Mirth and youth and young desire!
    Woods and groves are of thy dressing,
    Hill and dale doth boast thy blessing.
Thus we salute thee with our early song,
    And welcome thee and wish thee long.

INVOCATION TO SABRINA, FROM COMUS

    SABRINA fair!
  Listen, where thou art sitting,
Under the glassy, cool, translucent wave,
  In twisted braids of lilies knitting
The loose train of thine amber-dripping hair,
Listen for dear honour's sake,
Goddess of the silver lake,
    Listen and save!
Listen, and appear to us,
In name of great Oceanus,
By the earth-shaking Neptune's mace,
And Tethys' grave majestic pace;
By hoary Nereus' wrinkled look,
And the Carpathian wizard's hook;
By scaly Triton's winding shell,
And old soothsaying Glaucus' spell;

John Milton

By Leucothea's lovely hands,
And her son that rules the strands;
By Thetis' tinsel-slippered feet,
And the songs of sirens sweet;
By dead Parthenope's dear tomb,
And fair Ligea's golden comb,
Wherewith she sits on diamond rocks
Sleeking her soft alluring locks;
By all the nymphs that nightly dance
Upon thy streams with wily glance;
Rise, rise, and heave thy rosy head
From thy coral-paven bed,
And bridle in thy headlong wave,
Till thou our summons answered have.
    Listen and save!

INVOCATION TO ECHO, FROM COMUS

SWEET Echo, sweetest Nymph, that liv'st unseen
    Within thine airy shell
By slow Meander's margent green,
And in the violet-embroidered vale,
    Where the love-lorn nightingale
Nightly to thee her sad song mourneth well;
Canst thou not tell me of a single pair
    That likest thy Narcissus are?
    O, if thou have
    Hid them in some flowery cave,
    Tell me but where,
Sweet Queen of Parley, daughter of the Sphere!
So mayest thou be translated to the skies,
And give resounding grace to all Heaven's harmonies.

128

John Milton

To the ocean now I fly,
And those happy climes that lie
Where day never shuts his eye,
Up in the broad fields of the sky.
There I suck the liquid air,
All amid the gardens fair
Of Hesperus, and his daughters three
That sing about the golden tree.
Along the crisped shades and bowers
Revels the spruce and jocund Spring;
The Graces and the rosy-bosomed Hours
Thither all their bounties bring.
There eternal Summer dwells,
And west winds with musky wing
About the cedarn alleys fling
Nard and cassia's balmy smells.
Iris there with humid bow
Waters the odorous banks, that blow
Flowers of more mingled hue
Than her purpled scarf can show,
And drenches with Elysian dew
(List, mortals, if your ears be true)
Beds of hyacinth and roses,
Where young Adonis oft reposes,
Waxing well of his deep wound.
In slumber soft, and on the ground
Sadly sits the Assyrian queen.
But far above, in spangled sheen,
Celestial Cupid, her famed son, advanced,
Holds his dear Psyche, sweet entranced,

James Graham, Marquis of Montrose

After her wandering labours long,
Till free consent the gods among
Make her his eternal bride,
And from her fair unspotted side
Two blissful twins are to be born,
Youth and Joy; so Jove hath sworn.

But now my task is smoothly done:
I can fly or I can run
Quickly to the green earth's end,
Where the bowed welkin slow doth bend,
And from thence can soar as soon
To the corners of the moon.
Mortals that would follow me,
Love Virtue; she alone is free,
She can teach ye how to climb
Higher than the sphery chime;
Or if feeble Virtue were,
Heaven itself would stoop to her.

JAMES GRAHAM, MARQUIS OF MONTROSE

1612-1650

THE VIGIL OF DEATH

LET them bestow on every airth a limb,
Then open all my veins, that I may swim
To thee, my Maker! in that crimson lake.
Then place my parboiled head upon a stake—
Scatter my ashes—strew them in the air:
Lord! since thou know'st where all these atoms are,
I'm hopeful thou'lt recover once my dust,
And confident thou'lt raise me with the just.

130

Richard Crashaw

RICHARD CRASHAW
1615(?)-1652

ON A PRAYER-BOOK SENT TO MRS. M. R.

Lo, here a little volume, but great book!
A nest of new-born sweets,
Whose native pages, 'sdaining
To be thus folded, and complaining
Of these ignoble sheets,
Affect more comely bands,
Fair one, from thy kind hands,
And confidently look
To find the rest
Of a rich binding in your breast!

It is in one choice handful, heaven; and all
Heaven's royal hosts encamped, thus small
To prove that true schools use to tell,
A thousand angels in one point can dwell.

It is love's great artillery,
Which here contracts itself, and comes to lie
Close couched in your white bosom; and from thence,
As from a snowy fortress of defence,
Against your ghostly foe to take your part,
And fortify the hold of your chaste heart.

It is an armoury of light;
Let constant use but keep it bright,
　You'll find it yields
To holy hands and humble hearts
　More swords and shields
Than sin hath snares, or hell hath darts.

Richard Crashaw

Only be sure
The hands be pure
That hold these weapons, and the eyes
Those of turtles, chaste, and true,
   Wakeful, and wise.
Here's a friend shall fight for you;
Hold but this book before your heart,
Let prayer alone to play his part.

But, O! the heart
That studies this high art
Must be a sure housekeeper,   -
And yet no sleeper.
Dear soul, be strong;
Mercy will come ere long,
And bring her bosom full of blessings,
Flowers of never-fading graces,
To make immortal dressings
For worthy souls, whose wise embraces
Store up themselves for Him who is alone
The Spouse of virgins, and the Virgin's Son.

But if the noble Bridegroom when He comes
Shall find the wandering heart from home,
   Leaving her chaste abode
   To gad abroad,
Amongst the gay mates of the god of flies
   To take her pleasure, and to play
   And keep the Devil's holy day;
To dance in the sunshine of some smiling,
   But beguiling

Richard Crashaw

Spheres of sweet and sugared lies,
  Some slippery pair
  Of false, perhaps, as fair,
Flattering, but forswearing, eyes;

Doubtless some other heart
    Will get the start
Meanwhile, and, stepping in before,
Will take possession of that sacred store
  Of hidden sweets, and holy joys,
Words which are not heard with ears—
  These tumultuous shops of noise—
  Effectual whispers, whose still voice
The soul itself more feels than hears;

Amorous languishments, luminous trances,
  Sights which are not seen with eyes,
Spiritual and soul-piercing glances
  Whose pure and subtle lightning flies
Home to the heart, and sets the house on fire
And melts it down in sweet desire,
    Yet does not stay
To ask the window's leave to pass that way;

Delicious deaths, soft exhalations
Of soul; dear and divine annihilations;
  A thousand unknown rites
  Of joys, and rarefied delights;

A hundred thousand goods, glories, and graces,
  And many a mystic thing,
  Which the divine embraces
Of the dear Spouse of spirits with them will bring
  For which it is no shame
That dull mortality must not know a name.

Richard Crashaw

Of all this store
Of blessings, and ten thousand more,
   If when He come
He find the heart from home,
   Doubtless He will unload
Himself some otherwhere,
   And pour abroad
   His precious sweets,
On the fair soul whom first He meets.

O fair ! O fortunate ! O rich ! O dear !
   O happy, and thrice happy she,
   Dear silver-breasted dove,
   Whoe'er she be,
   Whose early love
   With winged vows
Makes haste to meet her morning Spouse,
And close with His immortal kisses !
   Happy, indeed, who never misses
   To improve that precious hour,
     And every day
     Seize her sweet prey,
   All fresh and fragrant as He rises,
   Dropping, with a balmy shower,
   A delicious dew of spices.

O, let the blessful heart hold fast
Her heavenly armful, she shall taste
At once ten thousand paradises !
     She shall have power
     To rifle and deflower
The rich and roseal spring of those rare sweets,
   Which with a swelling bosom there she meets ;

Richard Crashaw

Boundless and infinite, bottomless treasures
    Of pure inebriating pleasures;
Happy proof she shall discover,
    What joy, what bliss,
    How many heavens at once it is,
To have a God become her lover!

TO THE MORNING

Satisfaction for Sleep

WHAT succour can I hope the Muse will send,
Whose drowsiness hath wronged the Muse's friend?
What hope, Aurora, to propitiate thee,
Unless the Muse sing my apology?
O! in that morning of my shame, when I
Lay folded up in sleep's captivity;
How at the sight didst thou draw back thine eyes,
Into thy modest veil! how didst thou rise
Twice dyed in thine own blushes, and didst run
To draw the curtains and awake the sun!
Who, rousing his illustrious tresses, came,
And seeing the loathed object, hid for shame
His head in thy fair bosom, and still hides
Me from his patronage; I pray, he chides;
And, pointing to dull Morpheus, bids me take
My own Apollo, try if I can make
His Lethe be my Helicon, and see
If Morpheus have a Muse to wait on me.
Hence 'tis my humble fancy finds no wings,
No nimble raptures, starts to heaven and brings
Enthusiastic flames, such as can give
Marrow to my plump genius, make it live
Dressed in the glorious madness of a muse,
Whose feet can walk the milky-way, and choose

135

Richard Crashaw

Her starry throne; whose holy heats can warm
The grave, and hold up an exalted arm
To lift me from my lazy urn, and climb
Upon the stooped shoulders of old Time,
And trace eternity.   But all is dead,
All these delicious hopes are buried
In the deep wrinkles of his angry brow,
Where mercy cannot find them; but, O thou
Bright lady of the morn, pity doth lie
So warm in thy soft breast, it cannot die;
Have mercy, then, and when he next doth rise,
O, meet the angry god, invade his eyes,
And stroke his radiant cheeks; one timely kiss
Will kill his anger, and revive my bliss.
So to the treasure of thy pearly dew
Thrice will I pay three tears, to show how true
My grief is; so my wakeful lay shall knock
At the oriental gates, and duly mock
The early lark's shrill orisons to be
An anthem at the day's nativity.
And the same rosy-fingered hand of thine,
That shuts night's dying eyes, shall open mine.
   But thou, faint god of sleep, forget that I
Was ever known to be thy votary.
No more my pillow shall thine altar be,
Nor will I offer any more to thee
Myself a melting sacrifice; I 'm born
Again a fresh child of the buxom morn,
Heir of the sun's first beams; why threat'st thou so?
Why dost thou shake thy leaden sceptre?   Go,
Bestow thy poppy upon wakeful woe,
Sickness and sorrow, whose pale lids ne'er know
Thy downy finger dwell upon their eyes;
Shut in their tears, shut out their miseries.

Richard Crashaw

LOVE, brave Virtue's younger brother,
Erst hath made my heart a mother.
She consults the anxious spheres,
To calculate her young son's years;
She asks if sad or saving powers
Gave omen to his infant hours;
She asks each star that then stood by
If poor Love shall live or die.

Ah, my heart, is that the way?
Are these the beams that rule thy day?
Thou know'st a face in whose each look
Beauty lays ope Love's fortune-book,
On whose fair revolutions wait
The obsequious motions of Love's fate.
Ah, my heart! her eyes and she
Have taught thee new astrology.
Howe'er Love's native hours were set,
Whatever starry synod met,
'Tis in the mercy of her eye,
If poor Love shall live or die.

If those sharp rays, putting on
Points of death, bid Love be gone;
Though the heavens in council sat
To crown an uncontrolled fate;
Though their best aspects twined upon
The kindest constellation,
Cast amorous glances on his birth,
And whispered the confederate earth

137

Richard Crashaw

To pave his paths with all the good
That warms the bed of youth and blood :—
Love has no plea against her eye ;
Beauty frowns, and Love must die.

But if her milder influence move,
And gild the hopes of humble Love ;—
Though heaven's inauspicious eye
Lay black on Love's nativity ;
Though every diamond in Jove's crown
Fixed his forehead to a frown ;—
Her eye a strong appeal can give,
Beauty smiles, and Love shall live.

O, if Love shall live, O where,
But in her eye, or in her ear,
In her breast, or in her breath,
Shall I hide poor Love from death?
For in the life aught else can give,
Love shall die, although he live.

Or, if Love shall die, O where,
But in her eye, or in her ear,
In her breath, or in her breast,
Shall I build his funeral nest?
While Love shall thus entombed lie,
Love shall live, although he die !

ON MR. G. HERBERT'S BOOK

*Entitled, ' The Temple of Sacred Poems,' sent to a
Gentlewoman*

KNOW you, fair, on what you look ?
Divinest love lies in this book,

Richard Crashaw

Expecting fire from your eyes,
To kindle this his sacrifice.
When your hands untie these strings,
Think you 've an angel by the wings ;
One that gladly will be nigh
To wait upon each morning sigh,
To flutter in the balmy air
Of your well perfumed prayer.
These white plumes of his he 'll lend you,
Which every day to heaven will send you,
To take acquaintance of the sphere,
And all the smooth-faced kindred there.
And though Herbert's name do owe
These devotions, fairest, know
That while I lay them on the shrine
Of your white hand, they are mine.

WISHES TO HIS SUPPOSED MISTRESS

WHOE'ER she be,
That not impossible She
  That shall command my heart and me :

Where'er she lie,
Locked up from mortal eye
In shady leaves of destiny :

Till that ripe birth
Of studied Fate stand forth, .
And teach her fair steps tread our earth :

Till that divine
Idea take a shrine
Of crystal flesh, through which to shine :

Richard Crashaw

Meet you her, my Wishes,
Bespeak her to my blisses,
And be ye called, my absent kisses.

I wish her beauty
That owes not all its duty
To gaudy tire, or glist'ring shoe-tie.

Something more than
Taffata or tissue can,
Or rampant feather, or rich fan.

More than the spoil
Of shop, or silkworm's toil,
Or a bought blush, or a set smile.

A face that's best
By its own beauty drest,
And can alone commend the rest.

A cheek where youth
And blood, with pen of truth,
Write what the reader sweetly rueth.

A cheek where grows
More than a morning rose,
Which to no box his being owes.

Lips where all day
A lover's kiss may play,
Yet carry nothing thence away.

Richard Crashaw

Looks that oppress
Their richest tires, but dress
And clothe their simple nakedness.

Eyes that displace
Their neighbour diamond, and out-face
That sunshine by their own sweet grace.

Tresses that wear
Jewels, but to declare
How much themselves more precious are ;

Whose native ray
Can tame the wanton day
Of gems that in their bright shades play.

Each ruby there,
Or pearl that dare appear,
Be its own blush, be its own tear.

A well-tamed heart,
For whose more noble smart
Love may be long choosing a dart.

Eyes that bestow
Full quivers on love's bow,
Yet pay less arrows than they owe.

Smiles that can warm
The blood, yet teach a charm,
That chastity shall take no harm.

Richard Crashaw

Blushes that bin
The burnish of no sin,
Nor flames of aught too hot within.

Joys that confess,
Virtue their mistress,
And have no other head to dress.

Fears fond and slight
As the coy bride's, when night
First does the longing lover right.

Tears quickly fled,
And vain, as those are shed
For a dying maidenhead.

Soft silken hours,
Open suns, shady bowers ;
'Bove all, nothing within that lowers.

Days that need borrow
No part of their good-morrow
From a fore-spent night of sorrow.

Days that in spite
Of darkness, by the light
Of a clear mind, are day all night.

Nights, sweet as they,
Made short by lovers' play,
Yet long by the absence of the day.

Richard Crashaw

Life, that dares send
A challenge to his end,
And when it comes, say, Welcome, friend !

Sydneian showers
Of sweet discourse, whose powers
Can crown old winter's head with flowers.

Whate'er delight
Can make day's forehead bright,
Or give down to the wings of night.

In her whole frame,
Have Nature all the name,
Art and ornament the shame.

Her flattery,
Picture and poesy,
Her counsel her own virtue be.

I wish her store
Of worth may leave her poor
Of wishes; and I wish——no more.

Now, if Time knows
That Her, whose radiant brows
Weave them a garland of my vows;

Her whose just bays
My future hopes can raise,
A trophy to her present praise;

Richard Crashaw

Her that dares be
What these lines wish to see;
I seek no further, it is She.

'Tis She, and here,
Lo! I unclothe and clear
My wishes' cloudy character.

May she enjoy it
Whose merit dare apply it,
But modesty dares still deny it!

Such worth as this is
Shall fix my flying wishes,
And determine them to kisses.

Let her full glory,
My fancies, fly before ye;
Be ye my fictions:—but her story.

QUEM VIDISTIS PASTORES, ETC.

A HYMN OF THE NATIVITY, SUNG BY THE SHEPHERDS

Chorus

COME, we shepherds whose blest sight
Hath met Love's noon in Nature's night;
Come lift we up our loftier song,
And wake the sun that lies too long.

Richard Crashaw

To all our world of well-stol'n joy
    He slept, and dreamt of no such thing,
While we found out Heaven's fairer eye,
    And kissed the cradle of our King;
Tell him he rises now too late
To show us aught worth looking at.

Tell him we now can show him more
    Than he e'er showed to mortal sight,
Than he himself e'er saw before,
    Which to be seen needs not his light:
Tell him, Tityrus, where th' hast been,
Tell him, Thyrsis, what th' hast seen.

Tityrus

Gloomy night embraced the place
    Where the noble infant lay:
The babe looked up, and showed His face;
    In spite of darkness it was day.
It was Thy day, sweet, and did rise,
Not from the East, but from Thine eyes.
Chorus.   It was Thy day, sweet, and did rise,
        Not from the East, but from Thine eyes.

Thyrsis

Winter chid aloud, and sent
    The angry North to wage his wars:
The North forgot his fierce intent,
    And left perfumes instead of scars.
By those sweet eyes' persuasive powers,
Where he meant frosts he scattered flowers.
Chorus.   By those sweet eyes' persuasive powers,
        Where he meant frosts he scattered flowers.

Richard Crashaw

Both

We saw Thee in Thy balmy nest,
   Young dawn of our eternal day;
We saw Thine eyes break from the East,
   And chase the trembling shades away:
We saw Thee, and we blest the sight,
We saw Thee by Thine own sweet light.

Tityrus

Poor world, said I, what wilt thou do
   To entertain this starry stranger?
Is this the best thou canst bestow—
   A cold and not too cleanly manger?
Contend the powers of heaven and earth,
To fit a bed for this huge birth.
Chorus.   Contend the powers of heaven and earth,
      To fit a bed for this huge birth.

Thyrsis

Proud world, said I, cease your contest,
   And let the mighty babe alone,
The phœnix builds the phœnix' nest,
   Love's architecture is his own.
The babe, whose birth embraves this morn,
Made His own bed ere He was born.
Chorus.   The babe, whose birth embraves this morn,
      Made His own bed ere He was born.

Tityrus

I saw the curled drops, soft and slow,
   Come hovering o'er the place's head,
Off'ring their whitest sheets of snow,
   To furnish the fair infant's bed.

Richard Crashaw

Forbear, said I, be not too bold,
Your fleece is white, but 'tis too cold.

Thyrsis

I saw th' obsequious seraphim
    Their rosy fleece of fire bestow,
For well they now can spare their wings,
    Since Heaven itself lies here below.
Well done, said I ; but are you sure
Your down, so warm, will pass for pure ?
Chorus.   Well done, said I ; but are you sure
        Your down, so warm, will pass for pure ?

Both

No, no, your King's not yet to seek
    Where to repose His royal head ;
See, see how soon His new-bloomed cheek
    'Twixt mother's breasts is gone to bed.
Sweet choice, said we ; no way but so,
Not to lie cold, yet sleep in snow !
Chorus.   Sweet choice, said we ; no way but so,
        Not to lie cold, yet sleep in snow !

Full Chorus

Welcome all wonders in one sight !
    Eternity shut in a span !
Summer in winter ! day in night !

Chorus

Heaven in earth ! and God in man !
Great little one, whose all-embracing birth
Lifts earth to Heaven, stoops Heaven to earth,

Richard Crashaw

Welcome, tho' nor to gold, nor silk,
　To more than Cæsar's birthright is:
Two sister seas of virgin's milk,
　With many a rarely-tempered kiss,
That breathes at once both maid and mother,
Warms in the one, cools in the other.

She sings Thy tears asleep, and dips
　Her kisses in Thy weeping eye;
She spreads the red leaves of Thy lips,
　That in their buds yet blushing lie.
She 'gainst those mother diamonds tries
The points of her young eagle's eyes.

Welcome—tho' not to those gay flies,
　Gilded i' th' beams of earthly kings,
Slippery souls in smiling eyes—
　But to poor shepherds, homespun things,
Whose wealth's their flocks, whose wit's to be
Well read in their simplicity.

Yet, when young April's husband show'rs
　Shall bless the fruitful Maia's bed,
We'll bring the first-born of her flowers,
　To kiss Thy feet and crown Thy head.
To Thee, dread Lamb! whose love must keep
The shepherds while they feed their sheep.

To Thee, meek Majesty, soft King
　Of simple graces and sweet loves!
Each of us his lamb will bring,
　Each his pair of silver doves!
At last, in fire of Thy fair eyes,
Ourselves become our own best sacrifice!

Richard Crashaw

MUSIC'S DUEL

Now westward Sol had spent the richest beams
Of noon's high glory, when, hard by the streams
Of Tiber, on the scene of a green plat,
Under protection of an oak, there sat
A sweet lute's master: in whose gentle airs
He lost the day's heat, and his own hot cares.
   Close in the covert of the leaves there stood
A nightingale, come from the neighbouring wood :—
The sweet inhabitant of each glad tree,
Their muse, their Syren, harmless Syren she,—
There stood she list'ning, and did entertain
The music's soft report, and mould the same
In her own murmurs, that whatever mood
His curious fingers lent, her voice made good.
The man perceived his rival, and her art ;
Disposed to give the light-foot lady sport,
Awakes his lute, and 'gainst the fight to come
Informs it, in a sweet *prœludium*
Of closer strains ; and ere the war begin
He slightly skirmishes on every string,
Charged with a flying touch ; and straightway she
Carves out her dainty voice as readily
Into a thousand sweet distinguished tones ;
And reckons up in soft divisions
Quick volumes of wild notes, to let him know
By that shrill taste she could do something too.
   His nimble hand's instinct then taught each string
A cap'ring cheerfulness ; and made them sing
To their own dance ; now negligently rash
He throws his arm, and with a long-drawn dash
Blends all together, then distinctly trips
From this to that, then, quick returning, skips

149

Richard Crashaw

And snatches this again, and pauses there.
She measures every measure, everywhere
Meets art with art; sometimes, as if in doubt—
Not perfect yet, and fearing to be out—
Trails her plain ditty in one long-spun note
Through the sleek passage of her open throat:
A clear unwrinkled song; then doth she point it
With tender accents, and severely joint it
By short diminutives, that, being reared
In controverting warbles evenly shared,
With her sweet self she wrangles; he, amazed
That from so small a channel should be raised
The torrent of a voice whose melody
Could melt into such sweet variety,
Strains higher yet, that, tickled with rare art,
The tattling strings—each breathing in his part—
Most kindly do fall out; the grumbling bass
In surly groans disdains the treble's grace;
The high-perched treble chirps at this, and chides
Until his finger—moderator—hides
And closes the sweet quarrel, rousing all,
Hoarse, shrill, at once: as when the trumpets call
Hot Mars to th' harvest of death's field, and woo
Men's hearts into their hands; this lesson, too,
She gives him back, her supple breast thrills out
Sharp airs, and staggers in a warbling doubt
Of dallying sweetness, hovers o'er her skill,
And folds in waved notes, with a trembling bill,
The pliant series of her slippery song;
Then starts she suddenly into a throng
Of short thick sobs, whose thund'ring volleys float
And roll themselves over her lubric throat
In panting murmurs, 'stilled out of her breast,
That ever-bubbling spring, the sugared nest

Richard Crashaw

Of her delicious soul, that there does lie
Bathing in streams of liquid melody,—
Music's best seed-plot; when in ripened ears
A golden-headed harvest fairly rears
His honey-dropping tops, ploughed by her breath,
Which there reciprocally laboureth.
In that sweet soil it seems a holy quire
Founded to th' name of great Apollo's lyre;
Whose silver roof rings with the sprightly notes
Of sweet-lipped angel-imps, that swill their throats
In cream of morning Helicon; and then
Prefer soft anthems to the ears of men,
To woo them from their beds, still murmuring
That men can sleep while they their matins sing;—
Most divine service! whose so early lay
Prevents the eyelids of the blushing day.
There might you hear her kindle her soft voice
In the close murmur of a sparkling noise,
And lay the ground-work of her hopeful song;
Still keeping in the forward stream so long,
Till a sweet whirlwind, striving to get out,
Heaves her soft bosom, wanders round about,
And makes a pretty earthquake in her breast;
Till the fledged notes at length forsake their nest,
Fluttering in wanton shoals, and to the sky,
Winged with their own wild echos, pratt'ling fly.
She opes the floodgate, and lets loose a tide
Of streaming sweetness, which in state doth ride
On the waved back of every swelling strain,
Rising and falling in a pompous train;
And while she thus discharges a shrill peal
Of flashing airs, she qualifies their zeal
With the cool epode of a graver note;
Thus high, thus low, as if her silver throat

Richard Crashaw

Would reach the brazen voice of war's hoarse bird ;
Her little soul is ravished ; and so poured
Into loose ecstasies, that she is placed
Above herself—music's enthusiast !
   Shame now and anger mixed a double stain
In the musician's face : Yet once again,
Mistress, I come. Now reach a strain, my lute,
Above her mock, or be for ever mute ;
Or tune a song of victory to me,
Or to thyself sing thine own obsequy !
So said, his hands sprightly as fire he flings,
And with a quivering coyness tastes the strings :
The sweet-lipped sisters, musically frighted,
Singing their fears, are fearfully delighted :
Trembling as when Apollo's golden hairs
Are fanned and frizzled in the wanton airs
Of his own breath, which, married to his lyre,
Doth tune the spheres, and make heaven's self look higher;
From this to that, from that to this, he flies,
Feels music's pulse in all her arteries ;
Caught in a net which there Apollo spreads,
His fingers struggle with the vocal threads,
Following those little rills, he sinks into
A sea of Helicon ; his hand does go
Those parts of sweetness which with nectar drop,
Softer than that which pants in Hebe's cup :
The humorous strings expound his learned touch
By various glosses ; now they seem to grutch
And murmur in a buzzing din, then gingle
In shrill-tongued accents, striving to be single ;
Every smooth turn, every delicious stroke,
Gives life to some new grace : thus doth he invoke
Sweetness by all her names ; thus, bravely thus—
Fraught with a fury so harmonious—

Richard Crashaw

The lute's light Genius now does proudly rise,
Heaved on the surges of swoll'n rhapsodies,
Whose flourish, meteor-like, doth curl the air
With flash of high-born fancies ; here and there
Dancing in lofty measures, and anon
Creeps on the soft touch of a tender tone,
Whose trembling murmurs, melting in wild airs,
Run to and fro, complaining his sweet cares ;
Because those precious mysteries that dwell
In music's ravished soul he dare not tell,
But whisper to the world : thus do they vary,
Each string his note, as if they meant to carry
Their master's blest soul, snatched out at his ears
By a strong ecstasy, through all the spheres
Of music's heaven ; and seat it there on high
In th' *empyræum* of pure harmony.
At length—after so long, so loud a strife
Of all the strings, still breathing the best life
Of blest variety, attending on
His fingers' fairest revolution,
In many a sweet rise, many as sweet a fall—
A full-mouthed diapason swallows all.

This done, he lists what she would say to this ;
And she, although her breath's late exercise
Had dealt too roughly with her tender throat,
Yet summons all her sweet powers for a note.
Alas, in vain ! for while, sweet soul, she tries
To measure all those wild diversities
Of chatt'ring strings, by the small size of one
Poor simple voice, raised in a natural tone,
She fails ; and failing, grieves ; and grieving, dies ;
She dies, and leaves her life the victor's prize,
Falling upon his lute.   O, fit to have—
That lived so sweetly—dead, so sweet a grave !

Richard Crashaw

Upon the Book and Picture of the Seraphical Saint
Teresa, as she is usually expressed with
a Seraphim beside her

WELL-MEANING readers! you that come as friends
And catch the precious name this piece pretends,
Make not too much haste t' admire
That fair-cheeked fallacy of fire.
That is a seraphim, they say,
And this the great Teresia.
Readers, be ruled by me, and make
Here a well-placed and wise mistake;
You must transpose the picture quite,
And spell it wrong to read it right;
Read Him for Her, and Her for Him,
And call the saint the seraphim.
    Painter, what didst thou understand
To put her dart into his hand?
See, even the years and size of him
Shows this the mother seraphim.
This is the mistress flame, and duteous he
Her happy fireworks, here, comes down to see:
O, most poor-spirited of men!
Had thy cold pencil kissed her pen,
Thou couldst not so unkindly err
To show us this faint shade for her.
Why, man, this speaks pure mortal frame,
And mocks with female frost love's manly flame;
One would suspect thou meant'st to paint
Some weak, inferior woman Saint.
But, had thy pale-faced purple took
Fire from the burning cheeks of that bright book,

154

Richard Crashaw

Thou wouldst on her have heaped up all
That could be found seraphical;
Whate'er this youth of fire wears fair,
Rosy fingers, radiant hair,
Glowing cheek, and glist'ring wings,
All those fair and flagrant things;
But, before all, that fiery dart
Had filled the hand of this great heart.

    Do, then, as equal right requires,
Since his the blushes be, and hers the fires,
Resume and rectify thy rude design,
Undress thy seraphim into mine;
Redeem this injury of thy art,
Give him the veil, give her the dart.

    Give him the veil, that he may cover
The red cheeks of a rivalled lover,
Ashamed that our world now can show
Nests of new Seraphims here below.

    Give her the dart, for it is she,
Fair youth, shoots both thy shaft and thee;
Say, all ye wise and well-pierced hearts
That live and die amidst her darts,
What is 't your tasteful spirits do prove
In that rare life of her and love?
Say and bear witness. Sends she not
A seraphim at every shot?
What magazines of immortal arms there shine!
Heav'n's great artillery in each love-spun line!
Give, then, the dart to her who gives the flame,
Give him the veil who gives the shame.

    But if it be the frequent fate
Of worst faults to be fortunate,
If all 's prescription, and proud wrong
Hearkens not to an humble song,

Richard Crashaw

For all the gallantry of him,
Give me the suff'ring seraphim.
His be the bravery of those bright things,
The glowing cheeks, the glistering wings,
The rosy hand, the radiant dart;
Leave her alone the flaming heart.
    Leave her that, and thou shalt leave her
Not one loose shaft, but Love's whole quiver.
For in Love's field was never found
A nobler weapon than a wound.
Love's passives are his activ'st part,
The wounded is the wounding heart.
O, heart! the equal poise of Love's both parts,
Big alike with wounds and darts,
Live in these conquering leaves, live all the same,
And walk through all tongues one triumphant flame!
Live here, great heart, and love, and die, and kill,
And bleed, and wound, and yield, and conquer still.
Let this immortal Life, where'er it comes,
Walk in the crowd of loves and martyrdoms.
Let mystic deaths wait on 't, and wise souls be
The love-slain witnesses of this life of thee.
O, sweet incendiary! show here thy art
Upon this carcass of a hard, cold heart;
Let all thy scattered shafts of light, that play
Among the leaves of thy large books of day,
Combined against this breast, at once break in
And take away from me myself and sin;
This gracious robbery shall thy bounty be,
And my best fortunes such fair spoils of me.
O, thou undaunted daughter of desires!
By all thy dower of lights and fires,
By all the eagle in thee, all the dove,
By all thy lives and deaths of love,

By thy large draughts of intellectual day,
And by thy thirst of love more large than they;
By all thy brim-filled bowls of fierce desire,
By thy last morning's draught of liquid fire,
By the full kingdom of that final kiss
That seized thy parting soul, and sealed thee His;
By all the heav'ns thou hast in Him,
Fair sister of the seraphim!
By all of Him we have in thee,
Leave nothing of myself in me:
Let me so read thy life that I
Unto all life of mine may die.

ABRAHAM COWLEY

1618-1667

ON THE DEATH OF MR. CRASHAW

POET and Saint! to thee alone are given
The two most sacred names of earth and heaven;
The hard and rarest union which can be,
Next that of Godhead with humanity.
Long did the muses banished slaves abide,
And built vain pyramids to mortal pride;
Like Moses, thou (though spells and charms withstand)
Hast brought them nobly back home to their Holy
    Land.
  Ah, wretched we, poets of earth! but thou
Wert living the same poet which thou'rt now.
Whilst angels sing to thee their airs divine,
And join in an applause so great as thine,
Equal society with them to hold,
Thou need'st not make new songs, but say the old.

Abraham Cowley

And they (kind spirits !) shall all rejoice to see
How little less than they exalted man may be.
    Still the old heathen gods in numbers dwell,
The heavenliest thing on earth still keeps up hell.
Nor have we yet quite purged the Christian land ;
Still idols here, like calves at Bethel, stand.
And though Pan's death long since all oracles broke,
Yet still in rhyme the fiend Apollo spoke :
Nay, with the worst of heathen dotage we
(Vain men !) the monster woman deify ;
Find stars, and tie our fates there in a face,
And paradise in them, by whom we lost it, place.
What different faults corrupt our muses thus !
Wanton as girls, as old wives fabulous !
    Thy spotless muse, like Mary, did contain
The boundless Godhead ; she did well disdain
That her eternal verse employed should be
On a less subject than eternity ;
And for a sacred mistress scorned to take
But her whom God Himself scorned not His spouse to
      make.
It (in a kind) her miracle did do ;
A fruitful mother was and virgin too.
    How well, blest swan, did Fate contrive thy death,
And make thee render up thy tuneful breath
In thy great Mistress' arms, thou most divine
And richest offering of Loretto's shrine !
Where, like some holy sacrifice to expire,
A fever burns thee, and love lights the fire.
Angels (they say) brought the famed chapel there,
And bore the sacred load in triumph through the air.
'Tis surer much they brought *thee* there, and they
And thou, their charge, went singing all the way.

    '   .   .   .   .   .   .

Abraham Cowley

Hail, bard triumphant! and some care bestow
On us, the poets militant below.
Opposed by our old enemy, adverse chance,
Attacked by envy and by ignorance,
Enchained by beauty, tortured by desires,
Exposed by tyrant love to savage beasts and fires.
Thou from low earth in nobler flames didst rise,
And, like Elijah, mount alive the skies.
Elisha-like (but with a wish much less,
More fit thy greatness and my littleness),
Lo, here I beg (I, whom thou once didst prove
So humble to esteem, so good to love)
Not that thy spirit might on me doubled be—
I ask but half thy mighty spirit for me;
And when my muse soars with so strong a wing,
'Twill learn of things divine, and first of thee, to sing.

HYMN TO THE LIGHT

FIRST-BORN of chaos, who so fair didst come
From the old Negro's darksome womb!
Which, when it saw the lovely child,
The melancholy mass put on kind looks and smiled!

Thou tide of glory which no rest dost know,
But ever ebb and ever flow!
Thou golden shower of a true Jove
Who does in thee descend, and Heaven to Earth make
love!

Hail, active Nature's watchful life and health!
Her joy, her ornament, and wealth!
Hail to thy husband, Heat, and thee!
Thou the world's beauteous Bride, the lusty Bride-
groom he.

Abraham Cowley

Say from what golden quivers of the sky
    Do all thy winged arrows fly?
    Swiftness and power by birth are thine :
From thy great Sire they came, thy Sire the Word
    Divine.

'Tis, I believe, this archery to show,
    That so much cost in colours thou
    And skill in painting dost bestow
,Upon thy ancient arms, the gaudy heavenly bow.

Swift as light thoughts their empty career run,
    Thy race is finished when begun.
    Let a post-angel start with thee,
And thou the goal of earth shalt reach as soon as he.

Thou, in the moon's bright chariot proud and gay,
    Dost thy bright wood of stars survey ;
    And all the year dost with thee bring
Of thousand flowery lights thine own nocturnal spring.

Thou, Scythian-like, dost round thy lands above
    The sun's gilt tent for ever move ;
    And still as thou in pomp dost go,
The shining pageants of the world attend thy show.

Nor amidst all these triumphs dost thou scorn
    The humble glow-worms to adorn,
    And with those living spangles gild
(O, greatness without pride !) the lilies of the field.

160

Abraham Cowley

Night and her ugly subjects thou dost fright,
    And sleep, the lazy owl of night;
    Ashamed and fearful to appear,
They screen their horrid shapes with the black hemi-
    sphere.

With them there hastes, and wildly takes the alarm
    Of painted dreams a busy swarm.
    At the first opening of thine eye
The various clusters break, the antic atoms fly.

The guilty serpents and obscener beasts
    Creep, conscious, to their secret rests;
    Nature to thee does reverence pay,
Ill omens and ill sights remove out of thy way.

At thy appearance, Grief itself is said
    To shake his wings and rouse his head:
    And cloudy Care has often took
A gentle beamy smile, reflected from thy look.

At thy appearance, Fear itself grows bold;
    Thy sunshine melts away his cold.
    Encouraged at the sight of thee,
To the cheek colour comes, and firmness to the knee.

Even Lust, the master of a hardened face,
    Blushes, if thou be 'st in the place,
    To darkness' curtain he retires,
In sympathising night he rolls his smoky fires.

When, goddess, thou lift'st up thy wakened head
    Out of the morning's purple bed,
    Thy quire of birds about thee play,
And all thy joyful world salutes the rising day.

Abraham Cowley

The ghosts and monster-spirits that did presume
    A body's privilege to assume,
    Vanish again invisibly,
And bodies gain again their visibility.

All the world's bravery that delights our eyes,
    Is but thy several liveries:
    Thou the rich dye on them bestow'st,
Thy nimble pencil paints this landscape as thou go'st.

A crimson garment in the rose thou wear'st,
    A crown of studded gold thou bear'st.
    The virgin lilies in their white
Are clad but with the lawn of almost naked light.

The violet, Spring's little infant, stands
    Girt in the purple swaddling-bands;
    On the fair tulip thou dost dote,
Thou cloth'st it in a gay and parti-coloured coat.

With flames condensed thou dost thy jewels fix,
    And solid colours in it mix:
    Flora herself envies to see
Flowers fairer than her own, and durable as she.

Ah goddess! would thou couldst thy hand withhold
    And be less liberal to gold;
    Didst thou less value to it give,
Of how much care (alas!) might'st thou poor man relieve.

To me the sun is more delightful far,
    And all fair days much fairer are.
    But few, ah, wondrous few there be
Who do not gold prefer, O goddess, even to thee!

Richard Lovelace

Through the soft ways of heaven, and air, and sea,
    Which open all their pores to thee;
    Like a clear river thou dost glide,
And with thy living streams through the close channels
    slide.

But where firm bodies thy free course oppose,
    Gently thy source the land o'erflows;
    Takes there possession, and does make,
Of colours mingled, Light, a thick and standing lake.

But the vast ocean of unbounded Day
    In the Empyrean Heaven does stay.
    Thy rivers, lakes, and springs below
From thence took first their rise, thither at last must
    flow.

RICHARD LOVELACE

1618-1658

TO LUCASTA ON GOING TO THE WARS

TELL me not, Sweet, I am unkind,
    That from the nunnery
Of thy chaste breast and quiet mind
    To war and arms I fly.

True; a new mistress now I chase,
    The first foe in the field;
And with a stronger faith embrace
    A sword, a horse, a shield.

Richard Lovelace

Yet this inconstancy is such
    As thou, too, shalt adore;
I could not love thee, dear, so much
    Loved I not honour more.

TO AMARANTHA

That she would dishevel her hair

AMARANTHA, sweet and fair,
Ah, braid no more that shining hair!
As my curious hand or eye
Hovering round thee, let it fly.

Let it fly as unconfined
As its calm ravisher the wind,
Who hath left his darling, th' east,
To wanton in that spicy nest.

Every tress must be confessed;
But neatly tangled at the best;
Like a clew of golden thread
Most excellently ravelled.

Do not, then, wind up that light
In ribands, and o'er cloud in night,
Like the sun in 's early ray;
But shake your head and scatter day.

Richard Lovelace

Paying her Obsequies to the chaste memory of my dearest
Cousin, Mrs. Bowes Barne

SEE what an undisturbed tear
 She weeps for *her* last sleep !
But viewing her, straight waked, a star,
 She weeps that she did weep.

Grief ne'er before did tyrannize
 On the honour of that brow,
And at the wheels of her brave eyes
 Was captive led, till now.

Thus for a saint's apostasy,
 The unimagined woes
And sorrows of the hierarchy
 None but an angel knows.

Thus for lost soul's recovery,
 The clapping of the wings
And triumph of this victory
 None but an angel sings.

So none but she knows to bemoan
 This equal virgin's fate ;
None but Lucasta can *her* crown
 Of glory celebrate.

Then dart on me, Chaste Light, one ray,
 By which I may descry
Thy joy clear through this cloudy day
 To dress my sorrow by.

Richard Lovelace

WHEN love with unconfined wings
   Hovers within my gates,
And my divine Althea brings
   To whisper at the grates;
When I lie tangled in her hair
   And fettered to her eye;
The birds that wanton in the air
   Know no such liberty.

When flowing cups run swiftly round
   With no allaying Thames,
Our careless heads with roses crowned,
   Our hearts with loyal flames;
When thirsty grief in wine we steep,
   When healths and draughts go free,
Fishes that tipple in the deep
   Know no such liberty.

When (like committed linnets) I
   With shriller throat shall sing
The sweetness, mercy, majesty
   And glories of my King;
When I shall voice aloud how good
   He is, how great should be,
Enlarged winds that curl the flood
   Know no such liberty.

Stone walls do not a prison make
   Nor iron bars a cage;
Minds innocent and quiet take
   That for an hermitage;

Richard Lovelace

If I have freedom in my love,
 And in my soul am free,
Angels alone that soar above
 Enjoy such liberty.

A GUILTLESS LADY IMPRISONED: AFTER PENANCED

HARK, fair one, how whate'er here is
Doth laugh and sing at thy distress,
Not out of hate to thy relief,
But joy—to enjoy thee, though in grief.

See! that which chains you, you chain here,
The prison is thy prisoner;
How much thy jailor's keeper art!
He binds thy hands, but thou his heart.

The gyves to rase so smooth a skin
Are so unto themselves within;
But, blest to kiss so fair an arm,
Haste to be happy with that harm;

And play about thy wanton wrist,
As if in them thou so wert dressed;
But if too rough, too hard they press,
O they but closely, closely kiss.

And as thy bare feet bless the way,
The people do not mock, but pray,
And call thee, as amazed they run,
Instead of prostitute, a nun.

167

Richard Lovelace

The merry torch burns with desire
To kindle the eternal fire,[1]
And lightly dances in thine eyes
To tunes of epithalamies.

The sheet tied ever to thy waist,
How thankful to be so embraced!
And see! thy very, very bands
Are bound to thee to bind such hands.

THE ROSE

SWEET, serene, sky-like flower,
Haste to adorn the bower;
From thy long cloudy bed,
Shoot forth thy damask head.

New-startled blush of Flora,
The grief of pale Aurora
(Who will contest no more),
Haste, haste to strew her floor!

Vermilion ball that's given
From lip to lip in Heaven;
Love's couch's coverled,
Haste, haste to make her bed.

Dear offspring of pleased Venus
And jolly, plump Silenus,
Haste, haste to deck the hair
Of the only sweetly fair!

[1] Evidently of love.

Andrew Marvell

See ! rosy is her bower,
Her floor is all this flower
Her bed a rosy nest
By a bed of roses pressed.

But early as she dresses,
Why fly you her bright tresses?
Ah! I have found, I fear,—
Because her cheeks are near.

ANDREW MARVELL

1620-1678

A HORATIAN ODE UPON CROMWELL'S RETURN FROM IRELAND

THE forward youth that would appear
Must now forsake his muses dear,
          Nor in the shadows sing
          His numbers languishing.
'Tis time to leave the books in dust,
And oil the unused armour's rust,
          Removing from the wall
          The corselet of the hall.
So restless Cromwell could not cease
In the inglorious arts of peace,
          But through adventurous war
          Urged his active star ;
And, like the three-forked lightning, first
Breaking the clouds where it was nurst,
          Did thorough his own side
          His fiery way divide ;
(For 'tis all one to courage high,
The emulous, or enemy,

Andrew Marvell

And with such to enclose
Is more than to oppose ;)
Then burning through the air he went,
And palaces and temples rent ;
And Cæsar's head at last
Did through his laurels blast.
'Tis madness to resist or blame
The force of angry heaven's flame ;
And if we would speak true,
Much to the man is due,
Who, from his private gardens, where
He lived reserved and austere,
As if his highest plot
To plant the bergamot,
Could by industrious valour climb
To ruin the great work of Time,
And cast the kingdoms old
Into another mould.
Though Justice against Fate complain
And plead the ancient rights in vain
(But those do hold or break,
As men are strong or weak),
Nature, that hateth emptiness,
Allows of penetration less,
And therefore must make room
Where greater spirits come.
What field of all the civil war
Where his were not the deepest scar ?
And Hampton shows what part
He had of wiser art ;
Where, twining subtle fears with hope,
He wove a net of such a scope
That Charles himself might chase
To Carisbrook's narrow case,

Andrew Marvell

That thence the royal actor borne
The tragic scaffold might adorn,
        While round the armed bands
        Did clap their bloody hands;
He nothing common did, or mean,
Upon that memorable scene,
        But with his keener eye
        The axe's edge did try;
Nor called the gods with vulgar spite
To vindicate his helpless right,
        But bowed his comely head
        Down, as upon a bed.
This was that memorable hour,
Which first assured the forced power;
        So, when they did design
        The capitol's first line,
A bleeding head, where they begun,
Did fright the architects to run;
        And yet in that the State
        Foresaw its happy fate.
And now the Irish are ashamed
To see themselves in one year tamed;
        So much one man can do,
        That does both act and know.
They can affirm his praises best,
And have, though overcome, confessed
        How good he is, how just,
        And fit for highest trust;
Nor yet grown stiffer with command,
But still in the republic's hand
        (How fit he is to sway,
        That can so well obey!)
He to the Commons' feet presents
A kingdom for his first year's rents;

Andrew Marvell

And, what he may, forbears
His fame, to make it theirs;
And has his sword and spoil ungirt,
To lay them at the Public's skirt:
So when the falcon high
Falls heavy from the sky,
She, having killed, no more doth search,
But on the next green bough to perch;
Where, when he first does lure,
The falconer has her sure.
What may not then our isle presume,
While victory his crest does plume?
What may not others fear,
If thus he crowns each year?
As Caesar, he, ere long, to Gaul,
To Italy a Hannibal,
And to all states not free
Shall climacteric be.
The Pict no shelter now shall find
Within his parti-coloured mind,
But, from this valour sad,
Shrink underneath the plaid;
Happy, if in the tufted brake
The English hunter him mistake,
Nor lay his hounds in near
The Caledonian deer.
But thou, the war's and fortune's son,
March indefatigably on,
And for the last effect,
Still keep the sword erect;
Beside the force it has to fright
The spirits of the shady night;
The same arts that did gain
A power, must it maintain.

Andrew Marvell

SEE with what simplicity
This nymph begins her golden days !
In the green grass she loves to lie,
And there with her fair aspect tames
The wilder flowers, and gives them names ;
But only with the roses plays,
           And them does tell
What colours best become them, and what smell.

Who can foretell for what high cause
This darling of the gods was born ?
Yet this is she whose chaster laws
The wanton Love shall one day fear,
And, under her command severe,
See his bow broke, and ensigns torn.
           Happy who can
Appease this virtuous enemy of man !

O then let me in time compound
And parley with those conquering eyes,
Ere they have tried their force to wound ;
Ere with their glancing wheels they drive
In triumph over hearts that strive,
And them that yield but more despise :
           Let me be laid,
Where I may see the glories from some shade.

Meantime, whilst every verdant thing
Itself does at thy beauty charm,
Reform the errors of the Spring ;
Make that the tulips may have share

Andrew Marvell

Of sweetness, seeing they are fair,
And roses of their thorns disarm;
                    But most procure
That violets may a longer age endure.

But O young beauty of the woods,
Whom Nature courts with fruits and flowers,
Gather the flowers, but spare the buds;
Lest Flora, angry at thy crime
To kill her infants in their prime,
Should quickly make the example yours;
                    And, ere we see,
Nip, in the blossom, all our hopes in thee.

THE NYMPH COMPLAINING OF THE DEATH OF HER FAWN

THE wanton troopers riding by
Have shot my fawn, and it will die.
Ungentle men! they cannot thrive
Who killed thee.   Thou ne'er didst, alive,
Them any harm, alas! nor could
Thy death yet ever do them good.
I'm sure I never wished them ill,
Nor do I for all this, nor will.
But if my simple prayers may yet
Prevail with heaven to forget
Thy murder, I will join my tears
Rather than fail.   But O my fears!
It cannot die so.   Heaven's King
Keeps register of everything,
And nothing may we use in vain;
Even beasts must be with justice slain,
Else men are made their deodands.
Though they should wash their guilty hands

Andrew Marvell

In this warm life-blood which doth part
From thine, and wound me to the heart,
Yet could they not be clean, their stain
Is dyed in such a purple grain.
There is not such another in
The world, to offer for their sin.

Inconstant Sylvio, when yet
I had not found him counterfeit,
One morning (I remember well),
Tied in this silver chain and bell,
Gave it to me; nay, and I know
What he said then, I'm sure I do:
Said he, 'Look how your huntsman here
Hath taught a fawn to hunt his deer!'
But Sylvio soon had me beguiled;
This waxed tame while he grew wild,
And quite regardless of my smart
Left me his fawn, but took my heart.

Thenceforth I set myself to play
My solitary time away
With this; and, very well content,
Could so mine idle life have spent;
For it was full of sport, and light
Of foot and heart, and did invite
Me to its game; it seemed to bless
Itself in me; how could I less
Than love it? O, I cannot be
Unkind to a beast that loveth me!

Had it lived long, I do not know
Whether it too might have done so
As Sylvio did; his gifts might be
Perhaps as false, or more, than he.

Andrew Marvell

But I am sure, for aught that I
Could in so short a time espy,
Thy love was far more better than
The love of false and cruel man.

With sweetest milk and sugar first
I it at my own fingers nursed;
And as it grew, so every day
It waxed more white and sweet than they—
It had so sweet a breath! and oft
I blushed to see its foot more soft
And white—shall I say?—than my hand,
Nay, any lady's of the land!

It is a wondrous thing how fleet
'Twas on those little silver feet:
With what a pretty skipping grace
It oft would challenge me the race:—
And when 't had left me far away
'Twould stay, and run again, and stay;
For it was nimbler much than hinds,
And trod as if on the four winds.

I have a garden of my own,
But so with roses overgrown
And lilies, that you would it guess
To be a little wilderness:
And all the spring-time of the year
It only loved to be there.
Among the beds of lilies I
Have sought it oft, where it should lie;
Yet could not, till itself would rise,
Find it, although before mine eyes.

Andrew Marvell

For in the flaxen lilies' shade
It like a bank of lilies laid.
Upon the roses it would feed,
Until its lips e'en seemed to bleed,
And then to me 'twould boldly trip,
And print those roses on my lip.
But all its chief delight was still
On roses thus itself to fill,
And its pure virgin limbs to fold
In whitest sheets of lilies cold :—
Had it lived long, it would have been
Lilies without—roses within.

O help! O help! I see it faint
And die as calmly as a saint!
See how it weeps! the tears do come
Sad, slowly, dropping like a gum.
So weeps the wounded balsam ; so
The holy frankincense doth flow ;
The brotherless Heliades
Melt in such amber tears as these.

I in a golden vial will
Keep these two crystal tears, and fill
It, till it doth o'erflow, with mine,
Then place it in Diana's shrine.

Now my sweet fawn is vanished to
Whither the swans and turtles go ;
In fair Elysium to endure
With milk-white lambs and ermines pure.
O, do not run too fast, for I
Will but bespeak thy grave, and die.

Andrew Marvell

First my unhappy statue shall
Be cut in marble; and withal
Let it be weeping too; but there
The engraver sure his art may spare;
For I so truly thee bemoan
That I shall weep though I be stone,
Until my tears, still dropping, wear
My breast, themselves engraving there;
Then at my feet shalt thou be laid,
Of purest alabaster made;
For I would have thine image be
White as I can, though not as thee.

THE DEFINITION OF LOVE

My love is of a birth as rare
    As 'tis, for object, strange and high;
It was begotten by despair
    Upon impossibility.

Magnanimous despair alone
    Could show me so divine a thing,
Where feeble hope could ne'er have flown
    But vainly flapped its tinsel wing.

And yet I quickly might arrive
    Where my extended soul is fixed;
But fate does iron wedges drive,
    And always crowds itself betwixt.

For fate with jealous eyes does see
    Two perfect loves, nor lets them close;
Their union would her ruin be,
    And her tyrannic power depose.

Andrew Marvell

And therefore her decrees of steel
    Us as the distant poles have placed
(Though Love's whole world on us doth wheel),
    Not by themselves to be embraced,

Unless the giddy heaven fall,
    And earth some new convulsion tear,
And, us to join, the world should all
    Be cramped into a planisphere.

As lines, so loves oblique may well
    Themselves in every angle greet;
But ours, so truly parallel,
    Though infinite, can never meet.

Therefore the love which us doth bind,
    But fate so enviously debars,
Is the conjunction of the mind,
    And opposition of the stars.

THE GARDEN

Translated out of his own Latin

How vainly men themselves amaze
To win the palm, the oak, or bays,
And their incessant labours see
Crowned from some single herb or tree,
Whose short and narrow-verged shade
Does prudently their toils upbraid;
While all the flowers and trees do close
To weave the garlands of Repose.

Fair Quiet, have I found thee here,
And Innocence thy sister dear?
Mistaken long, I sought you then
In busy companies of men:

Andrew Marvell

Your sacred plants, if here below,
Only among the plants will grow :
Society is all but rude
To this delicious solitude.

No white nor red was ever seen
So amorous as this lovely green.
Fond lovers, cruel as their flame,
Cut in these trees their mistress' name :
Little, alas, they know or heed
How far these beauties her exceed !
Fair trees ! wheres'e'er your barks I wound,
No name shall, but your own, be found.

When we have run our passions' heat
Love hither makes his best retreat ;
The gods, who mortal beauty chase,
Still in a tree did end their race ;
Apollo hunted Daphne so
Only that she might laurel grow ;
And Pan did after Syrinx speed
Not as a nymph, but for a reed.

What wondrous life is this I lead !
Ripe apples drop about my head ;
The luscious clusters of the vine
Upon my mouth do crush their wine ;
The nectarine and curious peach
Into my hands themselves do reach ;
Stumbling on melons, as I pass,
Ensnared with flowers, I fall on grass.

Meanwhile the mind, from pleasure less,
Withdraws into its happiness ;

Andrew Marvell

The mind, that ocean where each kind
Does straight its own resemblance find;
Yet it creates, transcending these,
Far other worlds and other seas;
Annihilating all that's made
To a green thought in a green shade.

Here at the fountain's sliding foot
Or at some fruit-tree's mossy root,
Casting the body's vest aside
My soul into the boughs does glide;
There, like a bird, it sits and sings,
Then whets and claps its silver wings,
And, till prepared for longer flight,
Waves in its plumes the various light.

Such was that happy Garden-state
While man there walked without a mate:
After a place so pure and sweet,
What other help could yet be meet!
But 'twas beyond a mortal's share
To wander solitary there:
Two paradises 'twere in one,
To live in Paradise alone.

How well the skilful gardener drew
Of flowers and herbs this dial new!
Where, from above, the milder sun
Does through a fragrant zodiac run:
And, as it works, th' industrious bee
Computes its time as well as we.
How could such sweet and wholesome hours
Be reckoned, but with herbs and flowers?

HENRY VAUGHAN

1621-1695

THE DAWNING

AH! what time wilt Thou come? When shall
    that cry,
'The Bridegroom's coming!' fill the sky?
Shall it in the evening run,
When our words and works are done?
Or will Thy all-surprising light
        Break at midnight,
When either sleep or some dark pleasure
Possesseth mad man without measure?
Or shall these early, fragrant hours
        Unlock Thy bowers?
And with their blush of light descry
Thy locks crowned with eternity?
Indeed it is the only time
That with Thy glory best doth chime;
All now are stirring, every field
        Full hymns doth yield;
The whole creation shakes off night,
And for Thy shadow looks the light;
Stars now vanish without number,
Sleepy planets set and slumber,
The pursy clouds disband and scatter,
All expect some sudden matter;
Not one beam triumphs, but from far
        That morning star.
O at what time soever Thou,
Unknown to us, the heavens wilt bow,
And, with Thy angels in the van,

Henry Vaughan

Descend to judge poor careless man,
Grant I may not like puddle lie
In a corrupt security,
Where, if a traveller water crave,
He finds it dead, and in a grave;
But as this restless vocal spring
All day and night doth run and sing,
And, though here born, yet is acquainted
Elsewhere, and flowing keeps untainted;
So let me all my busy age
In Thy free services engage;
And though—while here—of force I must
Have commerce sometimes with poor dust,
And in my flesh, though vile and low,
As this doth in her channel flow,
Yet let my course, my aim, my love,
And chief acquaintance be above;
So when that day and hour shall come,
In which Thy Self will be the sun,
Thou 'lt find me dressed and on my way,
Watching the break of Thy great day.

CHILDHOOD

I CANNOT reach it; and my striving eye
Dazzles at it, as at eternity.

Were now that chronicle alive,
Those white designs which children drive,
And the thoughts of each harmless hour,
With their content too in my power,
Quickly would I make my path even,
And by mere playing go to heaven.

Henry Vaughan

Why should men love
A wolf, more than a lamb or dove?
Or choose hell-fire and brimstone streams
Before bright stars and God's own beams?
Who kisseth thorns will hurt his face,
But flowers do both refresh and grace;
And sweetly living—fie on men!—
Are, when dead, medicinal then;
If seeing much should make staid eyes,
And long experience should make wise;
Since all that age doth teach is ill,
Why should I not love childhood still?
Why, if I see a rock or shelf,
Shall I from thence cast down myself?
Or by complying with the world,
From the same precipice be hurled?
Those observations are but foul,
Which make me wise to lose my soul.

And yet the practice worldlings call
Business, and weighty action all,
Checking the poor child for his play,
But gravely cast themselves away.

Dear, harmless age! the short, swift span
Where weeping Virtue parts with man;
Where love without lust dwells, and bends
What way we please without self-ends.

An age of mysteries! which he
Must live twice that would God's face see;
Which angels guard, and with it play;
Angels! which foul men drive away.

184

Henry Vaughan

How do I study now, and scan
Thee more than e'er I studied man,
And only see through a long night
Thy edges and thy bordering light!
O for thy centre and mid-day!
For sure that is the narrow way!

SURE it was so. Man in those early days
    Was not all stone and earth;
He shined a little, and by those weak rays
    Had some glimpse of his birth.
He saw heaven o'er his head, and knew from whence
    He came, condemned, hither;
And, as first-love draws strongest, so from hence
    His mind sure progressed thither.
Things here were strange unto him; sweat and till;
    All was a thorn or weed;
Nor did those last, but—like himself—died still
    As soon as they did seed;
They seemed to quarrel with him; for that act,
    That fell him, foiled them all;
He drew the curse upon the world, and cracked
    The whole frame with his fall.
This made him long for home, as loth to stay
    With murmurers and foes;
He sighed for Eden, and would often say,
    'Ah! what bright days were those!'
Nor was heaven cold unto him; for each day
    The valley or the mountain
Afforded visits, and still Paradise lay
    In some green shade or fountain.

Henry Vaughan

Angels lay leiger here; each bush, and cell,
    Each oak and highway knew them:
Walk but the fields, or sit down at some well,
    And he was sure to view them.
Almighty Love! where art Thou now? mad man
    Sits down and freezeth on;
He raves, and swears to stir nor fire, nor fan,
    But bids the thread be spun.
I see Thy curtains are close-drawn; Thy bow
    Looks dim, too, in the cloud;
Sin triumphs still, and man is sunk below
    The centre, and his shroud.
All's in deep sleep and night: thick darkness lies
    And hatcheth o'er Thy people—
But hark! what trumpet's that? what angel cries
    'Arise! thrust in Thy sickle'?

THE NIGHT

    THROUGH that pure virgin shrine,
That sacred veil drawn o'er Thy glorious noon,
That men might look and live, as glow-worms shine,
    And face the moon:
    Wise Nicodemus saw such light
    As made him know his God by night.

    Most blest believer he!
Who in that land of darkness and blind eyes
Thy long-expected healing wings could see
    When Thou didst rise!
    And, what can never more be done,
    Did at midnight speak with the Sun!

Henry Vaughan

O, who will tell me where
He found Thee at that dead and silent hour?
What hallowed solitary ground did bear
So rare a flower;
Within whose sacred leaves did lie
The fulness of the Deity?

No mercy-seat of gold,
No dead and dusty cherub nor carved stone,
But His own living works did my Lord hold
And lodge alone;
Where trees and herbs did watch, and peep,
And wonder, while the Jews did sleep.

Dear night! this world's defeat;
The stop to busy fools; care's check and curb;
The day of spirits; my soul's calm retreat
Which none disturb!
Christ's progress, and His prayer-time;
The hours to which high Heaven doth chime.

God's silent, searching flight;
When my Lord's head is filled with dew, and all
His locks are wet with the clear drops of night;
His still, soft call;
His knocking-time; the soul's dumb watch,
When spirits their fair kindred catch.

Were my loud, evil days
Calm and unhaunted as is thy dark tent,
Whose peace but by some angel's wing or voice
Is seldom rent;
Then I in heaven all the long year
Would keep, and never wander here.

Henry Vaughan

But living where the sun
Doth all things wake, and where all mix and tire
Themselves and others, I consent and run
    To every mire ;
    And by this world's ill-guiding light,
    Err more than I can do by night.

    There is in God—some say—
A deep but dazzling darkness ; as men here
Say it is late and dusky, because they
    See not all clear.
    O for that night ! where I in Him
    Might live invisible and dim !

THE ECLIPSE

WHITHER, O whither didst Thou fly,
When I did grieve Thine holy eye?
When Thou didst mourn to see me lost,
And all Thy care and counsels crossed?
O do not grieve, where'er Thou art !
Thy grief is an undoing smart,
Which doth not only pain, but break
My heart, and makes me blush to speak.
Thy anger I could kiss, and will ;
But O Thy grief, Thy grief, doth kill !

THE RETREAT

HAPPY those early days when I
Shined in my angel infancy !
Before I understood this place
Appointed for my second race,
Or taught my soul to fancy ought

Henry Vaughan

But a white, celestial thought;
When yet I had not walked above
A mile or two from my first love,
And looking back, at that short space,
Could see a glimpse of his bright face;
When on some gilded cloud or flower
My gazing soul would dwell an hour,
And in those weaker glories spy
Some shadows of eternity;
Before I taught my tongue to wound
My conscience with a sinful sound,
Or had the black art to dispense
A several sin to every sense;
But felt through all this fleshly dress
Bright shoots of everlastingness.
   O how I long to travel back,
And tread again that ancient track!
That I might once more reach that plain
Where first I left my glorious train;
From whence the enlightened spirit sees
That shady city of palm-trees.
But ah! my soul with too much stay
Is drunk, and staggers in the way!
Some men a forward motion love,
But I by backward steps would move;
And, when this dust falls to the urn,
In that state I came, return.

THE WORLD OF LIGHT

THEY are all gone into the world of light,
   And I alone sit lingering here;
Their very memory is fair and bright,
     And my sad thoughts doth clear.

189

Henry Vaughan

It glows and glitters in my cloudy breast,
  Like stars upon some gloomy grove,
Or those faint beams in which this hill is drest,
  After the sun's remove.

I see them walking in an air of glory,
  Whose light doth trample on my days:
My days, which are at best but dull and hoary,
  Mere glimmering and decays.

O holy Hope! and high Humility,
  High as the heavens above!
These are your walks, and you have shewed them me,
  To kindle my cold love.

Dear, beauteous Death! the jewel of the just,
  Shining no where, but in the dark;
What mysteries do lie beyond thy dust,
  Could man outlook that mark!

He that hath found some fledged bird's nest, may know
  At first sight, if the bird be flown;
But what fair well or grove he sings in now,
  That is to him unknown.

And yet, as Angels in some brighter dreams
  Call to the soul, when man doth sleep:
So some strange thoughts transcend our wonted themes,
  And into glory peep.

If a star were confined into a tomb,
  Her captive flames must needs burn there;
But when the hand that locked her up gives room,
  She'll shine through all the sphere.

Scottish Ballads

O Father of eternal life, and all
    Created glories under Thee!
Resume Thy spirit from this world of thrall
    Into true liberty.

Either disperse these mists, which blot and fill
    My perspective still as they pass;
Or else remove me hence unto that hill
    Where I shall need no glass.

SCOTTISH BALLADS

HELEN OF KIRCONNELL

I WISH I were where Helen lies!
Night and day on me she cries;
O that I were where Helen lies
    On fair Kirconnell lea!

Curst be the heart that thought the thought,
And curst the hand that fired the shot,
When in my arms burd Helen dropt,
    And died for sake o' me!

O think na but my heart was sair
When my Love dropt down and spak nae mair;
I laid her down wi' meikle care
    On fair Kirconnell lea.

As I went down the water-side,
None but my foe to be my guide,
None but my foe to be my guide,
    On fair Kirconnell lea;

Scottish Ballads

I lighted down my sword to draw,
I hacked him in pieces sma',
I hacked him in pieces sma',
 For her that died for me.

O Helen fair, beyond compare!
I'll make a garland of thy hair
Shall bind my heart for evermair
 Until the day I die.

O that I were where Helen lies!
Night and day on me she cries;
Out of my bed she bids me rise,
 Says, 'Haste and come to me!'

O Helen fair! O Helen chaste!
If I were with thee, I were blest,
Where thou liest low and tak'st thy rest
 On fair Kirconnell lea.

I wish my grave were growing green,
A winding-sheet drawn ower my een,
And I in Helen's arms lying,
 On fair Kirconnell lea.

I wish I were where Helen lies!
Night and day on me she cries;
And I am weary of the skies,
 Since my Love died for me.

THE WIFE OF USHER'S WELL

THERE lived a wife at Usher's Well
 And a wealthy wife was she;
She had three stout and stalwart sons.
 And sent them over the sea.

Scottish Ballads

They hadna been a week from her,
    A week but barely ane,
When word came to the carlin wife
    That her three sons were gane.

They hadna been a week from her,
    A week but barely three,
When word came to the carlin wife
    That her sons she'd never see.

'I wish the wind may never cease,
    Nor fashes in the flood,
Till my three sons come hame to me,
    In earthly flesh and blood!'

It fell about the Martinmass,
    When nights are lang and mirk,
The carlin wife's three sons came hame,
    And their hats were of the birk.

It neither grew in syke nor ditch,
    Nor yet in ony sheugh;
But at the gates o' Paradise
    That birk grew fair eneugh.

'Blow up the fire, my maidens!
    Bring water from the well;
For a' my house shall feast this night,
    Since my three sons are well.'

And she has made to them a bed,
    She's made it large and wide;
And she's ta'en her mantle her about,
    Sat down at the bedside.

N

Scottish Ballads

Up then crew the red, red cock,
    And up and crew the grey ;
The eldest to the youngest said,
    ' 'Tis time we were awa ! '

The cock he hadna crawed but once,
    And clapped his wings at a',
When the youngest to the eldest said,
    ' Brother, we must awa.'

' The cock doth craw, the day doth daw,
    The channerin' worm doth chide ;
Gin we be mist out o' our place,
    A sair pain we maun bide.

' Fare ye weel, my mother dear !
    Fareweel to barn and byre !
And fare ye weel, the bonny lass
    That kindles my mother's fire ! '

THE DOWIE DENS OF YARROW

LATE at e'en, drinking the wine
    And e'er they paid the lawing,
They set a combat them between,
    To fight it in the dawing.

' O stay at hame, my noble lord,
    O stay at hame, my marrow !
My cruel brother will you betray
    On the dowie houms of Yarrow.'

' O fare ye weel, my lady gay !
    O fare ye weel, my Sarah !
For I maun gae, though I ne'er return
    Frae the dowie banks of Yarrow.'

Scottish Ballads

She kissed his cheek, she kaimed his hair,
    As oft she had done before, O ;
She belted him with his noble brand,
    And he's awa to Yarrow.

As he gaed up the Terries' bank,
    I wot he gaed with sorrow,
Till down in a den he spied nine armed men
    On the dowie houms of Yarrow.

'O, come ye here to part your land,
    The bonnie forest thorough ?
Or come ye here to wield your brand
    On the dowie houms of Yarrow ?'

'I come not here to part my land,
    And neither to beg or borrow ;
I come to wield my noble brand
    On the bonnie banks of Yarrow.

'If I see all, ye're nine to ane ;
    An' that's an unequal marrow :
Yet will I fight, while lasts my brand,
    On the bonnie banks of Yarrow.'

Four has he hurt, and five has slain,
    On the bloody braes of Yarrow ;
Till that stubborn knight came him behind,
    And ran his body thorough.

'Gae hame, gae hame, good brother John,
    And tell your sister Sarah,
To come and lift her leafu' lord ;
    He's sleeping sound on Yarrow.'

Scottish Ballads

'Yestreen I dreamed a dolefu' dream ;
    I fear there will be sorrow !
I dreamed I pu'ed the heather green
    With my true love, on Yarrow.

'O gentle wind that bloweth south
    From where my love repaireth,
Convey a kiss from his dear mouth,
    And tell me how he fareth.

'But in the glen strive armed men ;
    They 've wrought me dule and sorrow ;
They 've slain—the comeliest knight they 've
      slain—
    He bleeding lies on Yarrow.'

As she sped down yon high, high hill,
    She gaed wi' dule and sorrow,
And in the den spied ten slain men,
    On the dowie banks of Yarrow.

She kissed his cheek, she kaimed his hair,
    She searched his wounds all thorough,
She kissed them till her lips grew red,
    On the dowie houms of Yarrow.

'Now haud your tongue, my daughter dear,
    For a' this breeds but sorrow ;
I 'll wed ye to a better lord
    Than him ye lost on Yarrow.'

'O haud your tongue, my father dear,
    Ye mind me but of sorrow ;
A fairer rose did never bloom
    Than now lies cropped on Yarrow.'

Scottish Ballads

THERE came a ghost to Marg'ret's door,
　　With many a grievous groan ;
And aye he tirled at the pin,
　　But answer made she none.

' Is that my father Philip ?
　　Or is 't my brother John ?
Or is 't my true-love Willie,
　　From Scotland new come home ? '

' 'Tis not thy father Philip,
　　Nor yet thy brother John,
But 'tis thy true-love Willie
　　From Scotland new come home.

' O sweet Marg'ret, O dear Marg'ret !
　　I pray thee speak to me ;
Give me my faith and troth, Marg'ret,
　　As I gave it to thee.'

' Thy faith and troth thou 's never get,
　　Nor it will I thee lend,
Till that thou come within my bower
　　And kiss me cheek and chin.'

' If I should come within thy bower,
　　I am no earthly man ;
And should I kiss thy ruby lips
　　Thy days would not be lang.

197

Scottish Ballads

'O sweet Marg'ret! O dear Marg'ret,
   I pray thee speak to me;
Give me my faith and troth, Marg'ret,
   As I gave it to thee.'

'Thy faith and troth thou's never get,
   Nor it will I thee lend,
Till thou take me to yon kirk-yard,
   And wed me with a ring.'

'My bones are buried in yon kirk-yard
   Afar beyond the sea;
And it is but my spirit, Marg'ret,
   That's now speaking to thee.'

She stretched out her lily-white hand
   And for to do her best:
'Hae, there's your faith and troth, Willie;
   God send your soul good rest.'

Now she has kilted her robe o' green
   A piece below her knee,
And a' the live-lang winter night
   The dead corp followed she.

'Is there any room at your head, Willie,
   Or any room at your feet?
Or any room at your side, Willie,
   Wherein that I may creep?'

'There's nae room at my head, Marg'ret,
   There's nae room at my feet;
There's nae room at my side, Marg'ret,
   My coffin's made so meet.'

Scottish Ballads

Then up and crew the red red cock,
 And up and crew the grey;
' 'Tis time, 'tis time, my dear Marg'ret,
 That you were gane awa.'

THE king sits in Dumfermline toun,
 Drinking the blude-red wine;
'O whare will I get a skeely skipper
 To sail this new ship o' mine?'

O up and spake an eldern knight,
 Sat at the king's right knee;
'Sir Patrick Spens is the best sailor
 That ever sailed the sea.'

Our king has written a braid letter
 And sealed it with his hand,
And sent it to Sir Patrick Spens
 Was walking on the strand.

'To Noroway, to Noroway,
 To Noroway ower the faem;
The king's daughter o' Noroway
 'Tis thou must bring her hame.'

The first word that Sir Patrick read
 So loud loud laughed he;
The neist word that Sir Patrick read
 The tear blinded his e'e.

Scottish Ballads

'O wha is this has done this deed
   And tauld the king o' me,
To send us out, at this time o' year,
   To sail upon the sea?

'Be it wind, be it weet, be it hail, be it sleet,
   Our ship must sail the faem;
The king's daughter o' Noroway
   'Tis we must fetch her hame.'

They hoysed their sails on Monenday morn,
   Wi' a' the speed they may;
They hae landed in Noroway
   Upon a Wodensday.

They hadna been a week, a week,
   In Noroway but twae,
When that the lords o' Noroway
   Began aloud to say:

'Ye Scottishmen spend a' our king's goud,
   And a' our queenis fee.'
'Ye lee, ye lee, ye liars loud!
   Fu' loud I hear ye lee.

'For I have brought as much white monie
   As gane my men and me,
And I hae brought a half-fou of gude red gould
   Out o'er the sea wi' me.

'Make ready, make ready, my merry men a'!
   Our good ship sails the morn.'
'Now ever alack, my master dear,
   I fear a deadly storm.
200

Scottish Ballads

'I saw the new moon late yestreen
  Wi' the auld moon in her arm;
And if we gang to sea, master,
  I fear we'll come to harm.'

They hadna sailed a league, a league,
  A league but barely three,
When the lift grew dark, and the wind blew loud,
  And gurly grew the sea.

The ankers brak, and the top-mast lap,
  It was sic a deadly storm;
And the waves cam o'er the broken ship
  Till a' her sides were torn.

'O where will I get a gude sailor
  To tak the helm in hand,
Till I get up to the tall top-mast,
  To see if I can spy land?'

'O here am I, a sailor gude,
  To tak the helm in hand,
Till you go up to the tall top-mast,
  But I fear you'll ne'er spy land.'

He hadna gaen a step, a step
  A step but barely ane,
When a boult flew out of our goodly ship,
  And the salt sea it came in.

'Gae fetch a web o' the silken claith,
  Another o' the twine,
And wap them into our ship's side,
  And let nae the sea come in.'

Scottish Ballads

They fetched a web o' the silken claith,
  Another o' the twine,
And they wapped them round that gude ship's side,
  But still the sea came in.

O laith, laith were our gude Scots lords
  To wet their cork-heeled shoon;
But lang or a' the play was played
  They wat their hats aboon.

And mony was the feather bed
  That floated on the faem;
And mony was the gude lord's son
  That never mair came hame.

The ladyes wrang their fingers white,
  The maidens tore their hair,
A' for the sake o' their true loves,—
  For them they'll see nae mair.

O lang, lang may the ladyes sit,
  Wi' their fans into their hand,
Before they see Sir Patrick Spens
  Come sailing to the strand!

And lang, lang may the maidens sit,
  With their goud kaims in their hair,
A' waiting for their ain dear loves!
  For them they'll see nae mair.

Half ower, half ower to Aberdour,
  'Tis fifty fathoms deep,
And there lies gude Sir Patrick Spens,
  Wi' the Scots lords at his feet!

Scottish Ballads

HAME! hame! hame! O hame fain wad I be!
O hame, hame, hame to my ain countrie.
When the flower is in the bud, and the leaf is on the
tree,
The lark shall sing me hame to my ain countrie.
Hame, hame, hame! O hame fain wad I be!
O hame, hame, hame to my ain countrie!

The green leaf o' loyalty's beginning now to fa';
The bonnie white rose it is withering an' a';
But we'll water it with the blude of usurping tyrannie,
And fresh it shall blaw in my ain countrie!
Hame, hame, hame! O hame fain wad I be!
O hame, hame, hame to my ain countrie!

O, there's nocht now frae ruin my countrie can save,
But the keys o' kind heaven, to open the grave,
That a' the noble martyrs wha died for loyaltie
May rise again and fight for their ain countrie.
Hame, hame, hame! O hame fain wad I be!
O hame, hame, hame to my ain countrie!

The great now are gane, who attempted to save;
The green grass is growing abune their graves;
Yet the sun through the mirk seems to promise to me
I'll shine on ye yet in your ain countrie.
Hame, hame, hame! O hame fain wad I be!
O hame, hame, hame to my ain countrie!

BORDER BALLAD

A LYKE-WAKE DIRGE

THIS ae nighte, this ae nighte,
Every nighte and alle,
Fire and sleet and candle-lighte,
And Christe receive thy saule.

When thou from hence away art past,
Every nighte and alle,
To Whinny-muir thou com'st at last;
And Christe receive thy saule.

If ever thou gavest hosen and shoon,
Every nighte and alle,
Sit thee down and put them on;
And Christe receive thy saule.

If hosen and shoon thou ne'er gav'st nane,
Every nighte and alle,
The whinnes sall prick thee to the bare bane;
And Christe receive thy saule.

From Whinny-muir when thou may'st pass,
Every nighte and alle,
To Brig o' Dread thou com'st at last,
And Christe receive thy saule.

From Brig o' Dread when thou may'st pass,
Every nighte and alle,
To Purgatory fire thou com'st at last,
And Christe receive thy saule.

John Dryden

If ever thou gavest meat or drink,
   Every nighte and alle,
The fire sall never make thee shrink;
   And Christe receive thy saule.

If meat and drink thou ne'er gav'st nane,
   Every nighte and alle,
The fire will burn thee to the bare bane,
   And Christe receive thy saule.

This ae nighte, this ae nighte,
   Every nighte and alle,
Fire and sleet and candle-lighte,
   And Christe receive thy saule.

JOHN DRYDEN

1631-1700

ODE

To the Pious Memory of the accomplished young lady,
Mrs. Anne Killigrew, excellent in the two sister arts
of Poesy and Painting

THOU youngest virgin-daughter of the skies,
   Made in the last promotion of the blest;
Whose palms, new-plucked from paradise,
In spreading branches more sublimely rise,
   Rich with immortal green, above the rest:
Whether, adopted to some neighbouring star,
Thou roll'st above us in thy wandering race,
   Or in procession fixed and regular
Moved with the heaven's majestic pace,
   Or called to more superior bliss,
Thou tread'st with seraphims the vast abyss:

John Dryden

Whatever happy region be thy place,
Cease thy celestial song a little space ;
Thou wilt have time enough for hymns divine,
Since heaven's eternal year is thine.
Hear, then, a mortal muse thy praise rehearse,
    In no ignoble verse,
But such as thy own voice did practise here,
When thy first-fruits of poesy were given
To make thyself a welcome inmate there ;
        While yet a young probationer
        And candidate of heaven.

    If by traduction came thy mind,
    Our wonder is the less to find
A soul so charming from a stock so good ;
Thy father was transfused into thy blood :
So wert thou born into the tuneful strain
(An early, rich and inexhausted vein).
    But if thy pre-existing soul
Was formed at first with myriads more,
    It did through all the mighty poets roll
Who Greek or Latin laurels wore,
And was that Sappho last, which once it was before.
    If so, then cease thy flight, O heaven-born mind !
Thou hast no dross to purge from thy rich ore :
    Nor can thy soul a fairer mansion find
    Than was the beauteous frame she left behind :
Return, to fill or mend the choir of thy celestial kind.

    May we presume to say that, at thy birth,
New joy was sprung in heaven as well as here on
        earth ?
For sure the milder planets did combine
On thy auspicious horoscope to shine,

John Dryden

And even the most malicious were in trine.
Thy brother angels at thy birth
   Strung each his lyre, and tuned it high,
   That all the people of the sky
Might know a poetess was born on earth;
      And then, if ever, mortal ears
      Had heard the music of the spheres.
   And if no clustering swarm of bees
On thy sweet mouth distilled their golden dew,
    'Twas that such vulgar miracles
    Heaven had not leisure to renew:
For all the best fraternity of love
Solemnized there thy birth, and kept thy holiday
   above.

    O gracious God! how far have we
Profaned Thy heavenly gift of poesy!
Made prostitute and profligate the Muse,
Debased to each obscene and impious use,
Whose harmony was first ordained above,
For tongues of angels and for hymns of love!
O wretched we! why were we hurried down
    This lubric and adulterate age
   (Nay, added fat pollutions of our own),
    To increase the steaming ordures of the stage?
What can we say to excuse our second fall?
Let this thy Vestal, heaven, atone for all!
Her Arethusan stream remains unsoiled,
Unmixed with foreign filth and undefiled;
Her wit was more than man, her innocence a child.
Art she had none, yet wanted none,
   For Nature did that want supply:
So rich in treasures of her own,
   She might our boasted stores defy:

John Dryden

Such noble vigour did her verse adorn
That it seemed borrowed, where 'twas only born.
Her morals, too, were in her bosom bred,
   By great examples daily fed,
What in the best of books, her father's life, she read.
    And to be read herself she need not fear;
    Each test and every light her muse will bear,
    Though Epictetus with his lamp were there.
    Even love (for love sometimes her muse expressed)
Was but a lambent flame which played about her
      breast,
    Light as the vapours of a morning dream;
   So cold herself, while she such warmth expressed,
    'Twas Cupid bathing in Diana's stream.

     .   .   .   .   .   .

When in mid-air the golden trump shall sound,
    To raise the nations underground;
    When in the valley of Jehosophat
The judging God shall close the book of Fate,
    And there the last assizes keep
    For those who wake and those who sleep;
    When rattling bones together fly
    From the four quarters of the sky;
When sinews o'er the skeletons are spread,
Those clothed with flesh, and life inspires the dead;
The sacred poets first shall hear the sound,
And foremost from the tomb shall bound,
For they are covered with the lightest ground;
And straight with inborn vigour, on the wing,
Like mountain larks, to the new morning sing.
There thou, sweet saint, before the choir shalt go,
As harbinger of heaven, the way to show,
The way which thou so well hast learned below.

APHRA BEHN

1640-1689

SONG, FROM ABDELAZAR

LOVE in fantastic triumph sat,
  Whilst bleeding hearts around him flowed,
For whom fresh pains he did create ;
  And strange tyrannic power he showed.
From thy bright eyes he took his fires,
  Which round about in sport he hurled ;
But 'twas from mine he took desires
  Enough to undo the amorous world.

From me he took his sighs and tears,
  From thee his pride and cruelty ;
From me his languishment and fears,
  And every killing dart from thee.
Thus thou and I the god have armed,
  And set him up a deity ;
But my poor heart alone is harmed,
  Whilst thine the victor is, and free.

JOSEPH ADDISON

1672-1719

HYMN

THE spacious firmament on high,
With all the blue ethereal sky,
And spangled heavens (a shining frame !)
Their great Original proclaim.

Alexander Pope

The unwearied sun from day to day
Doth his Creator's power display,
And publisheth to every land
The work of an almighty hand.

Soon as the evening shades prevail,
The moon takes up the wondrous tale,
And nightly to the listening earth
Repeats the story of her birth :
Whilst all the stars that round her burn,
And all the planets in their turn,
Confirm the tidings as they roll,
And spread the truth from pole to pole.

What though in solemn silence all
Move round this dark terrestrial ball?
What though no real voice nor sound
Amid their radiant orbs be found?
In Reason's ear they all rejoice,
And utter forth a glorious voice,
For ever singing as they shine,
' The hand that made us is divine.'

ALEXANDER POPE

1688-1744

ELEGY

To the Memory of an unfortunate Lady

WHAT beckoning ghost along the moonlight shade
Invites my steps, and points to yonder glade?
'Tis she!—but why that bleeding bosom gored?
Why dimly gleams the visionary sword?

Alexander Pope

O ever beauteous, ever friendly ! tell,
Is it in heaven a crime to love too well,
To bear too tender or too firm a heart,
To act a lover's or a Roman's part?
Is there no bright reversion in the sky,
For those who greatly think or bravely die?
Why bade ye else, ye Powers ! her soul aspire
Above the vulgar flight of low desire?
Ambition first sprung from your blest abodes,
The glorious fault of angels and of gods.
Thence to their images on earth it flows,
And in the breasts of kings and heroes glows.
Most souls, 'tis true, but peep out once an age,
Dull, sullen pris'ners in the body's cage;
Dim lights of life, that burn a length of years,
Useless, unseen, as lamps in sepulchres;
Like eastern kings, a lazy state they keep,
And close confined to their own palace, sleep.
   From these perhaps (ere Nature bade her die)
Fate snatched her early to the pitying sky.
As into air the purer spirits flow,
And sep'rate from their kindred dregs below;
So flew the soul to its congenial place,
Nor left one virtue to redeem her race.
   But thou, false guardian of a charge too good,
Thou mean deserter of thy brother's blood !
See on these ruby lips the trembling breath,
These cheeks now fading at the blast of death;
Cold is that breath which warmed the world before,
And those love-darting eyes must roll no more.
Thus, if Eternal Justice rules the ball,
Thus shall your wives, and thus your children fall:
On all the line a sudden vengeance waits,
And frequent hearses shall besiege your gates;

Alexander Pope

There passengers shall stand, and pointing say
(While the long fun'rals blacken all the way),
'Lo ! these were they whose souls the Furies steeled,
And cursed with hearts unknowing how to yield.
Thus unlamented pass the proud away,
The gaze of fools, and pageants of a day !
So perish all whose breasts ne'er learned to glow
For others' good, or melt at others' woe.'
    What can atone (O ever injured shade !)
Thy fate unpitied, and thy rites unpaid ?
No friend's complaint, no kind domestic tear
Pleased thy pale ghost, or graced thy mournful bier :
By foreign hands thy dying eyes were closed,
By foreign hands thy decent limbs composed,
By foreign hands thy humble grave adorned,
By strangers honoured and by strangers mourned.
What though no friends in sable weeds appear,
Grieve for an hour perhaps, then mourn a year,
And bear about the mockery of woe
To midnight dances, and the public show ?
What though no weeping loves thy ashes grace,
Nor polished marble emulate thy face ?
What though no sacred earth allow thee room,
Nor hallowed dirge be muttered o'er thy tomb ?
Yet shall thy grave with rising flow'rs be dressed,
And the green turf lie lightly on thy breast :
There shall the morn her earliest tears bestow,
There the first roses of the year shall blow ;
While angels with their silver wings o'ershade
The ground, now sacred by thy relics made.
    So peaceful rests, without a stone, a name,
What once had beauty, titles, wealth and fame.
How loved, how honoured once, avails thee not,
To whom related, or by whom begot ;

William Cowper

A heap of dust alone remains of thee :
'Tis all thou art, and all the proud shall be !
   Poets themselves must fall, like those they sung,
Deaf the praised ear, and mute the tuneful tongue.
Ev'n he whose soul now melts in mournful lays
Shall shortly want the gen'rous tear he pays ;
Then from his closing eyes thy form shall part,
And the last pang shall tear thee from his heart :
Life's idle business at one gasp be o'er,
The Muse forgot, and thou beloved no more !

WILLIAM COWPER

1731-1800

LINES ON RECEIVING HIS MOTHER'S PICTURE

O THAT those lips had language ! Life has passed
With me but roughly since I heard thee last.
Those lips are thine—thy own sweet smiles I see,
The same that oft in childhood solaced me ;
Voice only fails, else how distinct they say,
'Grieve not, my child—chase all thy fears away ! '
The meek intelligence of those dear eyes
(Blest be the art that can immortalise,
The art that baffles Time's tyrannic claim
To quench it) here shines on me still the same.
Faithful remembrancer of one so dear,
O welcome guest, though unexpected here !
Who bid'st me honour with an artless song,
Affectionate, a mother lost so long.
I will obey, not willingly alone,
But gladly, as the precept were her own :

William Cowper

And while that face renews my filial grief,
Fancy shall weave a charm for my relief,
Shall steep me in Elysian reverie,
A momentary dream, that thou art she.
  My mother! when I learnt that thou wast dead,
Say, wast thou conscious of the tears I shed?
Hovered thy spirit o'er thy sorrowing son,
Wretch even then, life's journey just begun?
Perhaps thou gav'st me, though unseen, a kiss;
Perhaps a tear, if souls can weep in bliss—
Ah, that maternal smile! it answers—yes.
I heard the bell tolled on thy burial day,
I saw the hearse that bore thee slow away,
And, turning from my nursery window, drew
A long, long sigh, and wept a last adieu!
But was it such?—It was.—Where thou art gone
Adieus and farewells are a sound unknown.
May I but meet thee on that peaceful shore
The parting word shall pass my lips no more!
Thy maidens, grieved themselves at my concern,
Oft gave me promise of thy quick return.
What ardently I wished, I long believed,
And, disappointed still, was still deceived,
By expectation every day beguiled,
Dupe of *to-morrow* even from a child.
Thus many a sad to-morrow came and went,
Till, all my stock of infant sorrow spent,
I learnt at last submission to my lot,
But though I less deplored thee, ne'er forgot.
  Where once we dwelt our name is heard no more,
Children not thine have trod my nursery floor;
And where the gardener Robin, day by day,
Drew me to school along the public way,
Delighted with my bauble coach, and wrapped

William Cowper

In scarlet mantle warm, and velvet-capt,
'Tis now become a history little known,
That once we called the pastoral house our own.
Short-lived possession ! but the record fair
That memory keeps of all thy kindness there,
Still outlives many a storm, that has effaced
A thousand other themes less deeply traced :
Thy nightly visits to my chamber paid
That thou might'st know me safe and warmly laid ;
Thy morning bounties ere I left my home,
The biscuit, or confectionary plum ;
The fragrant waters on my cheeks bestowed
By thy own hand, till fresh they shone and glowed ;
All this, and more endearing still than all,
Thy constant flow of love, that knew no fall,
Ne'er roughened by those cataracts and breaks,
That humour interposed too often makes ;
All this still legible in memory's page,
And still to be so till my latest age,
Adds joy to duty, makes me glad to pay
Such honours to thee as my numbers may ;
Perhaps a frail memorial, but sincere,
Not scorned in heaven, though little noticed here.
   Could Time, his flight reversed, restore the hours,
When, playing with thy vesture's tissued flowers,
The violet, the pink, the jessamine,
I pricked them into paper with a pin
(And thou wast happier than myself the while,
Wouldst softly speak, and stroke my head and smile),
Could those few pleasant days again appear,
Might one wish bring them, would I wish them here ?
I would not trust my heart—the dear delight
Seems so to be desired, perhaps I might—
But no—what here we call our life is such,

William Cowper

So little to be loved, and thou so much,
That I should ill requite thee to constrain
Thy unbound spirit into bonds again.
   Thou, as a gallant bark from Albion's coast
(The storms all weathered and the ocean crossed),
Shoots into port at some well-havened isle,
Where spices breathe, and brighter seasons smile,
There sits quiescent on the floods, that show
Her beauteous form reflected clear below,
While airs impregnated with incense play
Around her, fanning light her streamers gay ;
So thou, with sails how swift ! hast reached the
      shore,
'Where tempests never beat nor billows roar,'
And thy loved consort on the dangerous tide
Of life, long since has anchored at thy side.
But me, scarce hoping to attain that rest,
Always from port withheld, always distressed—
Me howling winds drive devious, tempest-tossed,
Sails ripped, seams opening wide, and compass lost,
And day by day some current's thwarting force
Sets me more distant from a prosperous course.
Yet, O the thought that thou art safe, and he !
That thought is joy, arrive what may to me.
My boast is not that I deduce my birth
From loins enthroned, and rulers of the earth ;
But higher far my proud pretensions rise—
The son of parents passed into the skies.
And now, farewell—Time unrevoked has run
His wonted course, yet what I wished is done.
By contemplation's help, not sought in vain,
I seem to have lived my childhood o'er again ;
To have renewed the joys that once were mine,
Without the sin of violating thine ;

Anna Laetitia Barbauld

And, while the wings of Fancy still are free,
And I can view this mimic show of thee,
Time has but half succeeded in his theft—
Thyself removed, thy power to soothe me left.

ANNA LAETITIA BARBAULD

1743-1825

LIFE

LIFE! I know not what thou art,
But know that thou and I must part;
And when, or how, or where we met,
I own to me's a secret yet.

Life! we've been long together
Through pleasant and through cloudy weather;
'Tis hard to part when friends are dear—
Perhaps 'twill cost a sigh, a tear;
—Then steal away, give little warning,
  Choose thine own time;
Say not Good-night—but in some brighter clime
  Bid me Good-morning.

WILLIAM BLAKE

1757-1828

THE LAND OF DREAMS

AWAKE, awake, my little boy!
Thou wast thy mother's only joy.
Why dost thou weep in thy gentle sleep?
Awake, thy Father does thee keep.

William Blake

'O, what land is the Land of Dreams,
What are its mountains and what are its streams?
O father, I saw my mother there,
Among the lilies by waters fair.

'Among the lambs clothed in white,
She walked with her Thomas in sweet delight;
I wept for joy, like a dove I mourn,
O, when shall I again return?'

Dear child, I also by pleasant streams
Have wandered all night in the Land of Dreams,
But though calm and warm the waters wide,
I could not get to the other side.

'Father, O Father! what do we here,
In this land of unbelief and fear?
The Land of Dreams is better far
Above the light of the morning star.'

THE PIPER

PIPING down the valleys wild,
   Piping songs of pleasant glee,
On a cloud I saw a child,
   And he laughing said to me :—

'Pipe a song about a lamb.'
   So I piped with merry cheer.
'Piper, pipe that song again.'
   So I piped; he wept to hear.

William Blake

'Drop thy pipe, thy happy pipe,
  Sing thy songs of happy cheer.'
So I sang the same again,
  While he wept with joy to hear.

'Piper, sit thee down and write
  In a book that all may read':
So he vanished from my sight,
  And I plucked a hollow reed;

And I made a rural pen,
  And I stained the water clear,
And I wrote my happy songs
  Every child may joy to hear.

HOLY THURSDAY

'TWAS on a Holy Thursday, their innocent faces clean,
Came children walking two and two, in red, and blue,
    and green;
Grey-headed beadles walked before, with wands as
    white as snow,
Till into the high dome of Paul's they like Thames
    waters flow.

O what a multitude they seemed, these flowers of
    London town!
Seated in companies they sit, with radiance all their
    own;
The hum of multitudes was there, but multitudes of
    lambs,
Thousands of little boys and girls raising their innocent
    hands,

William Blake

Now, like a mighty wind, they raise to heaven the voice
  of song,
Or like harmonious thunderings the seats of heaven
  among;
Beneath them sit the aged men, wise guardians of the
  poor.
Then cherish pity, lest you drive an angel from your
  door.

THE TIGER

TIGER, tiger, burning bright
In the forests of the night,
What immortal hand or eye
Could frame thy fearful symmetry?

In what distant deeps or skies
Burnt the fire of thine eyes?
On what wings dare he aspire?
What the hand dare seize the fire?

And what shoulder, and what art,
Could twist the sinews of thy heart?
And when thy heart began to beat,
What dread hand and what dread feet?

What the hammer? what the chain?
In what furnace was thy brain?
What the anvil? what dread grasp
Dare its deadly terrors clasp?

When the stars threw down their spears,
And watered heaven with their tears,
Did he smile his work to see?
Did He who made the lamb make thee?

William Blake

Tiger, tiger, burning bright
In the forests of the night,
What immortal hand or eye
Dare frame thy fearful symmetry?

TO THE MUSES

WHETHER on Ida's shady brow,
  Or in the chambers of the East,
The chambers of the sun, that now
  From ancient melody have ceased;

Whether in heaven ye wander fair,
  Or the green corners of the earth,
Or the blue regions of the air,
  Where the melodious winds have birth;

Whether on crystal rocks ye rove
  Beneath the bosom of the sea,
Wandering in many a coral grove,—
  Fair Nine, forsaking Poetry;

How have you left the ancient love
  That bards of old enjoyed in you!
The languid strings do scarcely move,
  The sound is forced, the notes are few.

LOVE'S SECRET   .

NEVER seek to tell thy love,
  Love that never told can be;
For the gentle wind doth move
  Silently, invisibly.

Robert Burns

I told my love, I told my love,
    I told her all my heart,
Trembling, cold, in ghastly fears
    Ah ! she did depart.

Soon after she was gone from me
    A traveller came by,
Silently, invisibly :
    He took her with a sigh.

ROBERT BURNS

1759-1796

TO A MOUSE

On turning her up in her nest with the plough,
November, 1785

WEE, sleekit, cow'rin', tim'rous beastie,
O what a panic's in thy breastie !
Thou need na start awa sae hasty,
           Wi' bickerin' brattle !
I wad be laith to rin an' chase thee
           Wi' murd'ring pattle !

I'm truly sorry man's dominion
Has broken Nature's social union,
An' justifies that ill opinion
           Which makes thee startle
At me, thy poor earth-born companion,
           An' fellow-mortal !

Robert Burns

I doubt na, whiles, but thou may thieve ;
What then? poor beastie, thou maun live !
A daimen-icker in a thrave
   'S a sma' request :
I 'll get a blessin' wi' the lave,
   And never miss 't !

Thy wee bit housie, too, in ruin !
Its silly wa's the win's are strewin' :
And naething, now, to big a new ane,
   O' foggage green !
An' bleak December's winds ensuin'
   Baith snell and keen !

Thou saw the fields laid bare an' waste,
An' weary winter comin' fast,
An' cozy here beneath the blast,
   Thou thought to dwell,
Till crash ! the cruel coulter past
   Out through thy cell.

That wee bit heap o' leaves and stibble
Has cost thee mony a weary nibble !
Now thou 's turned out, for a' thy trouble,
   But house or hald,
To thole the winter's sleety dribble
   An' cranreuch cauld !

But, mousie, thou art no thy lane
In proving foresight may be vain :
The best-laid schemes o' mice an' men
   Gang aft a-gley,
An' lea'e us nought but grief an' pain,
   For promised joy.

Robert Burns

Still thou art blest compared wi' me !
The present only toucheth thee :
But, och ! I backward cast my e'e
        On prospects drear !
An' forward though I canna see,
        I guess and fear !

THE FAREWELL

IT was a' for our rightfu' king
  We left fair Scotland's strand ;
It was a' for our rightfu' king
  We e'er saw Irish land,
      My dear,
  We e'er saw Irish land.

Now a' is done that man can do,
  And a' is done in vain ;
My love and native land farewell,
  For I maun cross the main,
      My dear,
  For I maun cross the main.

He turned him right and round about
  Upon the Irish shore ;
And gae his bridle-reins a shake,
  With Adieu for evermore,
      My dear,
  Adieu for evermore.

The sodger frae the wars returns,
  The sailor frae the main ;
But I hae parted frae my love,

William Wordsworth

Never to meet again,
My dear,
Never to meet again.

When day is gane, and night is come,
And a' folks bound to sleep;
I think on him that's far awa',
The lee-lang night, and weep,
My dear,
The lee-lang night, and weep.

WILLIAM WORDSWORTH

1770-1850

WHY ART THOU SILENT?

WHY art thou silent? Is thy love a plant
Of such weak fibre that the treacherous air
Of absence withers what was once so fair?
Is there no debt to pay, no boon to grant?
Yet have my thoughts for thee been vigilant,
Bound to thy service with unceasing care—
The mind's least generous wish a mendicant
For nought but what thy happiness could spare.
Speak !—though this soft warm heart, once free to
    hold
A thousand tender pleasures, thine and mine,
Be left more desolate, more dreary cold
Than a forsaken bird's-nest filled with snow
'Mid its own bush of leafless eglantine—
Speak, that my torturing doubts their end may
    know !

P   225

William Wordsworth

THOUGHTS OF A BRITON ON THE SUBJUGATION OF SWITZERLAND

Two Voices are there; one is of the Sea,
One of the Mountains; each a mighty voice:
In both from age to age thou didst rejoice,
They were thy chosen music, Liberty!
There came a tyrant, and with holy glee
Thou fought'st against him—but hast vainly striven:
Thou from thy Alpine holds at length art driven,
Where not a torrent murmurs heard by thee.
—Of one deep bliss thine ear hath been bereft;
Then cleave, O cleave to that which still is left—
For, high-souled Maid, what sorrow would it be
That Mountain floods should thunder as before,
And Ocean bellow from his rocky shore,
And neither awful Voice be heard by thee!

IT IS A BEAUTEOUS EVENING, CALM AND FREE

It is a beauteous evening, calm and free;
The holy time is quiet as a Nun
Breathless with adoration; the broad sun
Is sinking down in his tranquillity;
The gentleness of heaven is on the Sea;
Listen! the mighty Being is awake,
And doth with his eternal motion make
A sound like thunder—everlastingly.
Dear child! dear girl! that walkest with me here,
If thou appear untouched by solemn thought,
Thy nature is not therefore less divine:
Thou liest in Abraham's bosom all the year,
And worshipp'st at the Temple's inner shrine
God being with thee when we know it not.

William Wordsworth

ON THE EXTINCTION OF THE VENETIAN REPUBLIC

ONCE did She hold the gorgeous East in fee,
And was the safeguard of the West; the worth
Of Venice did not fall below her birth,
Venice, the eldest child of Liberty.
She was a maiden city, bright and free;
No guile seduced, no force could violate;
And when she took unto herself a mate,
She must espouse the everlasting Sea.
And what if she had seen those glories fade,
Those titles vanish, and that strength decay—
Yet shall some tribute of regret be paid
When her long life hath reached its final day;
Men are we, and must grieve when even the shade
Of that which once was great is passed away.

O FRIEND! I KNOW NOT

O FRIEND! I know not which way I must look
For comfort; being, as I am, oppressed
To think that now our life is only dressed
For show; mean handiwork of craftsman, cook,
Or groom!—We must run glittering like a brook
In the open sunshine, or we are unblessed;
The wealthiest man among us is the best;
No grandeur now in nature or in book
Delights us. Rapine, avarice, expense,—
This is idolatry; and these we adore;
Plain living and high thinking are no more;
The homely beauty of the good old cause
Is gone; our peace, our fearful innocence,
And pure religion breathing household laws.

William Wordsworth

SURPRISED by joy—impatient as the wind—
I turned to share the transport—O! with whom
But thee—deep buried in the silent tomb,
That spot which no vicissitude can find?
Love, faithful love, recalled thee to my mind—
But how could I forget thee? Through what power,
Even for the least division of an hour,
Have I been so beguiled as to be blind
To my most grievous loss!—That thought's return
Was the worst pang that sorrow ever bore,
Save one, one only, when I stood forlorn,
Knowing my heart's best treasure was no more;
That neither present time nor years unborn
Could to my sight that heavenly face restore.

TO TOUSSAINT L'OUVERTURE

TOUSSAINT, the most unhappy man of men!
Whether the all-cheering sun be free to shed
His beams around thee, or thou rest thy head
Pillowed in some dark dungeon's noisome den—
O miserable chieftain! where and when
Wilt thou find patience? Yet die not; do thou
Wear rather in thy bonds a cheerful brow:
Though fallen thyself, never to rise again,
Live and take comfort. Thou hast left behind
Powers that will work for thee: air, earth, and skies;
There's not a breathing of the common wind
That will forget thee; thou hast great allies;
Thy friends are exultations, agonies,
And love, and man's unconquerable mind.

228

William Wordsworth

WITH ships the sea was sprinkled far and nigh,
Like stars in heaven, and joyously it showed;
Some lying fast at anchor in the road,
Some veering up and down, one knew not why.
A goodly vessel did I then espy
Come like a giant from a haven broad;
And lustily along the bay she strode,
'Her tackling rich, and of apparel high.'
This ship was naught to me, nor I to her,
Yet I pursued her with a lover's look;
This ship to all the rest did I prefer:
When will she turn, and whither? She will brook
No tarrying; where she comes the winds must stir:
On went she—and due north her journey took.

THE WORLD

THE World is too much with us; late and soon,
Getting and spending, we lay waste our powers;
Little we see in Nature that is ours;
We have given our hearts away, a sordid boon!
This Sea that bares her bosom to the moon,
The winds that will be howling at all hours
And are up-gathered now like sleeping flowers,—
For this, for every thing, we are out of tune;
It moves us not.—Great God! I'd rather be
A Pagan suckled in a creed outworn,—
So might I, standing on this pleasant lea,
Have glimpses that would make me less forlorn;
Have sight of Proteus rising from the sea,
Or hear old Triton blow his wreathed horn.

William Wordsworth

UPON WESTMINSTER BRIDGE, SEPT. 3, 1802

EARTH has not anything to show more fair:
Dull would he be of soul who could pass by
A sight so touching in its majesty:
This city now doth like a garment wear
The beauty of the morning: silent, bare,
Ships, towers, domes, theatres, and temples lie
Open unto the fields, and to the sky,—
All bright and glittering in the smokeless air.
Never did sun more beautifully steep
In his first splendour valley, rock, or hill;
Ne'er saw I, never felt, a calm so deep!
The river glideth at his own sweet will:
Dear God! the very houses seem asleep;
And all that mighty heart is lying still!

WHEN I HAVE BORNE IN MEMORY

WHEN I have borne in memory what has tamed
Great nations; how ennobling thoughts depart,
What men change swords for ledgers, and desert
The student's bower for gold,—some fears unnamed
I had, my country!—am I to be blamed?
Now, when I think of thee, and what thou art,
Verily, in the bottom of my heart
Of those unfilial fears I am ashamed.
For dearly must we prize thee; we do find
In thee a bulwark for the cause of men;
And I by my affection was beguiled:
What wonder if a Poet now and then,
Among the many movements of his mind,
Felt for thee as a lover or a child!

William Wordsworth

THREE YEARS SHE GREW

THREE years she grew in sun and shower;
Then Nature said, ' A lovelier flower
On earth was never sown.
This child I to myself will take:
She shall be mine, and I will make
A lady of my own.

'Myself will to my darling be
Both law and impulse; and with me
The girl, in rock and plain,
In earth and heaven, in glade and bower,
Shall feel an overseeing power
To kindle or restrain.

'She shall be sportive as the fawn,
That wild with glee across the lawn
Or up the mountain springs;
And hers shall be the breathing balm,
And hers the silence and the calm
Of mute insensate things.

'The floating clouds their state shall lend
To her; for her the willow bend;
Nor shall she fail to see
Ev'n in the motions of the storm
Grace that shall mould the maiden's form
By silent sympathy.

William Wordsworth

'The stars of midnight shall be dear
To her, and she shall lean her ear
In many a secret place,
Where rivulets dance their wayward round,
And beauty born of murmuring sound
Shall pass into her face.

'And vital feelings of delight
Shall rear her form to stately height,
Her virgin bosom swell;
Such thoughts to Lucy I will give
While she and I together live
Here in this happy dell.'

Thus Nature spake.   The work was done—
How soon my Lucy's race was run!
She died, and left to me
This heath, this calm and quiet scene;
The memory of what has been,
And never more will be.

THE DAFFODILS

I WANDERED lonely as a cloud
That floats on high o'er vales and hills,
When all at once I saw a crowd,
A host of golden daffodils,
Beside the lake, beneath the trees,
Fluttering and dancing in the breeze.

William Wordsworth

Continuous as the stars that shine
And twinkle on the milky way,
They stretched in never-ending line
Along the margin of a bay :
Ten thousand saw I at a glance
Tossing their heads in sprightly dance.

The waves beside them danced, but they
Out-did the sparkling waves in glee :—
A Poet could not but be gay
In such a jocund company !
I gazed—and gazed—but little thought
What wealth the show to me had brought ;

For oft when on my couch I lie
In vacant or in pensive mood,
They flash upon that inward eye
Which is the bliss of solitude ;
And then my heart with pleasure fills,
And dances with the daffodils.

THE SOLITARY REAPER

BEHOLD her, single in the field,
Yon solitary Highland Lass !
Reaping and singing by herself ;
Stop here, or gently pass !
Alone she cuts and binds the grain
And sings a melancholy strain ;
O listen ! for the vale profound
Is overflowing with the sound.

William Wordsworth

No nightingale did ever chaunt
More welcome notes to weary bands
Of travellers in some shady haunt,
Among Arabian sands:
A voice so thrilling ne'er was heard
In spring-time from the cuckoo-bird,
Breaking the silence of the seas
Among the farthest Hebrides.

Will no one tell me what she sings?
Perhaps the plaintive numbers flow
For old, unhappy, far-off things,
And battles long ago:
Or is it some more humble lay,
Familiar matter of to-day?
Some natural sorrow, loss, or pain,
That has been and may be again?

Whate'er the theme, the maiden sang
As if her song could have no ending;
I saw her singing at her work,
And o'er the sickle bending;—
I listened, motionless and still;
And, as I mounted up the hill,
The music in my heart I bore
Long after it was heard no more.

ELEGIAC STANZAS

Suggested by a Picture of Peele Castle in a Storm

I was thy neighbour once, thou rugged pile!
Four summer weeks I dwelt in sight of thee:
I saw thee every day; and all the while
Thy form was sleeping on a glassy sea.

William Wordsworth

So pure the sky, so quiet was the air!
So like, so very like, was day to day!
Whene'er I looked, thy image still was there;
It trembled, but it never passed away.

How perfect was the calm! It seemed no sleep,
No mood, which season takes away or brings:
I could have fancied that the mighty Deep
Was even the gentlest of all gentle things.

Ah! then—if mine had been the painter's hand
To express what then I saw; and add the gleam,
The light that never was on sea or land,
The consecration, and the Poet's dream,—

I would have planted thee, thou hoary pile,
Amid a world how different from this!
Beside a sea that could not cease to smile;
On tranquil land, beneath a sky of bliss.

Thou shouldst have seemed a treasure-house divine
Of peaceful years: a chronicle of heaven;—
Of all the sunbeams that did ever shine
The very sweetest had to thee been given.

A picture had it been of lasting ease,
Elysian quiet, without toil or strife;
No motion but the moving tide; a breeze;
Or merely silent Nature's breathing life.

Such, in the fond illusion of my heart,
Such picture would I at that time have made;
And seen the soul of truth in every part,
A steadfast peace that might not be betrayed.

William Wordsworth

So once it would have been—'tis so no more;
I have submitted to a new control:
A power is gone which nothing can restore;
A deep distress hath humanized my soul.

Not for a moment could I now behold
A smiling sea, and be what I have been;
The feeling of my loss will ne'er be old;
This, which I know, I speak with mind serene.

Then, Beaumont, Friend! who would have been
    the friend
If he had lived, of him whom I deplore.
This work of thine I blame not, but commend;
This sea in anger, and that dismal shore.

O 'tis a passionate work!—yet wise and well,
Well chosen is the spirit that is here;
That hulk which labours in the deadly swell,
This rueful sky, this pageantry of fear!

And this huge Castle, standing here sublime,
I love to see the look with which it braves,—
Cased in the unfeeling armour of old time—
The lightning, the fierce wind, and trampling
    waves.

Farewell, farewell the heart that lives alone,
Housed in a dream, at distance from the kind!
Such happiness, wherever it be known,
Is to be pitied, for 'tis surely blind.

William Wordsworth

But welcome fortitude, and patient cheer,
And frequent sights of what is to be borne,—
Such sights, or worse, as are before me here !
Not without hope we suffer and we mourn.

TO H. C.

(Hartley Coleridge ; six years old.)

O THOU ! whose fancies from afar are brought;
Who of thy words dost make a mock apparel,
And fittest to unutterable thought
The breeze-like motion and the self-born carol ;
Thou fairy voyager ! that dost float
In such clear water that thy boat
May rather seem
To brood on air than on an earthly stream ;
Suspended in a stream as clear as sky,
Where earth and heaven do make one imagery ;
O blessed vision ! O happy child !
That art so exquisitely wild,
I think of thee with many fears
For what may be thy lot in future years.

I thought of times when pain might be thy guest,
Lord of thy house and hospitality ;
And grief, uneasy lover ! never rest
But when she sat within the touch of thee.
O ! too industrious folly !
O ! vain and causeless melancholy !
Nature will either end thee quite ;
Or, lengthening out thy season of delight,
Preserve for thee, by individual right,
A young lamb's heart among the full-grown flocks.

William Wordsworth

What hast thou to do with sorrow,
Or the injuries of to-morrow?
Thou art a dew-drop which the morn brings forth,
Not framed to undergo unkindly shocks;
Or to be trailed along the soiling earth;
A gem that glitters while it lives,
And no forewarning gives;
But, at the touch of wrong, without a strife
Slips in a moment out of life.

'TIS SAID THAT SOME HAVE DIED FOR LOVE

'Tis said that some have died for love:
And here and there a churchyard grave is found
In the cold North's unhallowed ground,
Because the wretched man himself had slain,—
His love was such a grievous pain.
And there is one whom I five years have known;
He dwells alone
Upon Helvellyn's side:
He loved——the pretty Barbara died,
And thus he makes his moan:
Three years had Barbara in her grave been laid,
When thus his moan he made:

'O move, thou cottage, from behind that oak!
Or let the aged tree uprooted lie,
That in some other way yon smoke
May mount into the sky!
The clouds pass on; they from the heavens depart:
I look—the sky is empty space;
I know not what I trace;
But, when I cease to look, my hand is on my heart.

William Wordsworth

'O what a weight is in these shades! Ye leaves,
When will that dying murmur be suppressed?
Your sound my heart of peace bereaves,
It robs my heart of rest.
Thou thrush, that singest loud—and loud and free,
Into yon row of willows flit,
Upon that alder sit;
Or sing another song, or choose another tree.

'Roll back, sweet rill! back to thy mountain bounds,
And there for ever be thy waters chained!
For thou dost haunt the air with sounds
That cannot be sustained;
If still beneath that pine-tree's ragged bough
Headlong yon waterfall must come,
O let it then be dumb!—
Be anything, sweet rill, but that which thou art now.

'Thou eglantine, whose arch so proudly towers
(Even like a rainbow spanning half the vale),
Thou one fair shrub—oh, shed thy flowers,
And stir not in the gale!
For thus to see thee nodding in the air,—
To see thy arch thus stretch and bend,
Thus rise and thus descend,—
Disturbs me, till the sight is more than I can bear.'

The man who makes this feverish complaint
Is one of giant stature, who could dance
Equipped from head to foot in iron mail.
Ah gentle love! if ever thought was thine
To store up kindred hours for me, thy face
Turn from me, gentle love! nor let me walk
Within the sound of Emma's voice, or know
Such happiness as I have known to-day.

239

William Wordsworth

THE PET LAMB

A Pastoral

THE dew was falling fast, the stars began to blink;
I heard a voice: it said, 'Drink, pretty creature, drink!'
And, looking o'er the hedge, before me I espied
A snow-white mountain lamb, with a maiden at its side.

No other sheep were near, the lamb was all alone,
And by a slender cord was tethered to a stone;
With one knee on the grass did the little maiden kneel,
While to that mountain lamb she gave its evening meal.

The lamb, while from her hand he thus his supper took,
Seemed to feast with head and ears; and his tail with
    pleasure shook.
'Drink, pretty creature, drink,' she said, in such a tone
That I almost received her heart into my own.

'Twas little Barbara Lewthwaite, a child of beauty rare!
I watched them with delight; they were a lovely pair.
Now with her empty can the maiden turned away;
But ere ten yards were gone, her footsteps did she stay.

Towards the lamb she looked; and from that shady
    place
I, unobserved, could see the workings of her face;
If Nature to her tongue could measured numbers bring,
Thus, thought I, to her lamb that little maid might
    sing:—

William Wordsworth

'What ails thee, young one? What? Why pull so at
    thy cord?
Is it not well with thee? Well both for bed and board?
Thy plot of grass is soft, and green as grass can be;
Rest, little young one, rest; what is't that aileth thee?

'What is it thou wouldst seek? What is wanting to
    thy heart?
Thy limbs, are they not strong? And beautiful thou art:
This grass is tender grass; these flowers they have no
    peers;
And that green corn all day is rustling in thy ears!

'If the sun be shining hot, do but stretch thy woollen
    chain,
This beech is standing by, its covert thou canst gain;
For rain and mountain storms, the like thou need'st
    not fear;—
The rain and storm are things which scarcely can come
    here.

'Rest, little young one, rest; thou hast forgot the day
When my father found thee first in places far away:
Many flocks were on the hills, but thou wert owned by
    none;
And thy mother from thy side for evermore was gone.

'He took thee in his arms, and in pity brought thee
    home:
A blessed day for thee! then whither wouldst thou
    roam?
A faithful nurse thou hast; the dam that did thee yean
Upon the mountain-tops no kinder could have been.

William Wordsworth

'Thou know'st that twice a day I have brought thee in
    this can
Fresh water from the brook, as clear as ever ran;
And twice in the day, when the ground is wet with dew,
I bring thee draughts of milk, warm milk it is, and new.

'Thy limbs will shortly be twice as stout as they are
    now,
Then I'll yoke thee to my cart like a pony in the
    plough;
My playmate thou shalt be; and when the wind is cold,
Our hearth shall be thy bed, our house shall be thy fold.

'It will not, will not rest!—poor creature, can it be
That 'tis thy mother's heart which is working so in thee?
Things that I know not of belike to thee are dear,
And dreams of things which thou canst neither see nor
    hear.

'Alas, the mountain-tops that look so green and fair!
I've heard of fearful winds and darkness that come
    there;
The little brooks, that seem all pastime and all play,
When they are angry roar like lions for their prey.

'Here thou need'st not dread the raven in the sky;
Night and day thou art safe,—our cottage is hard by.
Why bleat so after me? Why pull so at thy chain?
Sleep—and at break of day I will come to thee again!'

As homeward through the lane I went with lazy feet,
This song to myself did I oftentimes repeat;
And it seemed, as I retraced the ballad line by line,
That but half of it was hers, and one-half of it was mine.

William Wordsworth

Again, and once again did I repeat the song ;
'Nay,' said I, 'more than half to the damsel must
  belong,
For she looked with such a look, and she spake with
  such a tone,
That I almost received her heart into my own.'

STEPPING WESTWARD

*While my fellow-traveller and I were walking by the
side of Loch Katrine, one fine evening after sunset, in
our road to a hut where in the course of our tour we had
been hospitably entertained some weeks before, we met,
in one of the loneliest parts of that solitary region, two
well-dressed women, one of whom said to us, by way
of greeting, 'What, you are stepping westward?'*

'*What, you are stepping westward?*'—'*Yea.*'
—'Twould be a wildish destiny,
If we, who thus together roam
In a strange land, and far from home,
Were in this place the guests of chance ;
Yet who would stop, or fear t' advance,
Though home or shelter he had none,
With such a sky to lead him on?

The dewy ground was dark and cold ;
Behind, all gloomy to behold ;
And stepping westward seemed to be
A kind of heavenly destiny :
I liked the greeting ; 'twas a sound
Of something without place or bound ;
And seemed to give me spiritual right
To travel through that region bright.

William Wordsworth

The voice was soft, and she who spake
Was walking by her native lake;
The salutation had to me
The very sound of courtesy;
Its power was felt; and while my eye
Was fixed upon the glowing sky,
The echo of the voice enwrought
A human sweetness with the thought
Of travelling through the world that lay
Before me in my endless way.

THE CHILDLESS FATHER

'Up, Timothy, up with your staff and away!
Not a soul in the village this morning will stay;
The hare has just started from Hamilton's grounds,
And Skiddaw is glad with the cry of the hounds.'

—Of coats and of jackets grey, scarlet, and green,
On the slopes of the pastures all colours were seen;
With their comely blue aprons, and caps white as
   snow,
The girls on the hills made a holiday show.

The basin of boxwood,[1] just six months before,
Had stood on the table at Timothy's door;
A coffin through Timothy's threshold had passed;
One child did it bear, and that child was his last.

[1] In several parts of the north of England, when a funeral takes place, a basin full of sprigs of boxwood is placed at the door of the house from which the coffin is taken up, and each person who attends the funeral ordinarily takes a sprig of this boxwood, and throws it into the grave of the deceased.

244

William Wordsworth

Now fast up the dell came the noise and the fray,
The horse and the horn, and the ' hark ! hark away ! '
Old Timothy took up his staff, and he shut,
With a leisurely motion, the door of his hut.

Perhaps to himself at that moment he said,
'The key I must take, for my Helen is dead.'
But of this in my ears not a word did he speak,
And he went to the chase with a tear on his cheek.

ODE ON INTIMATIONS OF IMMORTALITY FROM
RECOLLECTIONS OF EARLY CHILDHOOD

THERE was a time when meadow, grove, and stream,
The earth, and every common sight
        To me did seem
        Apparelled in celestial light,
The glory and the freshness of a dream.
It is not now as it hath been of yore ;—
        Turn wheresoe'er I may,
        By night or day,
The things which I have seen I now can see no more.

        The rainbow comes and goes,
        And lovely is the rose ;
        ·The moon doth with delight
Look round her when the heavens are bare ;
        Waters on a starry night
        Are beautiful and fair ;
The sunshine is a glorious birth ;
But yet I know, where'er I go,
That there hath past away a glory from the earth.

William Wordsworth

Now, while the birds thus sing a joyous song,
  And while the young lambs bound
    As to the tabor's sound,
    To me alone there came a thought of grief:
    A timely utterance gave that thought relief,
      And I again am strong.
    The cataracts blow their trumpets from the steep;–
    No more shall grief of mine the season wrong:
    I hear the echoes through the mountains throng,
    The winds come to me from the fields of sleep,
      And all the earth is gay;
        Land and sea
      Give themselves up to jollity,
        And with the heart of May
    Doth every beast keep holiday;—
        Thou child of joy
Shout round me, let me hear thy shouts, thou happy
    Shepherd-boy!

Ye blessed Creatures, I have heard the call
    Ye to each other make; I see
The heavens laugh with you in your jubilee;
    My heart is at your festival,
    My head hath its coronal,
The fulness of your bliss, I feel—I feel it all.
        O evil day! if I were sullen
        While Earth herself is adorning
          This sweet May-morning;
        And the children are culling
          On every side,
        In a thousand valleys far and wide,
        Fresh flowers; while the sun shines warm
And the babe leaps up on his mother's arm:—

William Wordsworth

I hear, I hear, with joy I hear!
—But there's a tree, of many, one,
A single field which I have looked upon,
Both of them speak of something that is gone;
    The pansy at my feet
    Doth the same tale repeat:
Whither is fled the visionary gleam?
Where is it now, the glory and the dream?

Our birth is but a sleep and a forgetting;
The Soul that rises with us, our life's Star,
    Hath had elsewhere its setting
    And cometh from afar.
    Not in entire forgetfulness,
    And not in utter nakedness,
But trailing clouds of glory do we come
    From God, who is our home:
Heaven lies about us in our infancy!
Shades of the prison-house begin to close
    Upon the growing Boy,
But he beholds the light, and whence it flows,
    He sees it in his joy;
The Youth, who daily farther from the east
  Must travel, still is Nature's priest,
    And by the vision splendid
    Is on his way attended;
At length the Man perceives it die away
And fade into the light of common day.

Earth fills her lap with pleasures of her own;
Yearnings she hath in her own natural kind,
And, even with something of a mother's mind
    And no unworthy aim,

William Wordsworth

The homely nurse doth all she can
To make her foster-child, her inmate, Man,
　　Forget the glories he hath known,
And that imperial palace whence he came.

Behold the Child among his new-born blisses,
A six years' darling of a pigmy size!
See, where 'mid work of his own hand he lies,
Fretted by sallies of his mother's kisses,
With light upon him from his father's eyes!
See, at his feet, some little plan or chart,
Some fragment from his dream of human life,
Shaped by himself with newly-learned art;
　　A wedding or a festival,
　　A mourning or a funeral;
　　　And this hath now his heart,
　　And unto this he frames his song:
　　　Then will he fit his tongue
To dialogues of business, love, or strife;
　　　But it will not be long
　　　Ere this be thrown aside,
　　　And with new joy and pride
The little actor cons another part;
Filling from time to time his 'humorous stage'
With all the Persons, down to palsied Age,
That life brings with her in her equipage;
　　　As if his whole vocation
　　　Were endless imitation.

Thou, whose exterior semblance doth belie
　　　Thy soul's immensity;
Thou best philosopher, who yet dost keep
Thy heritage, thou eye among the blind

248

William Wordsworth

That, deaf and silent, read'st the eternal deep,
Haunted for ever by the eternal Mind,—
      Mighty Prophet! Seer blest!
      On whom those truths do rest
Which we are toiling all our lives to find,
In darkness lost, the darkness of the grave;
Thou, over whom thy Immortality
Broods like the day, a master o'er a slave,
A Presence which is not to be put by;
Thou little child, yet glorious in the might
Of heaven-born freedom on thy being's height,
Why with such earnest pains dost thou provoke
The years to bring the inevitable yoke,
Thus blindly with thy blessedness at strife?
Full soon thy soul shall have her earthly freight,
And custom lie upon thee with a weight
Heavy as frost, and deep almost as life!

      O joy! that in our embers
      Is something that doth live,
      That Nature yet remembers
      What was so fugitive!
The thought of our past years in me doth breed
Perpetual benediction: not, indeed,
For that which is most worthy to be blest,
Delight and liberty, the simple creed
Of Childhood, whether busy or at rest,
With new-fledged hope still fluttering in his
      breast:
      —Not for these I raise
      The song of thanks and praise;
   But for those obstinate questionings
   Of sense and outward things,

William Wordsworth

Fallings from us, vanishings;
  Blank misgivings of a creature
Moving about in worlds not realised,
High instincts, before which our mortal nature
Did tremble like a guilty thing surprised:
  But for those first affections,
  Those shadowy recollections,
      Which, be they what they may,
Are yet the fountain-light of all our day,
Are yet a master-light of all our seeing;
  Uphold us, cherish, and have power to make
Our noisy years seem moments in the being
Of the eternal Silence: truths that wake,
      To perish never;
Which neither listlessness, nor mad endeavour,
      Nor man nor boy,
Nor all that is at enmity with joy,
Can utterly abolish or destroy!
  Hence, in a season of calm weather,
    Though inland far we be,
Our souls have sight of that immortal sea
    Which brought us hither;
    Can in a moment travel thither—
And see the children sport upon the shore,
And hear the mighty waters rolling evermore.

Then sing, ye birds, sing, sing a joyous song!
    And let the young lambs bound
    As to the tabor's sound!
  We, in thought, will join your throng,
    Ye that pipe and ye that play,
    Ye that through your hearts to-day
    Feel the gladness of the May!

William Wordsworth

What though the radiance which was once so
  bright
Be now for ever taken from my sight,
    Though nothing can bring back the hour
Of splendour in the grass, of glory in the flower;
        We will grieve not, rather find
        Strength in what remains behind;
        In the primal sympathy
        Which, having been, must ever be;
        In the soothing thoughts that spring
        Out of human suffering;
        In the faith that looks through death,
In years that bring the philosophic mind.

And O, ye Fountains, Meadows, Hills, and
    Groves,
Forbode not any severing of our loves!
Yet in my heart of hearts I feel your might;
I only have relinquished one delight
To live beneath your more habitual sway:
I love the brooks which down their channels fret
Even more than when I tripped lightly as they;
The innocent brightness of a new-born day
      Is lovely yet;
The clouds that gather round the setting sun
Do take a sober colouring from an eye
That hath kept watch o'er man's mortality;
Another race hath been, and other palms are
    won.
Thanks to the human heart by which we live,
Thanks to its tenderness, its joys, and fears,
To me the meanest flower that blows can give
Thoughts that do often lie too deep for tears.

SIR WALTER SCOTT
1771-1832

PROUD MAISIE

PROUD Maisie is in the wood,
   Walking so early ;
Sweet Robin sits on the bush,
   Singing so rarely.

'Tell me, thou bonny bird,
   When shall I marry me ?'
'When six braw gentlemen
   Kirkward shall carry ye.'

'Who makes the bridal bed,
   Birdie, say truly ?'
'The grey-headed sexton
   That delves the grave duly.

'The glowworm o'er grave and stone
   Shall light thee steady ;
The owl from the steeple sing
   Welcome, proud lady.'

A WEARY LOT IS THINE

'A WEARY lot is thine, fair maid,
   A weary lot is thine !
To pull the thorn thy brow to braid,
   And press the rue for wine.

Sir Walter Scott

A lightsome eye, a soldier's mien,
  A feather of the blue,
A doublet of the Lincoln green—
  No more of me you knew,
        My Love !
No more of me you knew.

'This morn is merry June, I trow,
  The rose is budding fain ;
But she shall bloom in winter snow
  Ere we two meet again.'
He turned his charger as he spake
  Upon the river shore,
He gave the bridle-reins a shake,
  Said, 'Adieu for evermore,
        My Love !
And adieu for evermore.'

THE MAID OF NEIDPATH

O LOVERS' eyes are sharp to see,
  And lovers' ears in hearing ;
And love, in life's extremity,
  Can lend an hour of cheering.
Disease had been in Mary's bower
  And slow decay from mourning,
Though now she sits on Neidpath's tower
  To watch her love's returning.

All sunk and dim her eyes so bright,
  Her form decayed by pining,
Till through her wasted hand, at night,
  You saw the taper shining.

253

Samuel Taylor Coleridge

By fits a sultry hectic hue
  Across her cheek was flying;
By fits so ashy pale she grew
  Her maidens thought her dying.

Yet keenest powers to see and hear
  Seemed in her frame residing;
Before the watch-dog pricked his ear
  She heard her lover's riding;
Ere scarce a distant form was kenned
  She knew and waved to greet him,
And o'er the battlement did bend
  As on the wing to meet him.

He came—he passed—an heedless gaze
  As o'er some stranger glancing;
Her welcome, spoke in faltering phrase,
  Lost in his courser's prancing—
The castle-arch, whose hollow tone
  Returns each whisper spoken,
Could scarcely catch the feeble moan
  Which told her heart was broken.

SAMUEL TAYLOR COLERIDGE

1772-1834

KUBLA KHAN

In Xanadu did Kubla Khan
A stately pleasure-dome decree:
Where Alph, the sacred river, ran
Through caverns measureless to man
  Down to a sunless sea.
So twice five miles of fertile ground
With walls and towers were girdled round:

Samuel Taylor Coleridge

And there were gardens bright with sinuous rills
Where blossomed many an incense-bearing tree;
And here were forests ancient as the hills,
Enfolding sunny spots of greenery.
   But oh! that deep romantic chasm which slanted
Down the green hill athwart a cedarn cover!
A savage place! as holy and enchanted
As e'er beneath a waning moon was haunted
By woman wailing for her demon-lover!
And from this chasm, with ceaseless turmoil seething,
As if this earth in fast thick pants were breathing,
A mighty fountain momently was forced:
Amid whose swift half-intermitted burst
Huge fragments vaulted like rebounding hail,
Or chaffy grain beneath the thresher's flail;
And 'mid these dancing rocks at once and ever
It flung up momently the sacred river.
Five miles meandering with a mazy motion
Through wood and dale the sacred river ran,
Then reached the caverns measureless to man,
And sank in tumult to a lifeless ocean:
And, 'mid this tumult, Kubla heard from far
Ancestral voices prophesying war!

    The shadow of the dome of pleasure
      Floated midway on the waves;
     Where was heard the mingled measure
      From the fountain and the caves.
  It was a miracle of rare device,
A sunny pleasure-dome with caves of ice!
     A damsel with a dulcimer
      In a vision once I saw:
     It was an Abyssinian maid,
     And on her dulcimer she played,

Samuel Taylor Coleridge

Singing of Mount Abora.
Could I revive within me
Her symphony and song,
To such a deep delight 'twould win me,
That with music loud and long
I would build that dome in air,
That sunny dome! those caves of ice!
And all who heard should see them there,
And all should cry, Beware! Beware!
His flashing eyes, his floating hair!
Weave a circle round him thrice,
And close your eyes with holy dread,
For he on honey-dew hath fed,
And drunk the milk of Paradise.

YOUTH AND AGE

VERSE, a breeze 'mid blossoms straying,
Where Hope clung feeding, like a bee—
Both were mine! Life went a-maying
        With Nature, Hope, and Poesy,
        When I was young!
When I was young?—Ah, woeful when!
Ah! for the change 'twixt Now and Then!
This breathing house not built with hands,
This body that does me grievous wrong,
O'er aery cliffs and glittering sands
How lightly then it flashed along:
Like those trim skiffs, unknown of yore,
On winding lakes and rivers wide,
That ask no aid of sail or oar,
That fear no spite of wind or tide!
Nought cared this body for wind or weather
When Youth and I lived in't together.

Samuel Taylor Coleridge

Flowers are lovely ; Love is flower-like ;
Friendship is a sheltering tree ;
O ! the joys, that came down shower-like,
Of Friendship, Love, and Liberty,
      Ere I was old !
Ere I was old ? Ah woful Ere,
Which tells me, Youth 's no longer here !
O Youth ! for years so many and sweet,
'Tis known that thou and I were one,
I 'll think it but a fond conceit—
It cannot be that thou art gone !
Thy vesper-bell hath not yet tolled :—
And thou wert aye a masker bold !
What strange disguise hast now put on
To make believe that thou art gone ?
I see these locks in silvery slips,
This drooping gait, this altered size ;
But Spring-tide blossoms on thy lips,
And tears take sunshine from thine eyes !
Life is but Thought : so think I will
That Youth and I are house-mates still.
Dew-drops are the gems of morning,
But the tears of mournful eve,
Where no hope is, life's forewarning
That only serves to make us grieve,
      When we are old :
That only serves to make us grieve
With oft and tedious taking-leave,
Like some poor nigh-related guest .
That may not rudely be dismissed,
Yet hath out-stayed his welcome while,
And tells the jest without the smile.

Samuel Taylor Coleridge

In seven parts

ARGUMENT

How a ship having passed the Line was driven by storms to the cold Country towards the South Pole; and how from thence she made her course to the tropical Latitude of the Great Pacific Ocean; and of the strange things that befell; and in what manner the Ancient Mariner came back to his own Country.

PART I

IT is an ancient mariner,
And he stoppeth one of three.
'By thy long grey beard and glittering eye,
Now wherefore stopp'st thou me?

'The Bridegroom's doors are opened wide,
And I am next of kin;
The guests are met, the feast is set:
May'st hear the merry din.'

He holds him with his skinny hand,
'There was a ship,' quoth he.
'Hold off! unhand me, grey-beard loon!'
Eftsoons his hand dropt he.

He holds him with his glittering eye—
The Wedding-Guest stood still,
And listens like a three-years' child:
The mariner hath his will.

The Wedding-Guest sat on a stone:
He cannot choose but hear;
And thus spake on that ancient man,
The bright-eyed Mariner.

Samuel Taylor Coleridge

'The ship was cheered, the harbour cleared,
Merrily did we drop
Below the kirk, below the hill,
Below the lighthouse top.

'The sun came up upon the left,
Out of the sea came he !
And he shone bright, and on the right
Went down into the sea.

'Higher and higher every day,
Till over the mast at noon—'
The Wedding-Guest here beat his breast,
For he heard the loud bassoon.

The bride hath paced into the hall,
Red as a rose is she;
Nodding their heads before her goes
The merry minstrelsy.

The Wedding-Guest he beat his breast,
Yet he cannot choose but hear;
And thus spake on that ancient man,
The bright-eyed Mariner.

'And now the Storm-blast came, and he
Was tyrannous and strong:
He struck with his o'ertaking wings,
And chased us south along.

'With sloping masts and dipping prow
As who pursued with yell and blow
Still treads the shadow of his foe,

And forward bends his head,
The ship drove fast, loud roared the blast,
And southward aye we fled.

'And now there came both mist and snow,
And it grew wondrous cold :
And ice, mast-high, came floating by,
As green as emerald.

'And through the drifts the snowy clifts
Did send a dismal sheen :
Nor shapes of men nor beasts we ken—
The ice was all between.

'The ice was here, the ice was there,
The ice was all around :
It cracked and growled, and roared and howled,
Like noises in a swound !

'At length did cross an Albatross,
Thorough the fog it came ;
As it had been a Christian soul,
We hailed it in God's name.

'It ate the food it ne'er had eat,
And round and round it flew.
The ice did split with a thunder-fit ;
The helmsman steered us through !

'And a good south wind sprang up behind ;
The Albatross did follow,
And every day, for food or play,
Came to the mariner's hollo !

Samuel Taylor Coleridge

'In mist or cloud, on mast or shroud,
It perched for vespers nine;
Whiles all the night, through fog-smoke white,
Glimmered the white moon-shine.'

'God save thee, ancient Mariner!
From the fiends that plague thee thus!—
Why look'st thou so?'—With my cross-bow
I shot the Albatross.

PART II

The sun now rose upon the right:
Out of the sea came he,
Still hid in mist, and on the left
Went down into the sea.

And the good south wind still blew behind,
But no sweet bird did follow,
Nor any day for food or play
Came to the mariner's hollo!

And I had done a hellish thing,
And it would work 'em woe:
For all averred I had killed the bird
That made the breeze to blow.
Ah wretch! said they, the bird to slay,
That made the breeze to blow!

Nor dim nor red, like God's own head
The glorious Sun uprist:
Then all averred I had killed the bird
That brought the fog and mist.
'Twas right, said they, such birds to slay,
That bring the fog and mist.

Samuel Taylor Coleridge

The fair breeze blew, the white foam flew,
The furrow followed free;
We were the first that ever burst
Into that silent sea.

Down dropt the breeze, the sails dropt down,
'Twas sad as sad could be;
And we did speak only to break
The silence of the sea!

All in a hot and copper sky,
The bloody Sun, at noon,
Right up above the mast did stand,
No bigger than the Moon.

Day after day, day after day,
We stuck, nor breath nor motion;
As idle as a painted ship
Upon a painted ocean.

Water, water, every where,
And all the boards did shrink;
Water, water, every where
Nor any drop to drink.

The very deep did rot: O Christ!
That ever this should be!
Yea, slimy things did crawl with legs
Upon the slimy sea.

About, about, in reel and rout
The death-fires danced at night;
The water, like a witch's oils,
Burnt green, and blue and white.

Samuel Taylor Coleridge

And some in dreams assured were
Of the Spirit that plagued us so,
Nine fathom deep he had followed us
From the land of mist and snow.

And every tongue, through utter drought,
Was withered at the root;
We could not speak, no more than if
We had been choked with soot.

Ah! well a-day! what evil looks
Had I from old and young!
Instead of the cross, the Albatross
About my neck was hung.

PART III

There passed a weary time.   Each throat
Was parched, and glazed each eye.
A weary time! a weary time!
How glazed each weary eye—
When looking westward, I beheld
A something in the sky.

At first it seemed a little speck,
And then it seemed a mist;
It moved and moved, and took at last
A certain shape, I wist.

A speck, a mist, a shape, I wist!
And still it neared and neared:
As if it dodged a water-sprite,
It plunged and tacked and veered.

Samuel Taylor Coleridge

With throats unslaked, with black lips baked,
We could nor laugh nor wail;
Through utter drought all dumb we stood!
I bit my arm, I sucked the blood,
And cried, A sail! a sail!

With throats unslaked, with black lips baked,
Agape they heard me call:
Gramercy! they for joy did grin,
And all at once their breath drew in,
As they were drinking all.

See! see! (I cried) she tacks no more!
Hither to work us weal,
Without a breeze, without a tide,
She steadies with upright keel!

The western wave was all aflame,
The day was well nigh done;
Almost upon the western wave
Rested the broad bright Sun;
When that strange shape drove suddenly
Betwixt us and the Sun!

And straight the Sun was flecked with bars,
(Heaven's Mother send us grace!)
As if through a dungeon-grate he peered
With broad and burning face.

Alas! (thought I, and my heart beat loud)
How fast she nears and nears!
Are those her sails that glance in the Sun,
Like restless gossameres?

Samuel Taylor Coleridge

Are those her ribs through which the Sun
Did peer as through a grate?
And is that Woman all her crew?
Is that a Death? and are there two?
Is Death that woman's mate?

Her lips were red, her looks were free,
Her locks were yellow as gold,
Her skin was white as leprosy;
The Night-mare Life-in-Death was she,
Who thicks man's blood with cold.

The naked hulk alongside came,
And the twain were casting dice;
'The game is done! I've won! I've won!'
Quoth she, and whistles thrice.

The Sun's rim dips; the stars rush out:
At one stride comes the dark;
With far-heard whisper, o'er the sea,
Off shot the spectre-bark.

We listened and looked sideways up;
Fear at my heart, as at a cup,
My life-blood seemed to sip!
The stars were dim, and thick the night,
The steersman's face by his lamp gleamed white;
From the sails the dew did drip—
Till clomb above the eastern bar
The horned Moon, with one bright star
Within the nether tip.

One after one, by the star-dogged Moon,
Too quick for groan or sigh,
Each turned his face with a ghastly pang,
And cursed me with his eye.

Samuel Taylor Coleridge

Four times fifty living men,
(And I heard nor sigh nor groan)
With heavy thump, a lifeless lump,
They dropped down one by one.

The souls did from their bodies fly,—
They fled to bliss or woe!
And every soul it passed me by,
Like the whizz of my cross-bow!

PART IV

'I fear thee, ancient Mariner!
I fear thy skinny hand!
And thou art long, and lank, and brown,
As is the ribbed sea-sand.

'I fear thee and thy glittering eye,
And thy skinny hand so brown.'—
Fear not, fear not, thou Wedding-Guest!
This body dropt not down.

Alone, alone, all, all alone,
Alone on a wide wide sea!
And never a saint took pity on
My soul in agony.

The many men, so beautiful!
And they all dead did lie;
And a thousand thousand slimy things
Lived on; and so did I.

Samuel Taylor Coleridge

I looked upon the rotting sea,
And drew mine eyes away :
I looked upon the rotting deck,
And there the dead men lay.

I looked to heaven and tried to pray;
But or ever a prayer had gusht,
A wicked whisper came and made
My heart as dry as dust.

I closed my lids, and kept them close,
And the balls like pulses beat ;
For the sky and the sea, and the sea and the sky
Lay like a load on my weary eye,
And the dead were at my feet.

The cold sweat melted from their limbs,
Nor rot nor reek did they :
The look with which they looked on me
Had never passed away.

An orphan's curse would drag to hell
A spirit from on high ;
But oh! more horrible than that
Is the curse in a dead man's eye !
Seven days, seven nights, I saw that curse,
And yet I could not die.

The moving Moon went up the sky,
And nowhere did abide :
Softly she was going up,
And a star or two beside—

Samuel Taylor Coleridge

Her beams bemocked the sultry main,
Like April hoar-frost spread;
But where the ship's huge shadow lay,
The charmed water burnt alway
A still and awful red.

Beyond the shadow of the ship,
I watched the water-snakes:
They moved in tracks of shining white,
And when they reared, the elfish light
Fell off in hoary flakes.

Within the shadow of the ship
I watched their rich attire:
Blue, glossy green, and velvet black,
They coiled and swam: and every track
Was a flash of golden fire.

O happy living things! no tongue
Their beauty might declare;
A spring of love gushed from my heart,
And I blessed them unaware:
Sure my kind Saint took pity on me,
And I blessed them unaware.

The selfsame moment I could pray;
And from my neck so free
The Albatross fell off, and sank
Like lead into the sea.

PART V

O sleep! it is a gentle thing,
Beloved from pole to pole!

Samuel Taylor Coleridge

To Mary Queen the praise be given!
She sent the gentle sleep from Heaven,
That slid into my soul.

The silly buckets on the deck,
That had so long remained,
I dreamt that they were filled with dew;
And when I woke, it rained.

My lips were wet, my throat was cold,
My garments all were dank;
Sure I had drunken in my dreams,
And still my body drank.

I moved, and could not feel my limbs;
I was so light—almost
I thought that I had died in sleep,
And was a blessed ghost.

And soon I heard a roaring wind:
It did not come anear;
But with its sound it shook the sails,
That were so thin and sere.

The upper air burst into life!
And a hundred fire-flags sheen,
To and fro they were hurried about!
And to and fro, and in and out,
The wan stars danced between.

And the coming wind did roar more loud,
And the sails did sigh like sedge;
And the rain poured down from one black cloud;
The Moon was at its edge.

Samuel Taylor Coleridge

The thick black cloud was cleft, and still
The Moon was at its side :
Like waters shot from some high crag,
The lightning fell with never a jag,
A river steep and wide.

The loud wind never reached the ship,
Yet now the ship moved on !
Beneath the lightning and the Moon
The dead men gave a groan.

They groaned, they stirred, they all uprose,
Nor spake, nor moved their eyes ;
It had been strange, even in a dream,
To have seen those dead men rise.

The helmsman steered, the ship moved on ;
Yet never a breeze up blew ;
The mariners all 'gan work the ropes,
Where they were wont to do ;
They raised their limbs like lifeless tools—
We were a ghastly crew.

The body of my brother's son
Stood by me, knee to knee:
The body and I pulled at one rope
But he said nought to me.

'I fear thee, ancient Mariner !'
Be calm, thou Wedding-Guest !
'Twas not those souls that fled in pain,
Which to their corses came again,
But a troop of spirits blest:

Samuel Taylor Coleridge

For when it dawned—they dropped their arms,
And clustered round the mast;
Sweet sounds rose slowly through their mouths,
And from their bodies passed.

Around, around, flew each sweet sound,
Then darted to the Sun;
Slowly the sounds came back again,
Now mixed, now one by one.

Sometimes a-dropping from the sky
I heard the sky-lark sing;
Sometimes all little birds that are,
How they seemed to fill the sea and air
With their sweet jargoning!

And now 'twas like all instruments,
Now like a lonely flute;
And now it is an angel's song,
That makes the heavens be mute.

It ceased; yet still the sails made on
A pleasant noise till noon,
A noise like of a hidden brook
In the leafy month of June,
That to the sleeping woods all night
Singeth a quiet tune.

Till noon we quietly sailed on,
Yet never a breeze did breathe;
Slowly and smoothly went the ship,
Moved onward from beneath.

Samuel Taylor Coleridge

Under the keel nine fathom deep,
From the land of mist and snow,
The spirit slid : and it was he
That made the ship to go.
The sails at noon left off their tune,
And the ship stood still also.

The Sun, right up above the mast,
Had fixed her to the ocean :
But in a minute she 'gan stir,
With a short uneasy motion—
Backwards and forwards half her length
With a short uneasy motion.

Then like a pawing horse let go,
She made a sudden bound :
It flung the blood into my head,
And I fell down in a swound.

How long in that same fit I lay,
I have not to declare ;
But ere my living life returned,
I heard, and in my soul discerned,
Two voices in the air.

'Is it he?' quoth one, 'Is this the man?
By Him who died on cross,
With his cruel bow he laid full low
The harmless Albatross.

'The spirit who bideth by himself
In the land of mist and snow,
He loved the bird that loved the man
Who shot him with his bow.'

Samuel Taylor Coleridge

The other was a softer voice,
As soft as honey-dew:
Quoth he, 'The man hath penance done,
And penance more will do.'

PART VI

FIRST VOICE

'But tell me, tell me! speak again,
Thy soft response renewing—
What makes that ship drive on so fast?
What is the ocean doing?'

SECOND VOICE

'Still as a slave before his lord,
The ocean hath no blast;
His great bright eye most silently
Up to the moon is cast—

'If he may know which way to go;
For she guides him smooth or grim.
See, brother, see! how graciously
She looketh down on him.'

FIRST VOICE

'But why drives on that ship so fast,
Without or wave or wind?'

SECOND VOICE

'The air is cut away before,
And closes from behind.

s   253

Samuel Taylor Coleridge

'Fly, brother, fly! more high, more high!
Or we shall be belated:
For slow and slow that ship will go,
When the Mariner's trance is abated.'

I woke, and we were sailing on
As in a gentle weather:
'Twas night, calm night, the moon was high,
The dead men stood together.

All stood together on the deck,
For a charnel-dungeon fitter:
All fixed on me their stony eyes,
That in the Moon did glitter.

The pang, the curse, with which they died
Had never passed away;
I could not draw my eyes from theirs,
Nor turn them up to pray.

And now this spell was snapt: once more
I viewed the ocean green,
And looked far forth, yet little saw
Of what had else been seen—

Like one that on a lonesome road
Doth walk in fear and dread,
And having once turned round walks on,
And turns no more his head;
Because he knows a frightful fiend
Doth close behind him tread.

Samuel Taylor Coleridge

But soon there breathed a wind on me,
Nor sound nor motion made :
Its path was not upon the sea,
In ripple or in shade.

It raised my hair, it fanned my cheek
Like a meadow-gale of spring—
It mingled strangely with my fears,
Yet it felt like a welcoming.

Swiftly, swiftly flew the ship,
Yet she sailed softly too ;
Sweetly, sweetly blew the breeze—
On me alone it blew.

O ! dream of joy ! is this indeed
The lighthouse top I see ?
Is this the hill ? is this the kirk ?
Is this mine own countree ?

We drifted o'er the harbour bar,
And I with sobs did pray—
O let me be awake, my God !
Or let me sleep alway.

The harbour-bay was clear as glass,
So smoothly it was strewn !
And on the bay the moonlight lay,
And the shadow of the Moon.

The rock shone bright, the kirk no less
That stands above the rock :
The moonlight steeped in silentness
The steady weathercock.

Samuel Taylor Coleridge

And the bay was white with silent light,
Till, rising from the same,
Full many shapes, that shadows were,
In crimson colours came.

A little distance from the prow
Those crimson shadows were:
I turned my eyes upon the deck—
O, Christ ! what saw I there !

Each corse lay flat, lifeless and flat,
And, by the holy rood !
A man all light, a seraph-man,
On every corse there stood.

This seraph-band, each waved his hand :
It was a heavenly sight !
They stood as signals to the land,
Each one a lovely light ;

This seraph-band, each waved his hand,
No voice did they impart—
No voice ; but oh ! the silence sank
Like music on my heart.

But soon I heard the dash of oars,
I heard the Pilot's cheer ;
My head was turned perforce away,
And I saw a boat appear.

The Pilot and the Pilot's boy,
I heard them coming fast :
Dear Lord in Heaven ! it was a joy
The dead men could not blast.

I saw a third—I heard his voice:
It is the hermit good!
He singeth loud his godly hymns
That he makes in the wood.
He'll shrieve my soul, he'll wash away
The Albatross's blood.

PART VII

This Hermit good lives in that wood
Which slopes down to the sea.
How loudly his sweet voice he rears!
He loves to talk with marineres
That come from a far countree.

He kneels at morn, and noon, and eve,—
He hath a cushion plump:
It is the moss that wholly hides
The rotted old oak-stump.

The skiff-boat neared: I heard them talk:
'Why, this is strange, I trow!
Where are those lights, so many and fair,
That signal made but now?'

'Strange, by my faith!' the Hermit said—
'And they answered not our cheer!
The planks looked warped! and see those sails,
How thin they are and sere!
I never saw aught like to them,
Unless perchance it were

Samuel Taylor Coleridge

Brown skeletons of leaves that lag
My forest-brook along;
When the ivy-tod is heavy with snow,
And the owlet whoops to the wolf below,
That eats the she-wolf's young.'

'Dear Lord! it hath a fiendish look'—
(The Pilot made reply)
'I am a-feared'—'Push on, push on!'
Said the Hermit cheerily.

The boat came closer to the ship,
But I nor spake nor stirred;
The boat came close beneath the ship,
And straight a sound was heard.

Under the water it rumbled on,
Still louder and more dread;
It reached the ship, it split the bay;
The ship went down like lead.

Stunned by that loud and dreadful sound,
Which sky and ocean smote,
Like one that hath been seven days drowned
My body lay afloat;
But swift as dreams, myself I found
Within the Pilot's boat.

Upon the whirl, where sank the ship,
The boat spun round and round;
And all was still, save that the hill
Was telling of the sound.

Samuel Taylor Coleridge

I moved my lips—the Pilot shrieked
And fell down in a fit;
The holy Hermit raised his eyes,
And prayed where he did sit.

I took the oars : the Pilot's boy,
Who now doth crazy go,
Laughed loud and long, and all the while
His eyes went to and fro.
'Ha ! ha !' quoth he, 'full plain I see,
The Devil knows how to row.'

And now all in my own countree,
I stood on the firm land !
The Hermit stepped forth from the boat,
And scarcely he could stand.

'O shrieve me, shrieve me, holy man !'
The Hermit crossed his brow.
'Say quick,' quoth he, 'I bid thee say—
What manner of man art thou ?'

Forthwith this frame of mine was wrenched
With a woful agony,
Which forced me to begin my tale ;
And then it left me free.

Since then, at an uncertain hour,
That agony returns:
And till my ghastly tale is told,
This heart within me burns.

Samuel Taylor Coleridge

I pass, like night, from land to land ;
I have strange power of speech ;
That moment that his face I see,
I know the man that must hear me ;
To him my tale I teach.

What loud uproar bursts from that door !
The wedding-guests are there :
But in the garden-bower the bride
And bride-maids singing are :
And hark the little vesper-bell
Which biddeth me to prayer !

O Wedding-Guest ! this soul hath been
Alone on a wide wide sea :
So lonely 'twas, that God Himself
Scarce seemed there to be.

O sweeter than the marriage-feast,
'Tis sweeter far to me,
To walk together to the kirk
With a goodly company—

To walk together to the kirk,
And all together pray,
While each to his great Father bends,
Old men, and babes, and loving friends,
And youths and maidens gay !

Farewell, farewell ! but this I tell
To thee, thou Wedding-Guest !
He prayeth well who loveth well
Both man and bird and beast.

Walter Savage Landor '

He prayeth best who loveth best
All things both great and small;
For the dear God who loveth us,
He made and loveth all.

The Mariner, whose eye is bright,
Whose beard with age is hoar,
Is gone: and now the Wedding-Guest
Turned from the bridegroom's door.

He went like one that hath been stunned,
And is of sense forlorn ;
A sadder and a wiser man,
He rose the morrow-morn.

WALTER SAVAGE LANDOR

1775-1864

ROSE AYLMER

Ah, what avails the sceptred race,
    Ah, what the form divine !
What every virtue, every grace !
    Rose Aylmer, all were thine.

.

Rose Aylmer, whom these watchful eyes
    May weep, but never see,
A night of memories and of sighs
    I consecrate to thee.

EPITAPH

I STROVE with none, for none were worth my strife.
Nature I loved, and next to Nature, Art.
I warmed both hands before the fire of life;
It sinks, and I am ready to depart.

CHILD OF A DAY

CHILD of a day, thou knowest not
The tears that overflow thine urn,
The gushing eyes that read thy lot,
Nor, if thou knewest, could'st return!

And why the wish! the pure and blest
Watch, like thy mother, o'er thy sleep;
O peaceful night! O envied rest!
Thou wilt not ever see her weep.

THOMAS CAMPBELL

1767-1844

HOHENLINDEN

ON Linden, when the sun was low,
All bloodless lay the untrodden snow;
And dark as winter was the flow
Of Iser, rolling rapidly.

But Linden saw another sight,
When the drum beat at dead of night
Commanding fires of death to light
The darkness of her scenery.

282

Thomas Campbell

By torch and trumpet fast arrayed
Each horseman drew his battle-blade,
And furious every charger neighed
    To join the dreadful revelry.

Then shook the hills with thunder riven;
Then rushed the steed, to battle driven;
And louder than the bolts of Heaven
    Far flashed the red artillery.

But redder yet that light shall glow
On Linden's hills of stained snow;
And bloodier yet the torrent flow
    Of Iser, rolling rapidly.

'Tis morn; but scarce yon level sun
Can pierce the war-clouds, rolling dun,
Where furious Frank and fiery Hun
    Shout in their sulphurous canopy.

The combat deepens. On, ye Brave,
Who rush to glory or the grave!
Wave, Munich! all thy banners wave,
    And charge with all thy chivalry!

Few, few shall part, where many meet!
The snow shall be their winding-sheet,
And every turf beneath their feet
    Shall be a soldier's sepulchre.

EARL MARCH

EARL MARCH looked on his dying child,
    And, smit with grief to view her—
The youth, he cried, whom I exiled
    Shall be restored to woo her.

She's at the window many an hour
   His coming to discover:
And he looked up to Ellen's bower
   And she looked on her lover—

But ah! so pale, he knew her not,
   Though her smile on him was dwelling!
And am I then forgot—forgot?
   It broke the heart of Ellen.

In vain he weeps, in vain he sighs,
   Her cheek is cold as ashes;
Nor love's own kiss shall wake those eyes
   To lift their silken lashes.

CHARLES LAMB

1775-1835

HESTER

WHEN maidens such as Hester die,
Their place ye may not well supply,
Though ye among a thousand try
     With vain endeavour.
A month or more hath she been dead,
Yet cannot I by force be led
To think upon the wormy bed
     And her together.

A springy motion in her gait,
A rising step, did indicate
Of pride and joy no common rate
     That flushed her spirit:
I know not by what name beside

I shall it call: if 'twas not pride,
It was a joy to that allied
      She did inherit.

Her parents held the Quaker rule,
Which doth the human feeling cool;
But she was trained in Nature's school,
      Nature had blest her.
A waking eye, a prying mind,
A heart that stirs, is hard to bind;
A hawk's keen sight ye cannot blind,
      Ye could not Hester.

My sprightly neighbour! gone before
To that unknown and silent shore,
Shall we not meet, as heretofore,
      Some summer morning—
When from thy cheerful eyes a ray
Hath struck a bliss upon the day,
A bliss that would not go away,
      A sweet fore-warning?

ALLAN CUNNINGHAM

1784-1842

A WET SHEET AND A FLOWING SEA

A WET sheet and a flowing sea,
   A wind that follows fast
And fills the white and rustling sail
   And bends the gallant mast;
And bends the gallant mast, my boys,
   While like the eagle free
Away the good ship flies, and leaves
   Old England on the lee.

George Noel Gordon, Lord Byron

O for a soft and gentle wind!
　　I heard a fair one cry;
But give to me the snoring breeze
　　And white waves heaving high;
And white waves heaving high, my lads,
　　The good ship tight and free—
The world of waters is our home,
　　And merry men are we.

There's tempest in yon horned moon,
　　And lightning in yon cloud;
But hark the music, mariners!
　　The wind is piping loud;
The wind is piping loud, my boys,
　　The lightning flashes free—
While the hollow oak our palace is,
　　Our heritage the sea.

GEORGE NOEL GORDON, LORD BYRON

1788-1823

THE ISLES OF GREECE

The Isles of Greece, the Isles of Greece!
　　Where burning Sappho loved and sung,
Where grew the arts of war and peace,
　　Where Delos rose, and Phœbus sprung!
Eternal summer gilds them yet,
But all, except their sun, is set.

The Scian and the Teian muse,
　　The hero's harp, the lover's lute,
Have found the fame your shores refuse;

George Noel Gordon, Lord Byron

Their place of birth alone is mute
To sounds which echo further west
Than your sires' 'Islands of the Blest.'

The mountains look on Marathon,
   And Marathon looks on the sea;
And musing there an hour alone,
   I dreamed that Greece might still be free;
For, standing on the Persians' grave,
I could not think myself a slave.

A king sate on the rocky brow
   Which looks o'er sea-born Salamis;
And ships, by thousands, lay below,
   And men in nations;—all were his!
He counted them at break of day—
And when the sun set where were they?

And where are they? and where art thou,
   My country? On thy voiceless shore
The heroic lay is tuneless now—
   The heroic bosom beats no more!
And must thy lyre, so long divine,
Degenerate into hands like mine?

'Tis something, in the dearth of fame,
   Though linked among a fettered race
To feel at least a patriot's shame,
   Even as I sing, suffuse my face;
For what is left the poet here?
For Greeks a blush—for Greece a tear.

George Noel Gordon, Lord Byron

Must *we* but weep o'er days more blest?
    Must *we* but blush?—Our fathers bled.
Earth! render back from out thy breast
    A remnant of our Spartan dead!
Of the three hundred grant but three,
To make a new Thermopylæ!

What, silent still? and silent all?
    Ah! no;—the voices of the dead
Sound like a distant torrent's fall,
    And answer, 'Let one living head,
But one, arise,—we come, we come!'
'Tis but the living who are dumb.

In vain—in vain : strike other chords;
    Fill high the cup with Samian wine!
Leave battles to the Turkish hordes,
    And shed the blood of Scio's vine!
Hark! rising to the ignoble call—
How answers each bold bacchanal!

You have the Pyrrhic dance as yet,
    Where is the Pyrrhic phalanx gone?
Of two such lessons, why forget
    The nobler and the manlier one?
You have the letters Cadmus gave—
Think ye he meant them for a slave?

Fill high the bowl with Samian wine!
    We will not think of themes like these!
It made Anacreon's song divine:
    He served—but served Polycrates—
A tyrant; but our masters then
Were still, at least, our countrymen.

George Noel Gordon, Lord Byron

The tyrant of the Chersonese
  Was freedom's best and bravest friend;
That tyrant was Miltiades!
  Oh! that the present hour would lend
Another despot of the kind!
Such chains as his were sure to bind.

Fill high the bowl with Samian wine!
  On Suli's rock, and Parga's shore,
Exists the remnant of a line
  Such as the Doric mothers bore;
And there, perhaps, some seed is sown,
The Heracleidan blood might own.

Trust not for freedom to the Franks—
  They have a king who buys and sells;
In native swords, and native ranks,
  The only hope of courage dwells;
But Turkish force, and Latin fraud,
Would break your shield, however broad.

Fill high the bowl with Samian wine!
  Our virgins dance beneath the shade—
I see their glorious black eyes shine;
  But gazing on each glowing maid,
My own the burning tear-drop laves,
To think such breasts must suckle slaves.

Place me on Sunium's marbled steep,
  Where nothing, save the waves and I,
May hear our mutual murmurs sweep;
  There, swan-like, let me sing and die:
A land of slaves shall ne'er be mine—
Dash down yon cup of Samian wine!

PERCY BYSSHE SHELLEY

1792-1822

HELLAS

THE world's great age begins anew,
  The golden years return,
The earth doth like a snake renew
  Her winter weeds outworn :
Heaven smiles, and faiths and empires gleam,
Like wrecks of a dissolving dream.

A brighter Hellas rears its mountains
  From waves serener far ;
A new Peneus rolls his fountains
  Against the morning star.
Where fairer Tempes bloom, there sleep
Young Cyclads on a sunnier deep.

A loftier Argo cleaves the main,
  Fraught with a later prize ;
Another Orpheus sings again,
  And loves, and weeps, and dies.
A new Ulysses leaves once more
Calypso for his native shore.

O write no more the tale of Troy,
  If earth Death's scroll must be !
Nor mix with Laian rage the joy
  Which dawns upon the free :
Although a subtler Sphinx renew
Riddles of death Thebes never knew.

Percy Bysshe Shelley

Another Athens shall arise,
  And to remoter time
Bequeath, like sunset to the skies,
  The splendour of its prime;
And leave, if nought so bright may live,
All earth can take or Heaven can give.

   .   .   .   .   .

O cease! must hate and death return?
  Cease! must men kill and die?
Cease! drain not to its dregs the urn
  Of bitter prophecy.
The world is weary of the past,
O might it die or rest at last!

WILD WITH WEEPING

My head is wild with weeping for a grief
  Which is the shadow of a gentle mind.
I walk into the air (but no relief
  To seek,—or haply, if I sought, to find;
It came unsought); to wonder that a chief
  Among men's spirits should be cold and blind.

TO THE NIGHT

Swiftly walk over the western wave,
     Spirit of Night!
Out of the misty eastern cave
Where, all the long and lone daylight,
Thou wovest dreams of joy and fear
Which make thee terrible and dear,—
     Swift be thy flight!

Percy Bysshe Shelley

Wrap thy form in a mantle grey
   Star-inwrought;
Blind with thine hair the eyes of Day,
Kiss her until she be wearied out:
Then wander o'er city and sea and land,
Touching all with thine opiate wand—
   Come, long-sought!

When I arose and saw the dawn,
   I sighed for thee;
When light rode high, and the dew was gone,
And noon lay heavy on flower and tree,
And the weary Day turned to his rest
Lingering like an unloved guest,
   I sighed for thee.

Thy brother Death came, and cried
   Wouldst thou me?
Thy sweet child Sleep, the filmy-eyed,
Murmured like a noon-tide bee,
Shall I nestle near thy side?
Wouldst thou me?—And I replied
   No, not thee!

Death will come when thou art dead,
   Soon, too soon—
Sleep will come when thou art fled;
Of neither would I ask the boon
I ask of thee, beloved Night—
Swift be thine approaching flight,
   Come soon, soon!

292

Percy Bysshe Shelley

HAIL to thee, blithe Spirit !
Bird thou never wert !
That from heaven, or near it,
Pourest thy full heart
In profuse strains of unpremeditated art.

Higher still and higher
From the earth thou springest,
Like a cloud of fire,
The blue deep thou wingest,
And singing still dost soar, and soaring ever singest.

In the golden lightning
Of the sunken sun
O'er which clouds are brightening,
Thou dost float and run
Like an unbodied joy whose race is just begun.

The pale purple even
Melts around thy flight:
Like a star of heaven
In the broad daylight
Thou art unseen, but yet I hear thy shrill delight ;

Keen as are the arrows
Of that silver sphere,
Whose intense lamp narrows
In the white dawn clear
Until we hardly see, we feel that it is there.

Percy Bysshe Shelley

All the earth and air
　　With thy voice is loud,
As, when night is bare,
　　From one lonely cloud
The moon rains out her beams, and heaven is over-
　　flowed.

What thou art we know not;
　　What is most like thee?
From rainbow clouds there flow not
　　Drops so bright to see
As from thy presence showers a rain of melody;—

Like a poet hidden
　　In the light of thought,
Singing hymns unbidden,
　　Till the world is wrought
To sympathy with hopes and fears it heeded not;

Like a high-born maiden
　　In a palace tower,
Soothing her love-laden
　　Soul in secret hour
With music sweet as love, which overflows her bower:

Like a glow-worm golden
　　In a dell of dew,
Scattering unbeholden
　　Its aërial hue
Among the flowers and grass, which screen it from the
　　view:

Percy Bysshe Shelley

Like a rose embowered
 In its own green leaves,
By warm winds deflowered,
 Till the scent it gives
Makes faint with too much sweet these heavy-winged
 thieves.

Sound of vernal showers
 On the twinkling grass,
Rain-awakened flowers,
 All that ever was
Joyous, and clear, and fresh, thy music doth surpass.

Teach us, sprite or bird,
 What sweet thoughts are thine :
I have never heard
 Praise of love or wine
That panted forth a flood of rapture so divine.

Chorus hymeneal
 Or triumphal chaunt
Matched with thine, would be all
 But an empty vaunt—
A thing wherein we feel there is some hidden want.

What objects are the fountains
 Of thy happy strain?
What fields, or waves, or mountains?
 What shapes of sky or plain?
What love of thine own kind? what ignorance of
 pain?

Percy Bysshe Shelley

With thy clear keen joyance
    Languor cannot be :
Shadow of annoyance
    Never came near thee :
Thou lovest ; but ne'er knew love's sad satiety.

Waking or asleep
    Thou of death must deem
Things more true and deep
    Than we mortals dream,
Or how could thy notes flow in such a crystal stream ?

We look before and after,
    And pine for what is not :
Our sincerest laughter
    With some pain is fraught :
Our sweetest songs are those that tell of saddest thought.

Yet if we could scorn
    Hate, and pride, and fear ;
If we were things born
    Not to shed a tear,
I know not how thy joy we ever should come near.

Better than all measures
    Of delightful sound,
Better than all treasures
    That in books are found,
Thy skill to poet were, thou scorner of the ground !

Teach me half the gladness
    That thy brain must know,
Such harmonious madness
    From my lips would flow,
The world should listen then, as I am listening now !

Percy Bysshe Shelley

TO THE MOON

ART thou pale for weariness
Of climbing heaven, and gazing on the earth,
Wandering companionless
Among the stars that have a different birth,—
And ever-changing, like a joyless eye
That finds no object worth its constancy?

THE QUESTION

I DREAMED that as I wandered by the way
  Bare Winter suddenly was changed to Spring,
And gentle odours led my steps astray,
  Mixed with a sound of waters murmuring
Along a shelving bank of turf, which lay
  Under a copse, and hardly dared to fling
Its green arms round the bosom of the stream,
But kissed it and then fled, as Thou mightest in dream.

There grew pied wind-flowers and violets,
  Daisies, those pearled Arcturi of the earth,
The constellated flower that never sets;
  Faint oxlips; tender blue-bells, at whose birth
The sod scarce heaved; and that tall flower that wets
  Its mother's face with heaven-collected tears,
When the low wind, its playmate's voice, it hears.

And in the warm hedge grew lush eglantine,
  Green cow-bind and the moonlight-coloured May,
And cherry-blossoms, and white cups, whose wine
  Was the bright dew yet drained not by the day;

297

Percy Bysshe Shelley

And wild roses, and ivy serpentine
  With its dark buds and leaves, wandering astray;
And flowers azure, black, and streaked with gold,
Fairer than any wakened eyes behold.

And nearer to the river's trembling edge
  There grew broad flag-flowers, purple pranked with
      white,
And starry river-buds among the sedge,
  And floating water-lilies, broad and bright,
Which lit the oak that overhung the hedge
  With moonlight beams of their own watery light;
And bulrushes, and reeds of such deep green
As soothed the dazzled eye with sober sheen.

Methought that of these visionary flowers
  I made a nosegay, bound in such a way
That the same hues, which in their natural bowers
  Were mingled or opposed, the like array
Kept these imprisoned children of the Hours
  Within my hand,—and then, elate and gay,
I hastened to the spot whence I had come
That I might there present it—O! to Whom?

THE WANING MOON

AND like a dying lady, lean and pale,
Who totters forth, wrapt in a gauzy veil,
Out of her chamber, led by the insane
And feeble wanderings of her fading brain,
The moon arose up in the murky east,
A white and shapeless mass.

Percy Bysshe Shelley

O WILD West Wind, thou breath of Autumn's being,
Thou, from whose unseen presence the leaves dead
Are driven, like ghosts from an enchanter fleeing,
Yellow, and black, and pale, and hectic red,
Pestilence-stricken multitudes! O thou
Who chariotest to their dark wintry bed
The winged seeds, where they lie cold and low,
Each like a corpse within its grave, until
Thine azure sister of the Spring shall blow
Her clarion o'er the dreaming earth, and fill
(Driving sweet buds like flocks to feed in air)
With living hues and odours plain and hill:
Wild Spirit, which art moving everywhere;
Destroyer and Preserver: Hear, oh hear!

Thou on whose stream, 'mid the steep sky's com-
    motion,
Loose clouds like earth's decaying leaves are shed,
Shook from the tangled boughs of heaven and ocean,
Angels of rain and lightning! there are spread
On the blue surface of thine airy surge,
Like the bright hair uplifted from the head
Of some fierce Maenad, even from the dim verge
Of the horizon to the zenith's height—
The locks of the approaching storm.   Thou dirge
Of the dying year, to which this closing.night
Will be the dome of a vast sepulchre,
Vaulted with all thy congregated might
Of vapours, from whose solid atmosphere
Black rain, and fire, and hail will burst: O hear!

Percy Bysshe Shelley

Thou who didst waken from his summer-dreams
The blue Mediterranean, where he lay,
Lulled by the coil of his crystalline streams,
Beside a pumice isle in Baiae's bay,
And saw in sleep old palaces and towers
Quivering within the wave's intenser day,
All overgrown with azure moss, and flowers
So sweet, the sense faints picturing them! Thou
For whose path the Atlantic's level powers
Cleave themselves into chasms, while far below
The sea-blooms and the oozy woods which wear
The sapless foliage of the ocean, know
Thy voice, and suddenly grow grey with fear
And tremble and despoil themselves: O hear!

If I were a dead leaf thou mightest bear;
If I were a swift cloud to fly with thee;
A wave to pant beneath thy power, and share
The impulse of thy strength, only less free
Than Thou, O uncontrollable! If even
I were as in my boyhood, and could be
The comrade of thy wanderings over heaven,
As then, when to outstrip thy skiey speed
Scarce seemed a vision,—I would ne'er have striven
As thus with thee in prayer in my sore need.
O! lift me as a wave, a leaf, a cloud!
I fall upon the thorns of life! I bleed!
A heavy weight of hours has chained and bowed
One too like thee—tameless, and swift, and proud.

Make me thy lyre, even as the forest is:
What if my leaves are falling like its own!
The tumult of thy mighty harmonies
Will take from both a deep autumnal tone,

Percy Bysshe Shelley

Sweet though in sadness.   Be thou, Spirit fierce,
My spirit! be thou me, impetuous one!
Drive my dead thoughts over the universe,
Like withered leaves, to quicken a new birth;
And, by the incantation of this verse,
Scatter, as from an unextinguished hearth
Ashes and sparks, my words among mankind
Be through my lips to unawakened earth
The trumpet of a prophecy!   O Wind,
If Winter comes, can Spring be far behind?

RARELY, RARELY COMEST THOU

RARELY, rarely comest thou,
    Spirit of Delight!
Wherefore hast thou left me now
    Many a day and night?
Many a weary night and day
'Tis since thou art fled away.

How shall ever one like me
    Win thee back again?
With the joyous and the free
    Thou wilt scoff at pain.
Spirit false! thou hast forgot
All but those who need thee not.

As a lizard with the shade
    Of a trembling leaf,
Thou with sorrow art dismayed;
    Even the sighs of grief

301

Reproach thee, that thou art not near,
And reproach thou wilt not hear.

Let me set my mournful ditty
    To a merry measure,
Thou wilt never come for pity,
    Thou wilt come for pleasure.
Pity then will cut away
Those cruel wings, and thou wilt stay.

I love all that thou lovest,
    Spirit of Delight!
The fresh Earth in new leaves drest,
    And the starry night,
Autumn evening, and the morn
When the golden mists are born.

I love snow, and all the forms
    Of the radiant frost;
I love waves, and winds, and storms—
    Everything almost
Which is Nature's, and may be
Untainted by man's misery.

I love tranquil solitude,
    And such society
As is quiet, wise and good;
    Between thee and me
What difference? but thou dost possess
The things I seek, not love them less.

I love Love,—though he has wings,
    And like light can flee,

Percy Bysshe Shelley

But above all other things,
    Spirit, I love thee—
Thou art love and life ! O come,
Make once more my heart thy home !

THE INVITATION, TO JANE

BEST and brightest, come away !
Fairer far than this fair Day,
Which, like thee to those in sorrow,
Comes to bid a sweet good-morrow
To the rough Year just awake
In its cradle on the brake.
The brightest hour of unborn Spring,
Through the winter wandering,
Found, it seems, the halcyon Morn
To hoar February born ;
Bending from Heaven, in azure mirth,
It kissed the forehead of the Earth,
And smiled upon the silent sea,
And bade the frozen streams be free,
And waked to music all their fountains,
And breathed upon the frozen mountains,
And like a prophetess of May
Strewed flowers upon the barren way,
Making the wintry world appear
Like one on whom thou smilest, dear.
Away, away, from men and towns,
To the wild wood and the downs—
To the silent wilderness
Where the soul need not repress

Its music, lest it should not find
An echo in another's mind,
While the touch of Nature's art
Harmonizes heart to heart.
I leave this notice on my door
For each accustomed visitor :—
'I am gone into the fields
To take what this sweet hour yields ;—
Reflection, you may come to-morrow,
Sit by the fireside with sorrow.—
You with the unpaid bill, Despair,—
You tiresome verse-reciter, Care,—
I will pay you in the grave,—
Death will listen to your stave.
Expectation, too, be off!
To-day is for itself enough ;
Hope in pity mock not Woe
With smiles, nor follow where I go ;
Long having lived on thy sweet food,
At length I find one moment's good
After long pain—with all your love,
This you never told me of.'

Radiant sister of the Day,
Awake! arise! and come away!
To the wild woods and the plains,
And the pools where winter rains
Image all their roof of leaves,
Where the pine its garland weaves
Of sapless green and ivy dun
Round stems that never kiss the sun ;
Where the lawns and pastures be,
And the sand-hills of the sea ;—

Where the melting hoar-frost wets
The daisy-star that never sets,
The wind-flowers, and violets,
Which yet join not scent to hue,
Crown the pale year weak and new ;
When the night is left behind
In the deep east, dun and blind,
And the blue noon is over us,
And the multitudinous
Billows murmur at our feet,
Where the earth and ocean meet,
And all things seem only one
In the universal sun.

THE RECOLLECTION

Now the last day of many days
All beautiful and bright as thou,
The loveliest and the last, is dead :
Rise, Memory, and write its praise !
Up—to thy wonted work ! come, trace
The epitaph of glory fled,
For nqw the earth has changed its face,
A frown is on the heaven's brow.

We wandered to the Pine Forest
   That skirts the Ocean's foam ;
The lightest wind was in its nest,
   The tempest in its home.
The whispering waves were half asleep,
   The clouds were gone to play,
And on the bosom of the deep
   The smile of heaven lay ;

Percy Bysshe Shelley

It seemed as if the hour were one
    Sent from beyond the skies
Which scattered from above the sun
    A light of Paradise!

We paused amid the pines that stood
    The giants of the waste,
Tortured by storms to shapes as rude
    As serpents interlaced,—
And soothed by every azure breath
    That under heaven is blown,
To harmonies and hues beneath,
    As tender as its own:
Now all the tree-tops lay asleep
    Like green waves on the sea,
As still as in the silent deep
    The ocean-woods may be.

How calm it was!—The silence there
    By such a chain was bound,
That even the busy woodpecker
    Made stiller with her sound
The inviolable quietness;
    The breath of peace we drew
With its soft motion made not less
    The calm that round us grew.
There seemed, from the remotest seat
    Of the white mountain waste
To the soft flower beneath our feet,
    A magic circle traced,—
A spirit interfused around,
    A thrilling silent life;
To momentary peace it bound
    Our mortal nature's strife;—

Percy Bysshe Shelley

And still I felt the centre of
   The magic circle there
Was one fair form that filled with love
   The lifeless atmosphere.

We paused beside the pools that lie
   Under the forest bough ;
Each seemed as 'twere a little sky
   Gulfed in a world below ;
A firmament of purple light
   Which in the dark earth lay,
More boundless than the depth of night
   And purer than the day—
In which the lovely forests grew
   As in the upper air,
More perfect both in shape and hue
   Than any spreading there.
There lay the glade and neighbouring lawn,
   And through the dark green wood
The white sun twinkling like the dawn
   Out of a speckled cloud.
Sweet views, which in our world above
   Can never well be seen,
Were imaged in the water's love
   Of that fair forest green :
And all was interfused beneath
   With an Elysian glow,
An atmosphere without a breath,
   A softer day below.
Like one beloved, the scene had lent
   To the dark water's breast
Its every leaf and lineament
   With more than truth exprest;

Until an envious wind crept by,
  Like an unwelcome thought
Which from the mind's too faithful eye
  Blots one dear image out.
—Though thou art ever fair and kind,
  The forests ever green,
Less oft is peace in Shelley's mind
  Than calm in waters seen!

.

ODE TO HEAVEN

Chorus of Spirits

FIRST SPIRIT

PALACE roof of cloudless nights!
Paradise of golden lights!
  Deep, immeasurable, vast,
Which art now and which wert then
  Of the present and the past,
Of the eternal where and when,
    Presence-chamber, temple, home,
    Ever canopying dome
  Of acts and ages yet to come!

Glorious shapes have life in thee,
Earth, and all earth's company;
  Living globes which ever throng
Thy deep chasms and wildernesses;
  And green worlds that glide along;
And swift stars with flashing tresses;
    And icy moons most cold and bright,
    And mighty suns beyond the night,
    Atoms of intensest light.

Percy Bysshe Shelley

Even thy name is as a God,
Heaven! for thou art the abode
  Of that power which is the glass
Wherein man his nature sees.
  Generations as they pass
Worship thee with bended knees.
    Their unremaining gods and they
    Like a river roll away:
    Thou remainest such alway.

SECOND SPIRIT

Thou art but the mind's first chamber,
Round which its young fancies clamber,
  Like weak insects in a cave,
Lighted up by stalactites;
  By the portal of the grave,
Where a world of new delights
    Will make thy best glories seem
    But a dim and noonday gleam
    From the shadow of a dream!

THIRD SPIRIT

Peace! the abyss is wreathed with scorn
At your presumption, atom-born!
  What is heaven, and what are ye
Who its brief expanse inherit?
  What are suns and spheres which flee
With the instinct of that spirit
    Of which ye are but a part?
    Drops which Nature's mighty heart
    Drives through thinnest veins. Depart!

Percy Bysshe Shelley

What is heaven? a globe of dew,
Filling in the morning new
  Some eyed flower whose young leaves waken
On an unimagined world:
  Constellated suns unshaken,
Orbits measureless are furled
   In that frail and fading sphere,
   With ten millions gathered there,
   To tremble, gleam, and disappear.

LIFE OF LIFE

LIFE of Life! thy lips enkindle
  With their love the breath between them;
And thy smiles before they dwindle
  Make the cold air fire; then screen them
In those looks, where whoso gazes
Faints, entangled in their mazes.

Child of Light! thy limbs are burning
  Thro' the vest which seeks to hide them;
As the radiant lines of morning
  Thro' the clouds ere they divide them;
And this atmosphere divinest
Shrouds thee wheresoe'er thou shinest.

Fair are others; none beholds thee,
  But thy voice sounds low and tender
Like the fairest, for it folds thee
  From the sight, that liquid splendour,
And all feel, yet see thee never,
As I feel now, lost for ever!

Percy Bysshe Shelley

Lamp of Earth! where'er thou movest
  Its dim shapes are clad with brightness,
And the souls of whom thou lovest
  Walk upon the winds with lightness,
Till they fail, as I am failing,
Dizzy, lost, yet unbewailing!

AUTUMN

A Dirge

THE warm sun is failing, the bleak wind is wailing,
The bare boughs are sighing, the pale flowers are dying,
            And the year
On the earth her death-bed, in a shroud of leaves dead,
            Is lying.
        Come, months, come away,
        From November to May,
        In your saddest array;
        Follow the bier
        Of the dead cold year,
And like dim shadows watch by her sepulchre.

The chill rain is falling, the nipt worm is crawling,
The rivers are swelling, the thunder is knelling
            For the year;
The blithe swallows are flown, and the lizards each gone
            To his dwelling;
        Come, months, come away;
        Put on white, black, and grey;
        Let your light sisters play—
        Ye, follow the bier
        Of the dead cold year,
And make her grave green with tear on tear.

Percy Bysshe Shelley

THE sun is warm, the sky is clear,
The waves are dancing fast and bright,
Blue isles and snowy mountains wear
The purple noon's transparent might:
The breath of the moist earth is light
Around its unexpanded buds;
Like many a voice of one delight—
The winds', the birds', the ocean-floods'—
The city's voice itself is soft like Solitude's.

I see the deep's untrampled floor
With green and purple sea-weeds strown;
I see the waves upon the shore
Like light dissolved in star-showers thrown:
I sit upon the sands alone;
The lightning of the noon-tide ocean
Is flashing round me, and a tone
Arises from its measured motion—
How sweet! did any heart now share in my emotion.

Alas! I have nor hope nor health,
Nor peace within nor calm around,
Nor that content, surpassing wealth,
The sage in meditation found,
And walked with inward glory crowned—
Nor fame, nor power, nor love, nor leisure;
Others I see whom these surround—
Smiling they live, and call life pleasure;
To me that cup has been dealt in another measure.

Percy Bysshe Shelley

Yet now despair itself is mild
Even as the winds and waters are;
I could lie down like a tired child,
And weep away the life of care
Which I have borne and yet must bear,—
Till death like sleep might steal on me,
And I might feel in the warm air
My cheek grow cold, and hear the sea
Breathe o'er my dying brain its last monotony.

DIRGE FOR THE YEAR

ORPHAN hours, the year is dead,
   Come and sigh, come and weep!
Merry hours, smile instead,
   For the year is but asleep.
See, it smiles as it is sleeping,
Mocking your untimely weeping.

As an earthquake rocks a corse
   In its coffin in the clay,
So White Winter, that rough nurse,
   Rocks the death-cold year to-day;
Solemn hours! wail aloud
For your mother in her shroud.

As the wild air stirs and sways
   The tree-swung cradle of a child,
So the breath of these rude days
   Rocks the year:—be calm and mild;
Trembling hours, she will arise
With new love within her eyes.

313

Percy Bysshe Shelley

January grey is here,
   Like a sexton by her grave;
February bears the bier,
   March with grief doth howl and rave.
And April weeps—but O, ye hours,
Follow with May's fairest flowers.

A WIDOW BIRD

A WIDOW bird sat mourning for her love
   Upon a wintry bough;
The frozen wind crept on above,
   The freezing stream below.

There was no leaf upon the forest bare,
   No flower upon the ground,
And little motion in the air
   Except the mill-wheel's sound.

THE TWO SPIRITS

First Spirit

O THOU, who plumed with strong desire
   Wouldst float above the earth, beware!
A shadow tracks the flight of fire—
   Night is coming!
Bright are the regions of the air,
And among the winds and beams
   It were delight to wander there—
   Night is coming!

314

Percy Bysshe Shelley

Second Spirit

The deathless stars are bright above ;
    If I would cross the shade of night,
Within my heart is the lamp of love,
        And that is day !
And the moon will smile with gentle light
On my golden plumes where'er they move ;
    The meteors will linger round my flight,
        And make night day.

First Spirit

But if the whirlwinds of darkness waken
    Hail, and lightning, and stormy rain ;
See, the bounds of the air are shaken—
        Night is coming !
The red swift clouds of the hurricane
Yon declining sun have overtaken ;
    The clash of the hail sweeps over the plain—
        Night is coming !

Second Spirit

I see the light, and I hear the sound ;
    I'll sail on the flood of the tempests dark,
With the calm within and the light around
        Which makes night day :
And then, when the gloom is deep and stark,
Look from thy dull earth, slumber-bound ;
    My moon-like flight thou then may'st mark
        On high, far away.

John Keats

Some say there is a precipice
    Where one vast pine is frozen to ruin
O'er piles of snow and chasms of ice
        'Mid Alpine mountains;
    And that the languid storm pursuing
That winged shape, for ever flies
    Round those hoar branches, aye renewing
        Its aëry fountains.

Some say, when nights are dry and clear,
    And the death-dews sleep on the morass,
Sweet whispers are heard by the traveller,
        Which make night day;
    And a silver shape, like his early love, doth pass
Up-borne by her wild and glittering hair,
    And when he awakes on the fragrant grass,
        He finds night day.

JOHN KEATS

1795-1821

LA BELLE DAME SANS MERCI

'O WHAT can ail thee, knight-at-arms,
    Alone and palely loitering?
The sedge has withered from the lake,
    And no birds sing.

'O what can ail thee, knight-at-arms!
    So haggard and so woe-begone?
The squirrel's granary is full,
    And the harvest's done.

John Keats

' I see a lily on thy brow
　　With anguish moist and fever-dew,
And on thy cheeks a fading rose
　　Fast withereth too.'

' I met a lady in the meads,
　　Full beautiful—a faery's child,
Her hair was long, her foot was light,
　　And her eyes were wild.

' I made a garland for her head,
　　And bracelets too, and fragrant zone ;
She looked at me as she did love,
　　And made sweet moan.

' I set her on my pacing steed
　　And nothing else saw all day long,
For sidelong would she bend, and sing
　　A faery's song.

' She found me roots of relish sweet,
　　And honey wild and manna-dew,
And sure, in language strange, she said,
　　" I love thee true."

' She took me to her elfin grot,
　　And there she wept and sighed full sore :
And there I shut her wild wild eyes
　　With kisses four.

' And there she lulled me asleep,
　　And there I dreamed—Ah ! woe betide !
The latest dream I ever dreamed
　　On the cold hill's side.

John Keats

'I saw pale kings and princes too,
    Pale warriors, death-pale were they all:
They cried—"La belle Dame sans Merci
    Hath thee in thrall!"

'I saw their starved lips in the gloam
    With horrid warning gaped wide,
And I awoke and found me here
    On the cold hill's side.

'And this is why I sojourn here
    Alone and palely loitering,
Though the sedge is withered from the lake,
    And no birds sing.'

ON FIRST LOOKING INTO CHAPMAN'S HOMER

MUCH have I travelled in the realms of gold,
    And many goodly states and kingdoms seen:
    Round many western islands have I been
Which bards in fealty to Apollo hold.

Oft of one wide expanse had I been told
    That deep-browed Homer ruled as his demesne:
    Yet did I never breathe its pure serene
Till I heard Chapman speak out loud and bold;

—Then felt I like some watcher of the skies
When a new planet swims into his ken;
Or like stout Cortez, when with eagle eyes

He stared at the Pacific—and all his men
Looked on each other with a wild surmise—
Silent, upon a peak in Darien.

John Keats

TO SLEEP

O SOFT embalmer of the still midnight,
  Shutting with careful fingers and benign
Our gloom-pleased eyes, embowered from the light,
  Enshaded in forgetfulness divine;
O soothest Sleep! if so it please thee, close,
  In midst of this thine hymn, my willing eyes,
Or wait the amen, ere thy poppy throws
  Around my bed its lulling charities;

Then save me, or the passed day will shine
  Upon my pillow, breeding many woes;
Save me from curious conscience, that still lords
  Its strength, for darkness burrowing like a mole;
Turn the key deftly in the oiled wards,
  And seal the hushed casket of my soul.

THE GENTLE SOUTH

AFTER dark vapours have oppressed our plains
  For a long dreary season, comes a day
  Born of the gentle South, and clears away
From the sick heavens all unseemly stains.
The anxious month, relieved from its pains,
  Takes as a long-lost sight the feel of May,
  The eyelids with the passing coolness play,
Like rose-leaves with the drip of summer rains.
The calmest thoughts come round us—as of leaves
  Budding; fruit ripening in stillness; autumn suns
Smiling at eve upon the quiet sheaves;
  Sweet Sappho's cheek; a sleeping infant's breath;
The gradual sand that through an hour-glass runs;
  A woodland rivulet; a poet's death.

319

John Keats

BRIGHT Star! would I were steadfast as thou art—
    Not in lone splendour hung aloft the night,
And watching with eternal lids apart,
    Like Nature's patient, sleepless Eremite,
The moving waters at their priest-like task
    Of pure ablution round earth's human shores,
Or gazing on the new soft-fallen mask
    Of snow upon the mountains and the moors—

No—yet still steadfast, still unchangeable,
    Pillowed upon my fair love's ripening breast,
To feel for ever its soft fall and swell,
    Awake for ever in a sweet unrest,
Still, still to hear her tender-taken breath,
And so live ever—or else swoon to death.

ODE TO A NIGHTINGALE

MY heart aches, and a drowsy numbness pains
    My sense, as though of hemlock I had drunk,
Or emptied some dull opiate to the drains
    One minute past, and Lethe-wards had sunk:
'Tis not through envy of thy happy lot,
    But being too happy in thine happiness,—
        That thou, light-winged Dryad of the trees,
            In some melodious plot
    Of beechen green, and shadows numberless,
        Singest of summer in full-throated ease.

John Keats

O for a draught of vintage! that hath been
  Cooled a long age in the deep-delved earth,
Tasting of Flora and the country green,
  Dance, and Provençal song, and sunburnt mirth!
O for a beaker full of the warm South,
  Full of the true, the blushful Hippocrene,
    With beaded bubbles winking at the brim,
      And purple-stained mouth;
  That I might drink, and leave the world unseen,
    And with thee fade into the forest dim:

Fade far away, dissolve, and quite forget
  What thou among the leaves hast never known,
The weariness, the fever, and the fret
  Here, where men sit and hear each other groan;
Where palsy shakes a few, sad, last grey hairs,
  Where youth grows pale, and spectre-thin, and dies;
    Where but to think is to be full of sorrow
      And leaden-eyed despairs;
  Where Beauty cannot keep her lustrous eyes,
    Or new Love pine at them beyond to-morrow.

Away! away! for I will fly to thee,
  Not charioted by Bacchus and his pards,
But on the viewless wings of Poesy,
  Though the dull brain perplexes and retards:
Already with thee! tender is the night,
  And haply the Queen-Moon is on her throne,
    Clustered around by all her starry Fays;
      But here there is no light,
  Save what from heaven is with the breezes blown
    Through verdurous glooms and winding mossy
      ways.

John Keats

I cannot tell what flowers are at my feet,
   Nor what soft incense hangs upon the boughs,
But, in embalmed darkness, guess each sweet
   Wherewith the seasonable month endows
The grass, the thicket, and the fruit-tree wild;
   White hawthorn, and the pastoral eglantine;
     Fast-fading violets covered up in leaves;
       And mid-May's eldest child,
   The coming musk-rose, full of dewy wine,
     The murmurous haunt of flies on summer eves.

Darkling I listen; and for many a time
   I have been half in love with easeful Death,
Called him soft names in many a mused rhyme,
   To take into the air my quiet breath;
Now more than ever seems it rich to die,
   To cease upon the midnight with no pain,
     While thou art pouring forth thy soul abroad
       In such an ecstasy!
   Still wouldst thou sing, and I have ears in vain—
     To thy high requiem become a sod.

Thou wast not born for death, immortal Bird!
   No hungry generations tread thee down;
The voice I hear this passing night was heard
   In ancient days by emperor and clown:
Perhaps the self-same song that found a path
   Through the sad heart of Ruth, when, sick for
      home,
     She stood in tears amid the alien corn;
      The same that oft-times hath
   Charmed magic casements, opening on the foam
     Of perilous seas, in faery lands forlorn.

John Keats

Forlorn! the very word is like a bell
  To toll me back from thee to my sole self!
Adieu! the Fancy cannot cheat so well
  As she is famed to do, deceiving elf.
Adieu! adieu! thy plaintive anthem fades
  Past the near meadows, over the still stream,
    Up the hill-side; and now 'tis buried deep
      In the next valley-glades:
Was it a vision or a waking dream?
  Fled is that music:—Do I wake or sleep?

ODE ON A GRECIAN URN

THOU still unravished bride of quietness,
  Thou foster-child of silence and slow time,
Sylvan historian, who canst thus express
  A flowery tale more sweetly than our rhyme:
What leaf-fringed legend haunts about thy shape
  Of deities or mortals, or of both,
    In Tempe or the dales of Arcady?
What men or gods are these? What maidens loth?
  What mad pursuit? What struggle to escape?
    What pipes and timbrels? What wild ecstasy?

Heard melodies are sweet, but those unheard
  Are sweeter; therefore, ye soft pipes, play on;
Not to the sensual ear, but, more endeared,
  Pipe to the spirit ditties of no tone:
Fair youth, beneath the trees thou canst not leave
  Thy song, nor ever can those trees be bare;
    Bold Lover, never, never canst thou kiss,
Though winning near the goal—yet do not grieve;
  She cannot fade, though thou hast not thy bliss,
    For ever wilt thou love, and she be fair!

John Keats

Ah, happy, happy boughs ! that cannot shed
  Your leaves, nor ever bid the Spring adieu ;
And happy melodist, unwearied,
  For ever piping songs for ever new ;
More happy love ! more happy, happy love !
  For ever warm and still to be enjoyed,
    For ever panting, and for ever young ;
All breathing human passion far above,
  That leaves a heart high-sorrowful and cloyed,
    A burning forehead and a parching tongue.

Who are these coming to the sacrifice ?
  To what green altar, O mysterious priest,
Lead'st thou that heifer lowing at the skies,
  And all her silken flanks with garlands drest ?
What little town by river or sea-shore,
  Or mountain-built with peaceful citadel,
    Is emptied of its folk, this pious morn ?
And, little town, thy streets for evermore
  Will silent be ; and not a soul to tell
    Why thou art desolate, can e'er return.

O Attic shape ! Fair attitude ! with brede
  Of marble men and maidens overwrought,
With forest branches and the trodden weed ;
  Thou, silent form, dost tease us out of thought
As doth eternity : Cold Pastoral !
  When old age shall this generation waste,
    Thou shalt remain, in midst of other woe
Than ours, a friend to man, to whom thou sayest,
  'Beauty is truth, truth beauty,—that is all
    Ye know on earth, and all ye need to know.'

John Keats

ODE TO AUTUMN

Season of mists and mellow fruitfulness,
Close bosom-friend of the maturing sun;
Conspiring with him how to load and bless
With fruit the vines that round the thatch-eaves run;
To bend with apples the mossed cottage-trees,
And fill all fruit with ripeness to the core;
To swell the gourd, and plump the hazel shells
With a sweet kernel; to set budding more,
And still more, later flowers for the bees,
Until they think warm days will never cease;
For Summer has o'erbrimmed their clammy cells.

Who hath not seen thee oft amid thy store?
Sometimes whoever seeks abroad may find
Thee sitting careless on a granary floor,
Thy hair soft-lifted by the winnowing wind;
Or on a half-reaped furrow sound asleep,
Drowsed with the fume of poppies, while thy hook
Spares the next swath and all its twined flowers:
And sometimes like a gleaner thou dost keep
Steady thy laden head across a brook;
Or by a cyder-press, with patient look,
Thou watchest the last oozings, hours by hours.

Where are the songs of Spring? Ay, where are they?
Think not of them, thou hast thy music too,—
While barred clouds bloom the soft-dying day
And touch the stubble-plains with rosy hue;
Then in a wailful choir the small gnats mourn

John Keats

Among the river-sallows, borne aloft
Or sinking as the light wind lives or dies;
And full-grown lambs loud bleat from hilly bourn;
Hedge-crickets sing; and now with treble soft
The red-breast whistles from a garden-croft;
And gathering swallows twitter in the skies.

ODE TO PSYCHE

O GODDESS! hear these tuneless numbers, wrung
    By sweet enforcement and remembrance dear,
And pardon that my secrets should be sung
    Even into thine own soft-conched ear:
Surely I dreamt to-day, or did I see
    The winged Psyche with awakened eyes?
I wandered in a forest thoughtlessly,
    And on the sudden, fainting with surprise,
Saw two fair creatures couched side by side
    In deepest grass, beneath the whispering roof
    Of leaves and trembled blossoms, where there ran
        A brooklet scarce espied:
'Mid hushed, cool-rooted flowers fragrant-eyed,
    Blue, silver-white, and budded Tyrian,
They lay calm-breathing on the bedded grass,
    Their arms embraced, and their pinions too;
    Their lips touched not, but had not bade adieu,
As if disjoined by soft-handed slumber,
And ready still past kisses to outnumber
    At tender eye-dawn of aurorean love:
        The winged boy I knew;
    But who wast thou, O happy, happy dove?
        His Psyche true!

John Keats

O latest-born and loveliest vision far
    Of all Olympus' faded hierarchy!
Fairer than Phoebe's sapphire-regioned star,
    Or Vesper, amorous glow-worm of the sky:
Fairer than these, though temple thou hast none,
        Nor altar heaped with flowers;
Nor Virgin-choir to make delicious moan
        Upon the midnight hours;
No voice, no lute, no pipe, no incense sweet
    From chain-swung censer teeming;
No shrine, no grove, no oracle, no heat
    Of pale-mouthed prophet dreaming.
O brightest! though too late for antique vows,
    Too, too late for the fond believing lyre,
When holy were the haunted forest boughs,
    Holy the air, the water, and the fire;
Yet even in these days so far retired
    From happy pieties, thy lucent fans,
    Fluttering among the faint Olympians,
I see and sing, by my own eyes inspired.
    So let me be thy choir, and make a moan
        Upon the midnight hours!
Thy voice, thy lute, thy pipe, thy incense sweet
    From swinged censer teeming;
Thy shrine, thy grove, thy oracle, thy heat
    Of pale-mouthed prophet dreaming.

Yes, I will be thy priest, and build a fane
    In some untrodden region of my mind,
Where branched thoughts, new-grown with pleasant
        pain,
    Instead of pines shall murmur in the wind;
Far, far around shall those dark-clustered trees
    Fledge the wild-ridged mountains steep by steep;

John Keats

And there by zephyrs, streams, and birds, and bees,
   The moss-lain Dryads shall be lulled to sleep;
And in the midst of this wide quietness
A rosy sanctuary will I dress
With the wreathed trellis of a working brain,
   With buds, and shells, and stars without a name.
With all the gardener Fancy e'er could feign,
   Who, breeding flowers, will never breed the same:
And there shall be for thee all soft delight
   That shadowy thought can win,
A bright torch, and a casement ope at night,
   To let the warm Love in!

ODE TO MELANCHOLY

No, no, go not to Lethe, neither twist
   Wolf's-bane, tight-rooted, for its poisonous wine;
Nor suffer thy pale forehead to be kissed
   By nightshade, ruby grape of Proserpine:
Make not your rosary of yew-berries,
   Nor let the beetle, nor the death-moth be
      Your mournful Psyche, nor the downy owl
A partner in your sorrow's mysteries;
   For shade to shade will come too drowsily,
      And drown the wakeful anguish of the soul.

But when the melancholy fit shall fall
   Sudden from heaven like a weeping cloud
That fosters the droop-headed flowers all,
   And hides the green hill in an April shroud;
Then glut thy sorrow on a morning rose,
   Or on the rainbow of a salt sand-wave;

Or on the wealth of globed peonies;
Or if thy mistress some rich anger shows,
  Emprison her soft hand, and let her rave,
    And feed deep, deep upon her peerless eyes.

She dwells with Beauty—Beauty that must die;
  And Joy, whose hand is ever at his lips
Bidding adieu; and aching Pleasure nigh,
  Turning to poison while the bee-mouth sips.
Ay, in the very temple of Delight
  Veiled Melancholy has her sovran shrine,
    Though seen of none save him whose strenuous
        tongue
Can burst Joy's grapes against his palate fine;
His soul shall taste the sadness of her might,
  And be among her cloudy trophies hung.

HARTLEY COLERIDGE

1796-1849

SHE IS NOT FAIR

SHE is not fair to outward view
  As many maidens be;
Her loveliness I never knew
  Until she smiled on me.
O then I saw her eye was bright,
A well of love, a spring of light.

But now her looks are coy and cold,
  To mine they ne'er reply,
And yet I cease not to behold
  The love-light in her eye:
Her very frowns are fairer far
Than smiles of other maidens are.

NOTES

EPITHALAMION.—Page 3.

WRITTEN by Spenser on his marriage in Ireland, in 1594, with Elizabeth Boyle of Kilcoran, who survived him, married one Roger Seckerstone, and was again a widow. Dr. Grosart seems to have finally decided the identity of the heroine of this great poem. It is worth while to explain, once for all, that I do not use the accented *e* for the longer pronunciation of the past participle. The accent is not an English sign, and, to my mind, disfigures the verse ; neither do I think it necessary to cut off the *e* with an apostrophe when the participle is shortened. The reader knows at a glance how the word is to be numbered ; besides, he may have his preferences where choice is allowed. In reading such a line as Tennyson's

'Dear as remembered kisses after death,'

one man likes the familiar sound of the word 'remembered' as we all speak it now ; another takes pleasure in the four light syllables filling the line so full. Tennyson uses the apostrophe as a rule, but neither he nor any other author is quite consistent.

ROSALYND'S MADRIGAL.—Page 21.

It may please the reader to think that this frolic, rich, and delicate singer was Shakespeare's very Rosalind. From Dr. Thomas Lodge's novel, *Euphues' Golden Legacy*, was taken much of the story, with some of the characters, and some few of the passages, of *As You Like It*.

ROSALINE.—Page 22.

This splendid poem (from the same romance), written on the poet's voyage to the Islands of Terceras and the Canaries, has the fire and freshness of the south and the sea ; all its colours are clear. The reader's ear will at once teach him to read the sigh 'heigh ho' so as to give the first syllable the time of two (long and short).

FAREWELL TO ARMS.—Page 25.

George Peele's four fine stanzas (which must be mentioned as dedicated to Queen Elizabeth, but are better without that dedication) exist

Notes

in another form, in the first person, and with some archaisms smoothed. But the third person seems to be far more touching, the old man himself having done with verse.

THE PASSIONATE SHEPHERD.—Page 28.

The sixth stanza is perhaps by Izaak Walton.

TAKE, O TAKE THOSE LIPS AWAY.—Page 44.

The author of this exquisite song is by no means certain. The second stanza ·is not with the first in Shakespeare, but it is in Beaumont and Fletcher.

KIND ARE HER ANSWERS.—Page 46.

These verses are a more subtle experiment in metre by the musician and poet, Campion, than even the following, *Laura*, which he himself sweetly commended as 'voluble, and fit to express any amorous conceit.' In *Kind are her Answers* the long syllables and the trochaic movement of the short lines meet the contrary movement of the rest, with an exquisite effect of flux and reflux. The 'dancers' whose time they sang must have danced (with Perdita) like 'a wave of the sea.'

DIRGE.—Page 44.

I have followed the usual practice in omitting the last and less beautiful stanza.

FOLLOW.—Page 49.

Campion's 'airs,' for which he wrote his words, laid rules too urgent upon what would have been a delicate genius in poetry. The airs demanded so many stanzas; but they gave his imagination leave to be away, and they depressed and even confused his metrical play, hurting thus the two vital spots of poetry. Many of the stanzas for music make an unlucky repeating pattern with the poor variety that a repeating wall-paper does not attempt. And yet Campion began again and again with the onset of a true poet. Take, for example, the poem beginning with the vitality of this line, 'touching in its majesty'—

'Awake, thou spring of speaking grace; mute rest becomes not thee!'

Who would have guessed that the piece was to close in a jogging stanza containing a reflection on the fact that brutes are speechless, with these two final lines—

'If speech be then the best of graces,
Doe it not in slumber smother!'

332

Notes

Campion yields a curious collection of beautiful first lines.

> 'Sleep, angry beauty, sleep and fear not me'

is far finer than anything that follows. So is there a single gloom in this—

> 'Follow thy fair sun, unhappy shadow!'

And a single joy in this—

> 'Oh, what unhoped-for sweet supply!'

Another solitary line is one that by its splendour proves Campion the author of *Cherry Ripe*—

> 'A thousand cherubim fly in her looks.'

And yet 'a thousand cherubim' is a line of a poem full of the dullest kind of reasoning—curious matter for music—and of the intricate knotting of what is a very simple thread of thought. It was therefore no easy matter to choose something of Campion's for a collection of the finest work. For an historical book of representative poetry the question would be easy enough, for there Campion should appear by his glorious lyric, *Cherry Ripe*, by one or two poems of profounder imagination (however imperfect), and by a madrigal written for the music (however the stanzas may flag in their quibbling). But the work of choosing among his lyrics for the sake of beauty shows too clearly the inequality, the brevity of the inspiration, and the poet's absolute disregard of the moment of its flight and departure. A few splendid lines may be reason enough for extracting a short poem, but must not be made to bear too great a burden.

When thou must Home.—Page 50.

Of the quality of this imaginative lyric there is no doubt. It is fine throughout, as we confess even after the greatness of the opening :—

> 'When thou must home to shades of underground,
> And there arrived, a new admired guest—'

It is as solemn and fantastic at the close as at this dark and splendid opening, and throughout, past description, Elizabethan. This single poem must bind Campion to that period without question; and as he lived thirty-six years in the actual reign of Elizabeth, and printed his *Book of Airs* with Rosseter two years before her death, it is by no violence that we give him the name that covers our earlier poets of the great age. *When thou must Home* is of the day of Marlowe. It has the qualities of great poetry, and especially the quality of keeping its simplicity; and it has a quality of great simplicity not at all child-like, but adult, large, gay, credulous, tragic, sombre, and amorous.

Notes

The Funeral.—Page 56.

Donne, too, is a poet of fine onsets. It was with some hesitation that I admitted a poem having the middle stanza of this Funeral; but the earlier lines of the last are fine.

Charis' Triumph.—Page 58.

The freshest of Ben Jonson's lyrics have been chosen. Obviously it is freshness that he generally lacks, for all his vigour, his emphatic initiative, and his overbearing and impulsive voice in verse. There is a stale breath in that hearty shout. Doubtless it is to the credit of his honesty that he did not adopt the country-phrases in vogue; but when he takes landscape as a task the effect is ill enough. I have already had the temerity to find fault, for a blunder of meaning, with the passage of a most famous lyric, where it says the contrary of what it would say—

> ' But might I of Jove's nectar sup
> I would not change for thine ; '

and for doing so have encountered the anger rather than the argument of those who cannot admire a pretty lyric but they must hold reason itself to be in error rather than allow that a line of it has chanced to get turned in the rhyming.

In Earth.—Page 64.

'I never saw anything,' says Charles Lamb, 'like this funeral dirge, except the ditty which reminds Ferdinand of his drowned father in the *Tempest*. As that is of the water, watery; so this is of the earth, earthy. Both have that intentness of feeling which seems to resolve itself into the element which it contemplates.'

Song.—Page 65.

All Drummond's poems seem to be minor poems, even at their finest, except only this. He must have known, for the creation of that poem, some more impassioned and less restless hour. It is, from the outset to the close, the sigh of a profound expectation. There is no division into stanzas, because its metre is the breath of life. One might wish that the English ode (roughly called ' Pindaric ') had never been written but with passion, for so written it is the most immediate of all metres; the shock of the heart and the breath of elation or grief are the law of the lines. It has passed out of the gates of the garden of stanzas, and walks (not astray) in the further freedom where all is interior law. Cowley, long afterwards, wrote this Pindaric ode, and wrote it coldly. But Drummond's (he calls it a song) can never again be forgotten. With admirable judgment it was set up at the very gate of that *Golden Treasury* we all know so well; and, therefore, generation after

Notes

generation of readers, who have never opened Drummond's poems, know this fine ode as well as they know any single poem in the whole of English literature. There was a generation that had not been taught by the *Golden Treasury*, and Cardinal Newman was of it. Writing to Coventry Patmore of his great odes, he called them beautiful but fragmentary; was inclined to wish that they might some day be made complete. There is nothing in all poetry more complete. Seldom is a poem in stanzas so complete but that another stanza might have made a final close; but a master's ode has the unity of life, and when it ends it ends for ever.

A poem of Drummond's has this auroral image of a blush: Anthea has blushed to hear her eyes likened to stars (habit might have caused her, one would think, to bear the flattery with a front as cool as the very daybreak), and the lover tells her that the sudden increase of her beauty is futile, for he cannot admire more: 'For naught thy cheeks that morn do raise.' What sweet, nay, what solemn roses!

Again:

> 'Me here she first perceived, and here a morn
> Of bright carnations overspread her face.'

The seventeenth century has possession of that 'morn' caught once upon its uplands; nor can any custom of aftertime touch its freshness to wither it.

To my Inconstant Mistress.—Page 75.

The solemn vengeance of this poem has a strange tone—not unique, for it had sounded somewhere in mediæval poetry in Italy—but in a dreadful sense divine. At the first reading, this sentence against inconstancy, spoken by one more than inconstant, moves something like indignation; nevertheless, it is menacingly and obscurely justified, on a ground as it were beyond the common region of tolerance and pardon.

The Pulley.—Page 91.

An editor is greatly tempted to mend a word in these exquisite verses. George Herbert was maladroit in using the word 'rest' in two senses. 'Peace' is not quite so characteristic a word, but it ought to take the place of 'rest' in the last line of the second stanza; so then the first line of the last stanza would not have this rather distressing ambiguity. The poem is otherwise perfect beyond description.

Misery.—Page 94.

George Herbert's work is so perfectly a box where thoughts 'compacted lie,' that no one is moved, in reading his rich poetry, to detach a line, so fine and so significant are its neighbours; nevertheless, it may be well to stop the reader at such a lovely passage as this—

> 'He was a garden in a Paradise.'

335

Notes

THE ROSE.—Page 99.

There is nothing else of Waller's fine enough to be admitted here; and even this, though unquestionably a beautiful poem, elastic in words and fresh in feeling, despite its wearied argument, is of the third-class. Greatness seems generally, in the arts, to be of two kinds, and the third rank is less than great. The wearied argument of *The Rose* is the almost squalid plea of all the poets, from Ronsard to Herrick: 'Time is short; they make the better bargain who make haste to love.' This thrifty business and essentially cold impatience was—time out of mind—unknown to the truer love; it is larger, illiberal, untender, and without all dignity. The poets were wrong to give their verses the message of so sorry a warning. There is only one thing that persuades you to forgive the paltry plea of the poet that time is brief—and that is the charming reflex glimpse it gives of her to whom the rose and the verse were sent, and who had not thought that time was brief.

L'ALLEGRO.—Page 109.

The sock represents the stage, in *L'Allegro*, for comedy, and the buskin, in *Il Penseroso*, for tragedy. Milton seems to think the comic drama in England needs no apology, but he hesitates at the tragic. The poet of *King Lear* is named for his sweetness and his wood-notes wild.

IL PENSEROSO.—Page 113.

It is too late to protest against Milton's display of weak Italian. *Pensieroso* is, of course, what he should have written.

LYCIDAS.—Page 119.

Most of the allusions in *Lycidas* need no explaining to readers of poetry. The geography is that of the western coasts from furthest north to Cornwall. Deva is the Dee; 'the great vision' means the apparition of the Archangel, St. Michael, at St. Michael's Mount; Namancos and Bayona face the mount from the continental coast; Bellerus stands for Belerium, the Land's End.

Arethusa and Mincius—Sicilian and Italian streams—represent the pastoral poetry of Theocritus and Virgil.

ON A PRAYER-BOOK.—Page 131.

'Fair and flagrant things'—Crashaw's own phrase—might serve for a brilliant and fantastic praise and protest in description of his own verses. In the last century, despite the opinion of a few, and despite the fact that Pope took possession of Crashaw's line—

'Obedient slumbers that can wake and weep,'

and for some time of the present century, the critics had a wintry word to blame him with. They said of George Herbert, of Lovelace,

Notes

of Crashaw, and of other light hearts of the seventeenth century—
not so much that their inspiration was in bad taste, as that no reader
of taste could suffer them. A better opinion on that company of
poets is that they had a taste extraordinarily liberal, generous, and
elastic, but not essentially lax: taste that gave now and then too
much room to play, but anon closed with the purest and exactest
laws of temperance and measure. The extravagance of Crashaw
is a far more lawful thing than the extravagance of Addison, whom
some believe to have committed none; moreover, Pope and all the
politer poets nursed something they were pleased to call a 'rage,'
and this expatiated (to use another word of their own) beyond all
bounds. Of sheer voluntary extremes it is not in the seventeenth
century conceit that we should seek examples, but in an eighteenth
century 'rage.' A 'noble rage,' properly provoked, could be backed to
write more trash than fancy ever tempted the half-incredulous sweet
poet of the older time to run upon. He was fancy's child, and the bard
of the eighteenth century was the child of common sense with straws
in his hair—vainly arranged there. The eighteenth century was
never content with a moderate mind; it invented 'rage'; it matched
rage with a flagrant diction mingled of Latin words and simple
English words made vacant and ridiculous, and these were the
worst; it was resolved to be behind no century in passion—nay, to
show the way, to fire the nations. Addison taught himself, as his
hero taught the battle, 'where to rage'; and in the later years of the
same literary age, Johnson summoned the lapsed and absent fury,
with no kind of misgiving as to the resulting verse. Take such a
phrase as 'the madded land'; there, indeed, is a word coined by the
noble rage as the last century evoked it. 'The madded land' is a
phrase intended to prove that the law-giver of taste, Johnson himself, could lodge the fury in his breast when opportunity occurred.
'And dubious title shakes the madded land.' It would be hard to
find anything, even in Addison, more flagrant and less fair.

Take *The Weeper* of Crashaw—his most flagrant poem. Its
follies are all sweet-humoured, they smile. Its beauties are a quick
and abundant shower. The delicate phrases are so mingled with
the flagrant that it is difficult to quote them without rousing that
general sense of humour of which any one may make a boast; and I
am therefore shy even of citing the 'brisk cherub' who has early
sipped the Saint's tear: 'Then to his music,' in Crashaw's divinely
simple phrase; and his singing 'tastes of this breakfast all day long.'
Sorrow is a queen, he cries to the Weeper, and when sorrow would
be seen in state, 'then is she drest by none but thee.' Then you come
upon the fancy, 'Fountain and garden in one face.' All places,
times, and objects are 'Thy tears' sweet opportunity.' If these
charming passages lurk in his worst poems, the reader of this
anthology will not be able to count them in his best. In the
Epiphany Hymn the heavens have found means

> 'To disinherit the sun's rise,
> Delicately to displace
> The day, and plant it fairer in thy face.'

337

Notes

To the Morning: Satisfaction for Sleep, is, all through, luminous. It would be difficult to find, even in the orient poetry of that time, more daylight or more spirit. True, an Elizabethan would not have had poetry so rich as in *Love's Horoscope*, but yet an Elizabethan would have had it no fresher. The *Hymn to St. Teresa* has the brevities which this poet—reproached with his *longueurs*—masters so well. He tells how the Spanish girl, six years old, set out in search of death : ' She 's for the Moors and Martyrdom. Sweet, not so fast !' Of many contemporary songs in pursuit of a fugitive Cupid, Crashaw's *Cupid's Cryer: out of the Greek*, is the most dainty. But if readers should be a little vexed with the poet's light heart and perpetual pleasure, with the late ripeness of his sweetness, here, for their satisfaction, is a passage capable of the great age that had lately closed when Crashaw wrote. It is in his summons to nature and art:

> ' Come, and come strong,
>   To the conspiracy of our spacious song !'

I have been obliged to take courage to alter the reading of the seventeenth and nineteenth lines of the *Prayer-Book*, so as to make them intelligible ; they had been obviously misprinted. I have also found it necessary to re-punctuate generally.

Wishes to his Supposed Mistress.—Page 139.

This beautiful and famous poem has its stanzas so carelessly thrown together that editors have allowed themselves a certain freedom with it. I have done the least I could, by separating two stanzas that repeated the rhyme, and by suppressing one that grew tedious.

On the Death of Mr. Crashaw.—Page 157.

This ode has been chosen as more nobly representative than that, better known, *On the Death of Mr. William Harvey*. In the Crashaw ode, and in the *Hymn to the Light*, Cowley is, at last, tender. But it cannot be said that his love-poems had tenderness. He wrote in a gay language, but added nothing to its gaiety. He wrote the language of love, and left it cooler than he found it. What the conceits of Lovelace and the rest—flagrant, not frigid—did not do was done by Cowley's quenching breath ; the language of love began to lose by him. But even then, even then, who could have foretold what the loss at a later day would be !

Hymn to the Light.—Page 159.

It is somewhat to be regretted that this splendid poem should show Cowley as the writer of the alexandrine that divides into two lines. For he it was who first used (or first conspicuously used) the alexandrine that is organic, integral, and itself a separate unit of metre. He first passed beyond the heroic line, or at least he first used the alexandrine freely, at his pleasure, amid heroic verse ; and after him

Notes ⟩

Dryden took possession and then Pope. But both these masters, when they wrote alexandrines, wrote them in the French manner, divided. Cowley, however, with admirable art, is able to prevent even an accidental pause, making the middle of his line fall upon the middle of some word that is rapid in the speaking and therefore indivisible by pause or even by any lingering. Take this one instance—

> 'Like some fair pine o'erlooking all the ignobler wood.'

If Cowley's delicate example had ruled in English poetry (and he surely had authority on this one point, at least), this alexandrine would have taken its own place as an important line of English metre, more mobile than the heroic, less fitted to epic or dramatic poetry, but a line liberally lyrical. It would have been the light, pursuing wave that runs suddenly, outrunning twenty, further up the sands than these, a swift traveller, unspent, of longer impulse, of more impetuous foot, of fuller and of hastier breath, more eager to speak, and yet more reluctant to have done. Cowley left the line with all this lyrical promise within it, and if his example had been followed, English prosody would have had in this a valuable bequest.

Cowley probably was two or three years younger than Richard Crashaw, and the alexandrine is to be found—to be found by searching—in Crashaw; and he took precisely the same care as Cowley that the long wand of that line should not give way in the middle—should be strong and supple and should last. Here are four of his alexandrines—

> 'Or you, more noble architects of intellectual noise.'

> 'Of sweets you have, and murmur that you have no more.'

> 'And everlasting series of a deathless song.'

> 'To all the dear-bought nations this redeeming name.'

A later poet—Coventry Patmore—wrote a far longer line than even these—a line not only speeding further, but speeding with a more celestial movement than Cowley or Crashaw heard with the ear of dreams.

'He unhappily adopted,' says Dr. Johnson as to Cowley's diction, 'that which was predominant.' 'That which was predominant' was as good a vintage of English language as the cycles of history have ever brought to pass.

To Lucasta.—Page 163.

Colonel Richard Lovelace, an enchanting poet, is hardly read, except for two poems which are as famous as any in our language. Perhaps the rumour of his conceits has frightened his reader. It must be granted they are now and then daunting; there is a poem on 'Princess Louisa Drawing' which is a very maze; the little paths of verse and fancy turn in upon one another, and the turns are

Notes

pointed with artificial shouts of joy and surprise. But, again, what a reader unused to a certain living symbolism will be apt to take for a careful and cold conceit is, in truth, a rapture—none graver, none more fiery or more luminous. But even to name the poem where these occur might be to deliver delicate and ardent poetry over to the general sense of humour, which one distrusts. Nor is Lovelace easy reading at any time (the two or three famous poems excepted). The age he adorned lived in constant readiness for the fiddler. Eleven o'clock in the morning was as good an hour as another for a dance, and poetry, too, was gay betimes, but intricate with figures. It is the very order, the perspective, as it were, of the movement that seems to baffle the eye, but the game was a free impulse. Since the first day danced with the first night, no dancing was more natural— at least to a dancer of genius. True, the dance could be tyrannous. It was an importunate fashion. When the Bishop of Hereford, compelled by Robin Hood, in merry Barnsdale, danced in his boots ('and glad he could so get away'), he was hardly in worse heart or trim than a seventeenth century author here and there whose original seriousness or work-a-day piety would have been content to go plodding flatfoot or halting, as the muse might naturally incline with him, but whom the tune, the grace, and gallantry of the time beckoned to tread a perpetual measure. Lovelace was a dancer of genius; nay, he danced to rest his wings, for he was winged, cap and heel. The fiction of flight has lost its charm long since. Modern art grew tired of the idea, now turned to commonplace, and painting took leave of the buoyant urchins—naughty cherub and Cupid together; but the seventeenth century was in love with that old fancy—more in love, perhaps, than any century in the past. Its late painters, whose human figures had no lack of weight upon the comfortable ground, yet kept a sense of buoyancy for this hovering childhood, and kept the angels and the loves aloft, as though they shook a tree to make a flock of birds flutter up.

Fine is the fantastic and infrequent landscape in Lovelace's poetry:

> 'This is the palace of the wood,
> And court o' the royal oak, where stood
> The whole nobility.'

In more than one place Lucasta's, or Amarantha's, or Laura's hair is sprinkled with dew or rain almost as freshly and wildly as in Wordsworth's line.

Lovelace, who loved freedom, seems to be enclosed in so narrow a book; yet it is but a 'hermitage.' To shake out the light and spirit of its leaves is to give a glimpse of liberty not to him, but to the world.

In *To Lucasta* I have been bold to alter, at the close, 'you' to 'thou.' Lovelace sent his verses out unrevised, and the inconsistency of pronouns is common with him, but nowhere else so distressing as in this brief and otherwise perfect poem. The fault is easily set right, and it seems even an unkindness not to lend him this redress, offered him here as an act of comradeship.

340

Notes

Lucasta Paying her Obsequies.—Page 165.

That errors should abound in the text of Lovelace is the more lamentable because he was apt to make a play of phrases that depend upon the precision of a comma—nay, upon the precision of the voice in reading. *Lucasta Paying her Obsequies* is a poem that makes a kind of dainty confusion between the two vestals—the living and the dead; they are 'equal virgins,' and you must assign the pronouns carefully to either as you read. This, read twice, must surely be placed amongst the loveliest of his lovely writings. It is a joy to meet such a phrase as 'her brave eyes.'

To Althea, from Prison.—Page 166.

This is a poem that takes the winds with an answering flight. Should they be 'birds' or 'gods' that wanton in the air in the first of these gallant stanzas? Bishop Percy shied at 'gods,' and with admirable judgment suggested 'birds,' an amendment adopted by the greater number of succeeding editors, until one or two wished for the other phrase again, as an audacity fit for Lovelace. But the Bishop's misgiving was after all justified by one of the MSS. of the poem, in which the 'gods' proved to be 'birds' long before he changed them. The reader may ask, what is there to choose between birds so divine and gods so light? But to begin with 'gods' would be to make an anticlimax of the close. Lovelace led from birds and fishes to winds, and from winds to angels.

'When linnet-like confined' is another modern reading. 'When, like committed linnets,' daunted the eighteenth century. Nevertheless, it is right seventeenth century, and is now happily restored; happily, because Lovelace would not have the word 'confined' twice in this little poem.

A Horatian Ode.—Page 169.

'He earned the glorious name,' says a biographer of Andrew Marvell (editing an issue of that poet's works which certainly has its faults), 'of the British Aristides.' The portly dulness of the mind that could make such a phrase, and having made, award it, is not, in fairness, to affect a reader's thought of Marvell himself nor even of his time. Under correction, I should think that the award was not made in his own age; he did but live on the eve of the day that cumbered its mouth with phrases of such foolish burden and made literature stiff with them. Andrew Marvell's political rectitude, it is true, seems to have been of a robustious kind; but his poetry, at its rare best, has a 'wild civility,' which might puzzle the triumph of him, whoever he was, who made a success of this phrase of the 'British Aristides.' Nay, it is difficult not to think that Marvell too, who was 'of middling stature, roundish-faced, cherry-cheeked,' a healthy and active rather than a spiritual Aristides, might himself

Notes

have been somewhat taken by surprise at the encounters of so subtle a muse. He, as a garden-poet, expected the accustomed Muse to lurk about the fountain-heads, within the caves, and by the walks and the statues of the gods, keeping the tryst of a seventeenth century convention in which there were certainly no surprises. And for fear of the commonplaces of those visits, Marvell sometimes outdoes the whole company of garden-poets in the difficult labours of the fancy. The reader treads with him a 'maze' most resolutely intricate, and is more than once obliged to turn back, having been too much puzzled on the way to a small, visible, plain, and obvious goal of thought.

And yet this poet two or three times did meet a Muse he had hardly looked for among the trodden paths; a spiritual creature had been waiting behind a laurel or an apple-tree. You find him coming away from such a divine ambush a wilder and a simpler man. All his garden had been made ready for poetry, and poetry was indeed there, but in unexpected hiding and in a strange form, looking rather like a fugitive, shy of the poet who was conscious of having her rules by heart, yet sweetly willing to be seen, for all her haste.

The political poems, needless to say, have an excellence of a different character and a higher degree. They have so much authentic dignity that 'the glorious name of the British Aristides' really seems duller when it is conferred as the earnings of the *Horatian Ode upon Cromwell's Return from Ireland* than when it inappropriately clings to Andrew Marvell, cherry-cheeked, caught in the tendrils of his vines and melons. He shall be, therefore, the British Aristides in those moments of midsummer solitude; at least, the heavy phrase shall then have the smile it never sought.

The Satires are, of course, out of reach for their inordinate length. The celebrated Satire on Holland certainly makes the utmost of the fun to be easily found in the physical facts of the country whose people 'with mad labour fished the land to shore.' The Satire on 'Flecno' makes the utmost of another joke we know of—that of famine. Flecno, it will be remembered, was a poet, and poor; but the joke of his bad verses was hardly needed, so fine does Marvell find that of his hunger. Perhaps there is no age of English satire that does not give forth the sound of that laughter unknown to savages—that craven laughter.

THE PICTURE OF T. C. IN A PROSPECT OF FLOWERS.—Page 173.

The presence of a furtive irony of the sweetest kind is the sure sign of the visit of that unlooked-for muse. With all spirit and subtlety does Marvell pretend to offer the little girl T. C. (the future 'virtuous enemy of man') the prophetic homage of the habitual poets. The poem closes with an impassioned tenderness not to be found elsewhere in Marvell.

Notes

THE DEFINITION OF LOVE.—Page 179.

The noble phrase of the *Horatian Ode* is not recovered again, high or low, throughout Marvell's book, if we except one single splendid and surpassing passage from *The Definition of Love*—

> 'Magnanimous despair alone
> Could show me so divine a thing.'

CHILDHOOD.—Page 183.

One of our true poets, and the first who looked at nature with the full spiritual intellect, Henry Vaughan was known to few but students until Mr. E. K. Chambers gave us his excellent edition. The tender wit and grave play of Herbert, Crashaw's lovely rapture, are all unlike this meditation of a soul condemned and banished into life. Vaughan's imagination suddenly opens a new window towards the east. The age seems to change with him, and it is one of the most incredible of all facts that there should be more than a century—and such a century!—from him to Wordsworth. The passing of time between them is strange enough, but the passing of Pope, Prior, and Gray—of the world, the world, whether reasonable or flippant or rhetorical—is more strange. Vaughan's phrase and diction seem to carry the light. *Il vous semble que cette femme dégage de la lumière en marchant ? Vous l'aimez!* says Marius in *Les Misérables* (I quote from memory), and it seems to be by a sense of light that we know the muse we are to love.

SCOTTISH BALLADS.—Page 191.

It was no easy matter to choose a group of representative ballads from among so many almost equally fine and equally damaged with thin places. Finally, it seemed best to take, from among the finest, those that had passages of genius—a line here and there of surpassing imagination and poetry—rare in even the best folk-songs. Such passages do not occur but in ballads that are throughout on the level of the highest of their kind. 'None but my foe to be my guide' so distinguishes *Helen of Kirconnell*; the exquisite stanza about the hats of birk, *The Wife of Usher's Well*; its varied refrain, *The Dowie Dens of Yarrow;* the stanza spoken by Margaret asking for room in the grave, *Sweet William and Margaret*; and a number of passages, *Sir Patrick Spens*, such as that. beginning, 'I saw the new moon late yestreen,' the stanza beginning 'O laith, laith were our gude Scots lords,' and almost all the stanzas following. *A Lyke Wake Dirge* is of surpassing quality throughout. I am sorry to have no room for Jamieson's version of *Fair Annie*, for *Edom o' Gordon*, for *The Dæmon Lover*, for *Edward, Edward*, and for the Scottish edition of *The Battle of Otterbourne*.

Notes

MRS. ANNE KILLIGREW.—Page 205.

This most majestic ode—one of the few greatest of its kind—is a model of noble rhythm and especially of cadence. To print it whole would be impossible, and one of the very few excisions in this book is made in the midst of it. Dryden, so adult and so far from simplicity, bears himself like a child who, having said something fine, caps it with something foolish. The suppressed part of the ode is silly with a silliness which Dryden's age chose to dodder in when it would. The deplorable 'rattling bones' of the closing section has a touch of it.

SONG, FROM ABDELAZAR.—Page 209.

It is a futile thing—and the cause of a train of futilities—to hail 'style' as though it were a separable quality in literature, and it is not in that illusion that the style of the opening of Aphra Behn's resounding song is to be praised. But it *is* the style—implying the reckless and majestic heart—that first takes the reader of these great verses.

HYMN.—Page 209.

Whether Addison wrote the whole of this or not,—and it seems that the inspired passages are none of his—it is to me a poem of genius, magical in spite of the limited diction.

ELEGY TO THE MEMORY OF AN UNFORTUNATE LADY.—Page 210.

Also in spite of limited diction—the sign of thought closing in, as it did fast close in during those years—are Pope's tenderness and passion communicated in this beautiful elegy. It would not be too much to say that all his passion, all his tenderness, and certainly all his mystery, are in the few lines at the opening and close. The *Epistle of Eloisa* is (artistically speaking) but a counterfeit. Yet Pope's *Elegy* begins by stealing and translating into the false elegance of altered taste that lovely and poetic opening of Ben Jonson's—

> 'What beckoning ghost, besprent with April dew,
> Hails me so solemnly to yonder yew?'

All the gravity, all the sweetness, one might fear, must be lost in such a change as Pope makes—

> 'What beckoning ghost along the moonlight shade
> Invites my steps, and points to yonder glade?'

Yet they are not lost. Pope's awe and ardour are authentic, and they prevail; the succeeding couplet—inimitably modulated, and of tragic dignity—proves, without delay, the quality of the poem. The poverty and coldness of the passage (towards the end), in which the roses and the angels are somewhat trivially sung, cannot mar so veritable an utterance. The four final couplets are the very glory of the English couplet.

Notes

LINES ON RECEIVING HIS MOTHER'S PICTURE.—Page 213.

Cowper, again, by the very directness of human feeling makes his narrowing English a means of absolutely direct communication. Of all his works (and this is my own mere and unshared opinion) this single one deserves immortality.

LIFE.—Page 217.

This fragment (the only fragment, properly so called, in the present collection) so pleased Wordsworth that he wished he had written the lines. They are very gently touched.

THE LAND OF DREAMS.—Page 217.

When Blake writes of sleep and dreams he writes under the very influence of the hours of sleep—with a waking consciousness of the wilder emotion of the dream. Corot painted so, when at summer dawn he went out and saw landscape in the hours of sleep.

SURPRISED BY JOY.—Page 229.

It is not necessary to write notes on Wordsworth's sonnets—the greatest sonnets in our literature; but it would be well to warn editors how they print this one sonnet; 'I wished to share the transport' is by no means an uncommon reading. Into the history of the variant I have not looked. It is enough that all the suddenness, all the clash and recoil of these impassioned lines are lost by that 'wished' in the place of 'turned.' The loss would be the less tolerable in as much as perhaps only here and in that heart-moving poem, *'Tis said that some have died for love*, is Wordsworth to be confessed as an impassioned poet.

STEPPING WESTWARD.—Page 243.

This and the preceding two exquisite poems of sympathy are far more justified, more recollected and sincere than is that more monumental composition, the famous poem of sympathy, *Hartleap Well*. The most beautiful stanzas of this poem last-named are so rebuked by the truths of nature that they must ever stand as obstacles to the straightforward view of sensitive eyes upon the natural world. Wordsworth shows us the ruins of an aspen-wood, a blighted hollow, a dreary place forlorn because an innocent creature, hunted, had there broken its heart in a leap from the rocks above; grass would not grow, nor shade linger there—

> 'This beast not unobserved by Nature fell,
> His death was mourned by sympathy divine.'

And the signs of that sympathy are cruelly asserted to be these arid woodland ruins—cruelly, because the common sight of the day

Notes

blossoming over the agonies of animals and birds is made less tolerable by such fictions. We have to shut our ears to the benign beauty of this stanza especially—

> 'The Being that is in the clouds and air,
>   That is in the green leaves among the groves,
> Maintains a deep and reverential care
>   For the unoffending creature whom He loves.'

We must shut our ears because the poet offers us, as a proof of that 'reverential care,' the visible alteration of nature at the scene of suffering—an alteration we are obliged to dispense with every day we pass in the woods. We are tempted to ask whether Wordsworth himself believed in a sympathy he asks us—upon such grounds! —to believe in? Did he think his faith to be worthy of no more than a fictitious sign or a false proof?

To choose from Wordsworth is to draw close a net with very large meshes—so that the lovely things that escape must doubtless cause the reader to protest; but the poems gathered here are not only supremely beautiful but exceedingly Wordsworthian.

YOUTH AND AGE.—Page 256.

Close to the marvellous *Kubla Khan*—a poem that wrests the secret of dreams and brings it to the light of verse—I place *Youth and Age* as the best specimen of Coleridge's poetry that is quite undelirious—to my mind the only fine specimen. I do not rate his undelirious poems highly, and even this, charming and nimble as it is, seems to me rather lean in thought and image. The tenderness of some of the images comes to a rather lamentable close; the likeness to 'some poor nigh-related guest' with the three lines that follow is too squalid for poetry, or prose, or thought.

THE RIME OF THE ANCIENT MARINER.—Page 258.

This poem is surely more full of a certain quality of extreme poetry—the simplest 'flower of the mind,' the most single magic— than any other in our language. But the reader must be permitted to call the story silly.

Page 265.

Coleridge used the sun, moon, and stars as a great dream uses them when the sleeping imagination is obscurely threatened with illness. All through *The Ancient Mariner* we see them like apparitions. It is a pity that he followed the pranks also of a dream when he impossibly placed a star *within* the tip of the crescent.

Page 266.

The likeness of 'the ribbed sea sand' is said to be the one passage actually composed by Wordsworth,—who according to the first plan should have written *The Ancient Mariner* with Coleridge—

Notes

'and perhaps the most beautiful passage in the poem,' adds one critic after another. It is no more than a good likeness, and has nothing whatever of the indescribable Coleridge quality.

Coleridge reveals, throughout this poem, an exaltation of the senses, which is the most poetical thing that can befall a simple poet. It is necessary only to refer, for sight, to the stanza on 'the moving Moon' at the bottom of page 267; for hearing, to the supernatural stanzas on page 271; and, for touch, to the line—

'And still my body drank.'

Rose Aylmer.—Page 281.

Never was a human name more exquisitely sung than in these perfect stanzas.

The Isles of Greece.—Page 286.

One really fine and poetic stanza—of course, the third; three stanzas that are good eloquence—the fourth, fifth, and seventh; and one that is a fair bit of argument—the tenth—may together perhaps carry the rest.

Hellas.—Page 290.

The profounder spirit of Shelley's poem yet leaves it a careless piece of work in comparison with Byron's. The two false rhymes at the outset may not be of great importance, but there is something annoying in the dissyllabic rhymes of the second stanza. Dissyllabic rhymes are beautiful and enriching when they fall in the right place; that is, where there is a pause for the second little syllable to stand. For example, they could not be better placed than they would have been at the end of the shorter lines of this same stanza, where they would have dropped into a part of the pause. Another sin of sheer heedlessness—the lapse of grammar in *The Skylark*, at the top of page 296—will remind the reader of the special habitual error of Drummond of Hawthornden.

The Waning Moon.—Page 298.

In these few lines the Shelley spirit seems to be more intense than in any other passage as brief.

Ode to the West Wind.—Page 299.

This magnificent poem is surely the greatest of a great poet's writings, and one of the most splendid poems on nature and on poetry in a literature resounding with odes on these enormous themes.

The Invitation.—Page 303.

No need to point to a poem that so shines as does this lucent verse.

347

Notes

LA BELLE DAME SANS MERCI.—Page 316.

Keats is here the magical poet, as he is the intellectual poet in the great sonnet following; and it is his possession or promise of both imaginations that proves him greater than Coleridge. In his day they seem to have found Coleridge to be a thinker in his poetry. To me he seems to have had nothing but senses, magic, and simplicity, and these he had to the utmost yet known to man. Keats was to have been a great intellectual poet, besides all that in fact he was.

ODE TO A NIGHTINGALE.—Page 320.

Of the five odes of Keats, the *Nightingale* is perhaps the most perfect, and certainly the most imaginative. But the *Grecian Urn* is the finest, even though it has fancy rather than imagination, for never was fancy more exquisite. The most conspicuous idea—the emptying of the town because its folk are away at play in the tale of the antique urn—is merely a fancy, and a most antic fancy—a prank; it is an irony of man, a rallying of art, a mockery of time, a burlesque of poetry, divine with tenderness. The six lines in which this fancy sports are amongst the loveliest in all literature: the 'little town,' the 'peaceful citadel,'—were ever simple adjectives more happy? But John Keats's final moral here is undeniably a failure; it says so much and means so little. The *Ode to Autumn* is an exterior ode, and not in so high a rank, but lovely and perfect. The *Psyche* I love the least, because its fancy is rather weak and its sentiment effusive. It has a touch of the deadly sickliness of *Endymion*. None the less does it remain just within the group of the really fine odes of English poets. The eloquent *Melancholy* more narrowly escapes exclusion from that group.

Printed by T. and A. CONSTABLE, Printers to Her Majesty
at the Edinburgh University Press

www.ingramcontent.com/pod-product-compliance
Lightning Source LLC
Chambersburg PA
CBHW030911270326
41929CB00008B/651